# ALL THE FIRST MINISTER'S MEN

David Black

# ALL THE FIRST MINISTER'S MEN

*Uncovering the Truth Behind the
Holyrood Scandal*

Foreword by Ian Hamilton QC

**Birlinn**

First published in 2001 by
Birlinn Limited
8 Canongate Venture
5 New Street
Edinburgh
EH8 8BH

www.birlinn.co.uk

ISBN 1 84158 167 4

British Library Cataloguing-in-Publication Data
A catalogue record is available on request
from the British Library

Typeset by Palimpsest Book Production Limited,
Polmont, Stirlingshire
Printed and bound by Omnia Books Ltd, Bishopbriggs

# CONTENTS

# ACKNOWLEDGEMENTS

In the course of writing this book I have had encouragement from many, but some long-standing influences deserve mention. Any views I now hold on Scotland's built environment began with committed questioners such as my mother and her sister, founder members of the Craigmillar Festival Society, who both knew about the value of history and art to those who are too often alienated from it. There were others like Moultrie Kelsall, Colin McWilliam, Jack Kane, Grace Durham and Frank Tindall, whose legacy can be measured in buildings saved and experience passed on, while in the last months of his life Nigel Tranter gave much advice and support.

I owe a more immediate debt to those of all political persuasions, and none, who provided valuable assistance. Mike Watson MSP and Sir David Steel, amongst others, could scarcely have approved of my activities, but were helpful nonetheless. The late Donald Dewar, while adamant that we could only agree to disagree on the issue, took the trouble to reply in person to my letters, which he need not have done. Paul Flynn MP kindly sent me a copy of his book on the Welsh leadership débâcle, an object lesson in how a dysfunctional historic event should be chronicled. Encouragement and comment was also forthcoming from Stephen Bayley, Tam Dalyell, the Duke of Hamilton, Peter Wilson, Bill Armstrong, Alexander Stoddart, George Rosie, Alex Salmond, Charles McKean, Bart Joziasse, Murray Tosh, Margo MacDonald, James Douglas Hamilton, Donald Gorrie, Alistair Guild, Ian Tuckett, Charles Prosser, John Clifford, Marion Ralls, Sebastian Tombs, Courtney Peyton, John Gifford, Andrew Ecclestone and many others. Miss Mary Mackenzie kept me constantly updated, while

David Walker advised on aspects of architectural history. Journalists' accounts have been indispensible. Some are named in the text, others not, but they all have my thanks. I am especially indebted to Lesley Riddoch, Paul Harris, Harry Reid, and David Taylor of *The Architects Journal*, and to Ian Hamilton for supplying a foreword at a moment's notice. In addition to those architects mentioned, there were many others who had insights to offer, as well as 'sources' whose private views were always gratefully received.

Thanks are due to all at Birlinn Limited and Palimpsest Book Production, and to super-efficient editor Morag Lyall, for making this book possible at all, as well as to Alison, Hugh, Adam and James for putting up with all the demands and distractions which having an author in the family must inevitably impose.

# FOREWORD

Britain has been generous to its former colonies. Will England be generous to Scotland when the break-up comes? To east and west the old Empire was sent on its way with good wishes and encouraging hand-outs. This wonderful book documents a different relationship. Downing Street and devolving Scotland are two equals drifting uneasily apart. From all the muddle one thing emerges: Downing Street has shafted us.

A Foreword is no place to précis the theme to follow. Suffice to say that England insisted on the Holyrood site for Scotland's new Parliament House. The Scots might have got delusions of nationhood from the wonderful and obvious site on Calton Hill. The cost of the subsequent chaos, now £250 million and rising, has to come not from UK funds, which pay for every English folly, and to which we Scots contribute handsomely – every penny of this English-imposed catastrophe has to come from the Scottish exchequer.

This book is more than a chronicle of folly. It is a wonderful romp of a read. I got through it in two long, almost breathless, sittings. David Black comes at it from every side. I defy any reader, except Tony Blair, not to give many a belly laugh at the record of how Labour re-branded itself. The chapter on Calton Hill should be made compulsory reading in every school.

Will lessons be learned? Mrs Liddell keeps telling us that we're a United Kingdom. Has she learned her own lesson? It means we Scots own a vast treasury of assets, including part of every state-owned building in London and elsewhere. They were all built during the Union and we contributed to their cost and upkeep. When we come to claim our share of Whitehall, we must not allow ourselves to be tricked as Scottish Labour has been tricked over our New Parliament House. This book is a roaring record of muddle and deceit. Start turning the pages. You won't stop until you reach the end.

Ian Hamilton
April 2001

# 1 Introduction
## *Putting a Parliament in its Place*

> *There can't be a crisis. I haven't got room in my schedule*
>
> Henry Kissinger

THE CHAOTIC ATTEMPT to build a 'signature' Scottish parliament building on the site of an old brewery in Edinburgh has been described as Scotland's version of London's Millennium Dome. This would be startling enough if it were true, but it isn't. 'Holyrood' is much, much worse than the Dome. It even eclipses Sydney's notorious Opera House, and might yet turn out to be the building with the highest budget overrun in recorded history.

As a political scandal, the Holyrood project has no parallel. There has been nothing quite like it in the long annals of British state architecture. It has also been the running sore of the devolution process. Despite this, Scotland's political establishment has clung tenaciously to the vestigial remnants of the late Enric Miralles' upturned boats vision, or rather to a grossly distorted remake of his vision. Our politicians and bureaucrats have struggled in vain to fend off criticism by imposing *omertà* on open debate. They have also demonstrated an alarming capacity for being economical with the truth as the scandal continues to oscillate between tragedy and farce.

Compared to the débâcle at Greenwich, the facts speak for themselves. The Dome ended up costing £758 million, having risen from a planned £580 million, a rise of 30 per cent. Although the devolution white paper had estimated a Scottish parliament at £40 million, the Scottish Office, in its eagerness to undermine the converted former Royal High

School, at one point produced a base-line estimate which stated that a parliament might be built for as little as £10 million. Three years later the total cost of avoiding the existing parliament building on Edinburgh's Calton Hill, which is what this bizarre exercise has been all about, was set to top £300 million. At 3,000 per cent over budget, Holyrood promises to be in a class of its own, all right, if only in financial terms.

That's only part of the story. This money has to be found. Comparing Holyrood with the Dome on a like-for-like basis requires a demographic adjustment. The Dome is an all-UK affair, built in the name of 60 million people, where Holyrood's costs have been devolved to a country of 5 million. This is a sobering enough thought, but it now seems likely that a project that at one time had been costed as low as £10 million could end up costing around £300 million – a thirty-fold increase. Apply this multiple to the Dome and a truly terrifying picture emerges. However you look at it, £580 million times thirty equals a mind-boggling £17.4 *billion*. No need to pinch yourself: that wasn't a misprint. It was just the kind of simple arithmetic our political establishment would rather you didn't trouble yourself with. Reflect, for a moment, on how Mr Mandelson would have fared if *his* project had taken this cost trajectory. His political ruin was brought about when a relatively modest £1 million pay-out for the Dome's faith zone was linked to a passport application. Meanwhile, Holyrood's meter was nudging towards £300 million as misinformation and deceit were elevated to a high art, though somehow no one in either Edinburgh or Westminster seemed to be responsible.

Next, think about the financing. The Dome was largely squandering lottery takings and *baksheesh* from corporate sponsors where Holyrood will come from budget revenue, and Scottish taxpayers must bear *all* the cost. Even with expenditure spread over three to four years it will impact measurably in a country with western Europe's worst health and poverty indices. Financial resources that could have

been used for schools, hospitals, transport, rural assistance, housing, economic regeneration and the arts will be
diverted to a project that doesn't even have the virtue of
democratic legitimacy.

But it doesn't end there. Why did we take on Holyrood in
the first place? We didn't need it, after all. There was already
a parliament on Edinburgh's Calton Hill, one of Europe's
most spectacular urban sites. It had been converted by
the Callaghan government from an outstanding neo-Greek
building designed by Thomas Hamilton, the old Royal
High School, ahead of the 1979 referendum. It needed
refurbishing and electronically upgrading, but the 150 dark
green leather seats in its oval debating chamber were ready
and waiting for the first intake of MSPs.

In time, perhaps, MSPs would have deemed it unsuitable,
and quite possibly would have built something else to meet
their needs. They might even have chosen to go somewhere else altogether. Leith, Glasgow, Stirling, Dingwall,
Ecclefechan: *where* is not the issue; rather it's a question
of *how*, and that should involve an accountable process of
decision-making, which, in the case of Holyrood, is precisely
what we were denied.

So what should have happened? The democratic option
was self-evident. MSPs, duly elected, should quite simply
have been given an opportunity to put the issue to a vote
without any outside interference from Westminster. They
could have taken their time, and appropriate expert advice,
technical and financial. They could also have consulted their
constituents. If, after due consideration, 'New Parliament
House' on Calton Hill had been deemed inadequate they
could have looked at *all* the alternative sites, rather than a
rationed list fixed in secret by Scottish civil servants in collusion with Downing Street. There was a massive landholding
at Greenside Place on the hill's north flank. It was ignored.
Why? There was the vacant 1960s hulk of New St Andrew's
House which could have been beneficially demolished. It,
too, was ignored. Again, why? Either of these locations could
have accommodated an internationally acclaimed signature

building while Hamilton's *tour de force*, retaining its iconic role within this wider parliamentary precinct, could have become a cabinet office, a civic forum, or a complex of committee rooms. None of this was allowed to happen, and not because it wasn't feasible or desirable. There was only one reason: Calton Hill's symbolism had to be wiped out.

Whatever one thinks of devolution *per se*, there can be no doubt that the Calton Hill location was practical, as well as aesthetically inspiring. We had one of the finest historic buildings in the country ready for use directly opposite another, 1930s St Andrew's House, where the senior civil servants of the Scottish Office were based. It overlooked Scotland's principal railway station, to which it had potential dedicated access, and was surrounded by available land and vacant buildings in need of alternative uses. It was an outdoor pantheon celebrating the giants of the Scottish Enlightenment, and included Regent Terrace, the city's diplomatic quarter. This was, in anyone's language, a parliament precinct which lacked only one thing: a parliament.

The former brewery land at Holyrood, by contrast, was a planner's nightmare. Set on low ground within the medieval core of a UNESCO World Heritage Site, it had obvious access problems and was surrounded by listed buildings. The old brewery groundworkings included a labyrinth of aquifers and tunnels which would require costly stabilisation. As a place where you *shouldn't* construct a large, institutional edifice it was exemplary. On the other hand, as the sort of residential urban regeneration area described in the 1989 Edinburgh Old Town report, and latterly in the Canongate masterplan by the Edinburgh architect John Hope, it offered tremendous opportunities for high-quality sustainable development.

Perhaps the most extraordinary aspect of the Holyrood fiasco was that it just wasn't necessary. Dreamed up entirely by politicians and civil servants, it had nothing to do with the 'settled will' of an electorate which, immediately after the declaration of the referendum result, fully expected to see Thomas Hamilton's Doric masterpiece on Calton Hill being brought into service as their parliament. When our politicians, for no good reason, unaccountably shell out an amount of revenue tñat is the equivalent of 2p out of the 3p variable charge allowed for under the devolution settlement – Michael Forsyth's famous 'Tartan Tax' – something is obviously amiss. This isn't simply a scandal about a building. It is a failure of our politics, both north and south of the border, and we should know about it, if only to stop it happening again.

The London-based media, preoccupied by the Millennium Dome débâcle (perhaps understandably, since so many editors were snarled up at Stratford Station on that fateful millennium eve!), have paid little heed to the Holyrood scandal, though there has been some informed comment from specialist journalists such as Jonathan Glancey in the *Guardian* and Gavin Stamp in the *Telegraph*, while *Private Eye* has covered the high points. We should be neither surprised nor worried by this low level of interest, for with devolution comes detachment. Scotland's affairs, viewed from a newsroom overlooking the Thames, are hardly going to be given priority rating. Like Chamberlain's Czechoslovakia we are now a little country, far away, and if we allow our elected representatives to make a mess of things we only have ourselves to blame.

Yet the problems of Holyrood are unlikely to remain Scotland's alone, for it was not a Scottish idea in the first place. There are several constitutional chickens out there, and they roost in Downing Street as well as Edinburgh. Scotland's MSPs may not exactly have covered themselves in glory over this issue, but the very least that can be said in their defence is that they had no say in the primary decisions. Under the doctrine of collective responsibility the UK Cabinet Office is the authority that brought the project into being. The Prime Minister himself has stated that all matters relating to Holyrood and its costs are the responsibility of the Scottish parliament. But how can this be, when the site was purchased, the architect hired, the project team put in place, and the first contracts let before the parliament existed?

Nor do the constitutional complications end there. If Scottish civil servants have a case to answer, they must answer to the UK Cabinet Office, where the scheme originated. Under the devolution settlement, civil service discipline is a matter reserved to Westminster. The Chief Secretary to the Cabinet Office Sir Richard Wilson would hardly be well placed if he had to censure his Edinburgh colleagues for complying with a decision that they had inherited from him. This may explain why they have been getting away with so much. The Downing Street linkage also calls into question the issue of payment. Why is the liability for a Downing Street decision falling exclusively on the Scottish budget? As for an answer to this perfectly straightforward question, expect there none. Neither the Prime Minister nor the Chancellor have room for manoeuvre, with sharp-eyed Conservative opponents taking a less than sanguine view of the notion that HM Treasury might assist the Scottish executive. New Labour, eager to keep faith with middle England's electorate, is unlikely to court a backlash from the shires by offering to bail out Holyrood.

As moral tales go, Holyrood is multi-faceted in its Aristotelian complexity, but for many it is summed up by the apparent intransigence of one man, Scotland's inaugural First Minister, the late Donald Dewar. The reality behind that common perception is opaque, but once penetrated tells us things about causes and motivations which the First Minister himself was at times only vaguely aware of. On the few occasions when we did exchange views I gained an impression of a man who refused (albeit with unfailing courtesy) to admit he was wrong. How was it that, as matters went from bad to worse, a politician of his status and experience allowed himself to be carried along by a project that ultimately could only have damaged his reputation? It seemed at times that just as Macbeth was 'so steept in blood' he felt compelled to continue with his folly, so Donald Dewar was in thrall to a series of events that were spinning out of control. Holyrood's story is a grim human drama, as well as a political scandal.

Then there's the architecture. This book tries to unravel the genesis of a building which, at the time of writing, doesn't exist. Writing this, I can only reflect on the first hesitant signs on the ground of a structure that we are assured will be ready in 2003, by which time it may be possible to judge, on the basis of its design and functionality, whether it was worth all the suffering and expense.

In the pages following, Holyrood is the starting point in a journey that transcends our own historic period and national boundaries. When politicians take it upon themselves to create monuments what are they actually doing? Is it a striving for legitimacy, a substitute for genuine policy, an assertion of real confidence, or a gesture of self-importance by a political élite indulging its own imagined magnificence through the medium of showpiece architecture? Or was the idea behind this Westminster-authored building really rooted in the disingenuous belief that power devolved is power retained? In other words, is Holyrood ultimately a last-gasp symbol of British democratic centralism masquerading as devolution, rather than a symbol of devolution itself?

The problem is not architecture, but the means by which it arrives. Those who wield power are entitled, perhaps even morally obliged, to bequeath a profound and lasting legacy of public buildings. The nobility of purpose implicit in Barry and Pugin's Palace of Westminster or Jefferson's Washington are visible reminders of this fact.

On the other hand an expensive signature building is not always, by definition, a pure expression of the democratic ideal. Consider Ceausescu's Bucharest, Speer's Berlin, or that modernist icon, Terragni's Casa del Fascio, by Lake Como. The buildings, as such, are mere volumes in space; some, like Terragni's, are beautiful, others not. It is their purpose and intent which provides 'meaning'. The Holyrood parliament building will have a particular look and style which we, and future generations, may judge on aesthetic merit. But meaning is another matter altogether. The result of an undemocratic act of iconoclasm, it owes its existence to the fact that a small coterie of civil servants and politicians were determined not to allow Scotland's new parliament to convene on Calton Hill. Holyrood may turn out to be a most wonderful modern building (though this is unlikely, given the limitations of the site, the tragic death of the architect, and the frantic budget paring) but it is inevitably condemned by its lack of democratic credentials.

In an age of warlords, when power came through force, large-scale buildings had a very specific meaning and cultural purpose. At that time architecture was used to confer legitimacy. In seventeenth-century Scotland, a quasi-tribal state largely abandoned by its Stuart monarchs, power and architecture were inseparable. The Duke of Lauderdale's great turreted castle of Thirlestane, for example, was a bombastic puff for his status and authority. The Holyrood parliament building is intended to capture a hint of neo-baroque bluster in its own way, as an edifice created by edict, but this hardly accords with the spirit of devolution. It is an anachronism before it has even been built, a denial, rather than an endorsement, of modern democratic process.

The difference between the two cases is that while Lauderdale, the ruthless demagogue, seemed to know exactly what he was about, our present ruling coalition has been so clueless about the purpose and meaning of their Holyrood project that they are more likely to undermine their legitimacy than anything else. As a chilling evocation of a tyrant's craving for power Thirlestane is a stunning success; as an emblem of the democratic will of the Scottish people Holyrood can only be regarded as a disastrous failure.

## 2 Donald Goes to Holyrood
### *The Democratic Inversion*

*He that builds a fair house upon an ill seat committeth
himself to prison*

Francis Bacon: 'Of Buildings'

THIS STORY IS about a political choice and its consequences.
In May 1997 the Labour Party swept into office with a manifesto commitment to devolution in Scotland and Wales. The
following September Scotland's electorate overwhelmingly
endorsed the new government's proposal to establish a parliament with tax-raising powers in Edinburgh. It was widely
anticipated that the first intake of Scottish parliamentary
representatives since 1707 would occupy 'New Parliament
House', a neoclassical building of some 25,000 square feet
on Edinburgh's Calton Hill. It was not to be.

The chances are that had the former Royal High School,
set in its grounds of two and a half acres, become Scotland's
parliament it might eventually have been found inadequate
on its own in terms of space and circulation. Meetings of
the Scottish Grand Committee had shown its strengths as
a debating chamber, but its weakness – a lack of space for
the press and visiting public – was also evident. The true
potential of the stunning classical building which a previous
Labour government had converted into a parliament in 1978
lay in its wider setting, where there was a substantial
surplus of vacant land and redundant buildings in an area
that just happened to be one of the most exciting civic
precincts in the world. Finding more space, or building a
new, state-of-the-art debating chamber nearby, would have
presented few problems.

But even before the general election hidden forces were

hard at work as meetings took place between Scottish
Office civil servants and Edinburgh council officials. Word
got around that certain mandarins and politicians were
unhappy about the potency of all this symbolism. Finally, on
29 September 1997, Donald Dewar announced at a Charter
88 fringe meeting at Labour's Brighton conference that he
was in effect going to ditch Calton Hill. Mr Dewar, his
mandarins and Downing Street wanted a waterfront 'signature' building in Leith more in tune with the rebranding
ethos of Mr Blair's new Britain. Influential forces within the
Scottish Labour Party, including MPs, privately denounced
this as a blatant 'dumbing-down' exercise imposed from
above. Edinburgh's Labour finance convener Brian Weddell
offered a prescient view about the government 'making a
hasty decision it might live to regret'. Mr Dewar's Leith
choice was, in effect, sunk by the party itself.

Yet a return to Calton Hill was not to be tolerated,
such was the strength of establishment hostility towards
it. For both the Scottish Office hierarchy and Labour's upper
echelons another site was considered essential. Holyrood
emerged, seemingly the perfect compromise, or, more accu-
rately, a convenient spoiler, for it was in central Edinburgh,
yet it wasn't Calton Hill. Politically expedient it may have
been, but in every other way it was the worst location
imaginable. An old brewery surrounded by historic buildings in a UNESCO World Heritage Site, it was notoriously
difficult to access. In terms of planning, sustainability, architectural flexibility and the potential damage to a setting that
included the ecologically important green space of Arthur's
Seat and Holyrood Park, it was a patently unsuitable parcel
of land for any large-scale public project.

Nor was it simply a matter of a site: it was the manner
in which the decision was being made. If this was meant
to be about a home for a devolved parliament, why was it
being decided by a London minister acting with the benefit
of collective cabinet responsibility? In Scotland the notion
that popular democracy lies at the heart of national identity
is a simple fact of history. A Reformation in the sixteenth

century, the emigration of a king in the seventeenth, and the loss of parliamentary sovereignty in the eighteenth, delivered much influence to the middle-class intelligentsia. By the literate nineteenth century political awareness was widespread throughout society. Scotland's democratic instinct has ancient roots. An embryonic notion of democracy is even expressed in the 1320 Declaration of Arbroath in which the 'community of the realm' reserved the right to remove the king (then Robert the Bruce) from office as a 'subverter' should he fail to discharge his duties.

For a London cabinet minister to assume imperial authority in deciding where a *devolved* legislature would conduct its business was a non-sequitur at odds with the currents of Scottish history. The closest precedent was in Helsinki, where Russia's Tsar Nicholas, under pressure from his pan-Slavists, vetoed Eliel Saarinen's proposal for a semi-autonomous Finnish parliament building. It was a damning comparison. Worse still, this London-imposed decision was uncomfortably redolent of that notorious faux pas of the 1980s, Mrs Thatcher's poll tax, the very measure which, in undermining confidence in the Conservatives, had helped to propel Labour into office in the first place.

Even the name of the site was questionable. 'Holyrood' was a useful label in so far as it was poached from a neighbouring royal palace and ancient abbey, and so conferred a measure of bogus respectability on the new institution, yet the real Holyrood is a very specific area around the royal precinct which once lay outside the jurisdiction of the city. It was a well-known debtors' sanctuary whose inhabitants had included the author Thomas de Quincey. Holyrood is identified to this day by brass markers, and the former brewery site lies outside its perimeter at the Watergate, a more accurate name geographically though, for obvious reasons, one unlikely to have much political appeal.* Apart from the American connotations, the Watergate had

---

* In the interests of clarity, the term 'Holyrood' will be used throughout to identify the project at the Watergate.

served a grim role in Edinburgh's past, being the point at which Charles I entered the city when the storm clouds of Cromwellian revolution were gathering, and where the rebellious Marquess of Montrose, shackled in a cart, was taken uphill to the Mercat Cross for his execution. It was also an appropriately sobering thought that the actor Ian 'Francis Urquhart' Richardson of *House of Cards* fame had his first job as an office boy in that same brewery.

In theory a line was drawn under the Holyrood débâcle on 5 April 2000 when the Scottish parliament, meeting in its temporary chamber on the Mound, voted by a majority of nine to press on with First Minister Dewar's scheme at the foot of Edinburgh's Canongate. In practice we weren't even halfway into the woods, never mind out of them. This was the second full debate on the building, and it was characterised on the ruling Labour and Liberal Democrat coalition side not so much by a thoughtful consideration of architectural issues as by a fevered search for an expedient fix. An amendment to Presiding Officer Steel's motion was moved by Labour's Gordon Jackson. Trumpeted more in hope than expectation, this stated that the project would be completed within a total budget of £ 195 million by late 2002.

A distinguished Queen's Counsel, Mr Jackson seemed not so much fired up with enthusiasm for the disaster-prone project as charged with salvaging his leader's reputation. He was eminently qualified. Many tabloid readers still recall his exploits as champion of Woofie the dog, saved by a moving courtroom peroration. Mr Dewar, too, needed his help. If Holyrood was scuttled the First Minister was almost certain to go with it. The prospect of a change of Labour leadership in the lead-up to a UK general election was not a happy one. Donald Dewar, whatever his faults, was a respected and experienced political operator.

Gordon Jackson was himself no stranger to controversy. Colourful private life apart, there was the small matter of how he came to be Govan's MSP in the first place. According to press reports at the time his selection had been no easy matter. Local resistance had culminated in the resignation of five members of the branch party, including its chairman, and the defection of a councillor to the SNP. Perceived in some quarters as Donald Dewar's place-man parachuted in to carry the New Labour message to one of the darker Old Labour fastnesses of west central Scotland, he now had it in his power to return the favour.

Mr Jackson's plea in mitigation was explicable within the context of the well-oiled Labour machine where displays of loyalty are part of the *modus vivendi*. Not so the role of Presiding Officer Sir David Steel, who according to Murray Ritchie in the *Herald* had made an arrangement with Mr Dewar days before the debate. The general perception that Sir David's function equated in some way to that of Speaker of the Commons Betty Boothroyd as a politically neutral mediating chairman fell to pieces when he stepped out from behind his desk and delivered an impassioned defence of the First Minister's beleaguered project, ending with words more appropriate to a field marshal at the Somme: 'Courage, brothers, do not stumble!'

In the event Holyrood was salvaged, and so too, it then seemed, was Mr Dewar's reputation. Forget buildings. Forget budgets. Labour's performance was desultory, the object of the exercise plain to see. This was a classic vote of confidence in a man whose future was seriously at risk. Holyrood's opponents made one cogent point after another, but the outcome was a foregone conclusion. The result predictably split along party lines, with only one Labour MSP (the congenitally honourable John McAllion) voting against the absurd extravagance of a scheme that was patently out of control. As far as the traditions of parliamentary debate were concerned, we had hit an all-time low.

Throughout the debate attention focused on the Liberal Democrats, since it was one of their number, Donald Gorrie, who had tabled the amendment to give consideration to all available sites. Mr Gorrie, who for reasons of honest conviction found himself cast in the role of Scotland's Martin Bell, did his best in the circumstances, but he clearly knew that his mission was doomed. The evening before, word had got out that the dealmakers had fixed everything. There would be a majority of between eight and ten. Individual Liberal Democrat MSPs later denied being pressurised, but the high-level arrangement had supplied the required majority. In some ways, this complicity was difficult to comprehend in a party that could ill-afford to give its largely rural constituents the impression that it was a creature of Labour's central-belt barons, particularly since, only weeks earlier, Lib Dem minds had been concentrated by their Ayr by-election disaster. Here was an opportunity to make a timely gesture of independence from Labour's machine politics, yet it was an opportunity all but three of them chose to miss.

And so Donald Dewar scraped through for the second time in a year, but his troubles were far from over. A parliament subjected to the rigours of national press coverage is rather different from a council meeting in some burgh chambers where, on a good day, the local cub reporter might look in. There were, quite simply, too many journalists who could see what was going on, too many professionals who were aware that the project was out of control, and too many MSPs who felt that Holyrood was a dangerous distraction which could ultimately undermine the devolution process itself. Was one man's arrogant determination worth such a price?

In Catalonia they have a word: *seny*. This carries a dual meaning. Used by a Catalan it denotes native wisdom and steadfastness; the equivalent, perhaps, of the Scots *smeddum*. Used by a Castilian, on the other hand, it is pejorative, suggesting arrogance, hubris and cussed determination. Linguists may take issue with this, but, if accurate, it captures a critical aspect of the Holyrood controversy, and since the conceptual building in question originates in Barcelona it is even more appropriate. The late Donald Dewar fell victim to *seny* when he ruled out Calton Hill as Scotland's parliament site at Labour's 1997 Brighton conference, and *seny* would pursue him remorselessly throughout his time as First Minister, but the *seny*, as we shall discover in due course, was not entirely his.

This second debate of April 2000, like the first of June 1999, was another Pyrrhic victory on the road to disaster. Mr Dewar secured a nine-vote majority and was visibly relieved, but his success came with sinister qualifications. His 'robust' figure of £109 million in the earlier debate had turned out to be no such thing when a 'lost' additional £27 million suddenly appeared. The reality was that press reports of the scheme reaching £230 million were now borne out by the facts. The obvious conclusion, namely that either the First Minister had lied to parliament, or that civil servants had witheld information from the First Minister, met with a breathtaking response. Yes, he had been deceived, but rightly so, he claimed, since his civil servants were only 'protecting' him from bad news.

The after-effects were almost surreal. A First Minister held in highest esteem by the electorate was pinning his defence on a confession of ignorance. Holyrood at this point stopped being an architectural vision and became a damage-containment exercise, the goal being to remove blame from all concerned. Brian Stewart of RMJM, architects of Victoria Quay, and government development chief John Gibbons left by the rear entrance deep in conversation as Donald Dewar strode up the back staircase pursued by a microphone-waving radio journalist. Labour MSPs emerged in sullen groups. They were, said one, off to a Christmas party. In April? Yes, I was assured. Confused turkeys, perhaps? Whatever, it didn't look as if it would be much of a do for Donald's less than exultant victors. Then came a bunch of nationalists, not remotely disconsolate; indeed, one announced that they were all heading off to the Jolly Judge for a celebratory drink. And who could blame them? They had just been handed a spectacular propaganda gift!

What exactly was going on here? The tactic was obvious. Labour's strategists had resorted to risk-assessment. They had, as they saw it, two options, each a white-knuckle gamble. Either stick with the leader, strong-arm the back-benchers, and ask the Lib Dems to vote with them. Or abandon Holyrood, and leave the First Minister open to the sort of ridicule that could destroy his political career. They had flunked the opportunity to devise an exit strategy which, no doubt, Gordon Jackson could have put together, if asked.

They didn't give themselves much of a choice, and the reason was plain to see. Labour was taking a hammering, and the need to close ranks behind a beleaguered leader was compelling. The party had already alienated many journalists after Alastair Campbell, Tony Blair and Donald Dewar had launched into Scotland's media for its off-message attitudes. A by-election disaster at Ayr had brought panic. Labour's poll ratings had plummeted, and the project was part of the problem. 'IS DEWAR DIGGING HIS OWN GRAVE AT HOLYROOD?' ran the headline over a *Scotland on Sunday* investigation. Subsequent events were to imbue those words with a more sombre significance than anyone then could possibly have guessed.

The simple fact was that, despite everything. Donald Dewar was Scottish Labour's best asset, with a charisma no other front-bencher could begin to match. He had clearly done himself little good with his obstinacy over Holyrood, but still commanded a level of public affection that brought his party much badly needed residual support. The alternatives as leader lacked the 'recognition factor' which he had enjoyed for years and, more to the point, they would have been out of their depth against Alex Salmond, whose formidable debating style and relaxed television manner had helped to make the SNP a serious political force. Donald Dewar was both tough and trusted. His hesitant manner, the bookish demeanour, the stern-but-fair image of a dominie were traits that served him well. A friend of the late John Smith, he had served under Wilson, and came with just enough Old Labour credentials to allay the Scottish voters' incipient distrust of the Blair regime. His spin-doctors found him unspinnable, yet that fact alone, in distancing him from the marketing style of Millbank's modernisers, added to his reputation at home.

Nor was Donald Dewar's political survival a matter of mere local interest for Scotland. The last thing Downing Street needed ahead of an election was the humiliating resignation of devolution's standard-bearer and an SNP surge in the polls. Middle England may have been the ground on which the 1997 election was fought, but for Labour the bulwark vote of the Scots and the Welsh secures the foundations of power. If these loyalties crumble the entire Westminster edifice is weakened. After the débâcle over Alun Michael in Wales it was even more important to consolidate Labour's core support in Scotland.

The *realpolitik* of the debate of April 2000, as in the debate of June 1999, was that Labour's Scottish troops had been given their marching orders, and being off-message would simply not be tolerated. The sole dissident was to be John McAllion, already beyond the pale, who assured me that no pressure was applied in his case. In other cases, a great deal of pressure was applied in what was technically billed a 'free vote'.

Yet this enforced support for Labour's Holyrood project was anything but risk-free. The constituents of most Labour MSPs were hardly cheerleaders for cash-squandering *leitmotiv* gestures, and Holyrood was becoming an embarrassment. A change of tone became noticeable as talk of an exciting 'architectural vision' and 'a building for the new Scotland' gave way to dark (and usually vague) warnings about the contractual liabilities of cancellation. The priority now was to keep the project on track and minimise the damage from the continuing adverse publicity by playing down the crisis.

Holyrood had assumed a momentum of its own, and the public looked on in disbelief. With this single, profligate decision the wittering on about 'inclusiveness' took on a decidedly hollow ring. You don't get much more exclusive than sixty-eight MSPs voting to set themselves up in a palatial signature building costing the same as a whole portfolio of hospitals and schools. As Simon Hoggart said on Radio 4's *Westminster Hour* to MSP Jamie Stone (a Lib Dem who had supported Labour's case) you could buy every one of Scotland's MSPs a Highland sporting estate for less!

While Labour politicians struggled with their increasingly less credible explanations the SNP and the Conservatives were spared the indignity of making excuses to their constituents. The Holyrood scandal had given both parties clear propaganda advantages, in particular the SNP. Where the nationalists of MacDiarmid's era were considered feckless romantics, the post-devolution brand, compared to Labour's confused ranks, took on the comforting air of safe centre-left Scandinavian social democrats in spite of their own *penchant* for disharmony. They didn't have to call in expensive image-consultants to create this reassuring persona. The Holyrood extravaganza was doing it for them.

Meanwhile the Conservatives, who had all but ceased to exist as a force in Scottish politics in May 1997, perked up. They'd spoken wistfully of a comeback then, and nobody, themselves included, believed a word of it. Suddenly, with the member for Ayr safely ensconced, they talked not just of survival, but actually dared to contemplate revival. Again, much of the credit for this was due to the Holyrood project.

The Ayr by-election held three weeks before the April debate exposed the damage both Labour and the Liberal Democrats were doing to themselves over Holyrood. In a Labour-held constituency where cutbacks in welfare provision for the elderly was a hot issue, the electorate were unimpressed by the notion that MSPs intended to set themselves up in palatial grandeur at the taxpayer's expense. The Conservatives gained their first non-list MSP while Labour was knocked into third place after the SNP, causing a wave of horror which even reached Westminster. One excited psephologist quickly extrapolated an all-Scotland result: if this performance were repeated in a general election the party would be devasted and the main beneficiaries would be the nationalists. A System Three poll taken the week before the debate confirmed Labour's worst fears when the SNP gained a four-point lead, its first since the parliament had opened. This raised the 'doomsday' question. Had Donald Dewar and the Holyrood fiasco taken us to the edge of the independence abyss?

This is a serious point, with serious implications, for although a building scandal in a relatively small north European city may seem like a parochial matter, it inevitably benefits the very cause that devolution was designed to marginalise: nationalism. This, together with Welsh alienation and the swings of middle England, could clearly affect Labour's prospects. It could also tip the balance towards Scottish independence. Whether you consider the break-up of Great Britain a good or bad thing, it would certainly be one of history's more momentous events, with repercussions extending well beyond our own boundaries, like the wingbeats of the butterfly. How would US foreign policy be affected, for example, if there was no Britain on the UN Security Council?

So much for the politics. What about the project itself? The debate of 5 April 2000, far from resolving matters, only raised more questions. It isn't as if we had the beginnings of a building, or even a completed design. Like a *Don Quixote* castle in the air, it remained little more than a concept. There was also a dramatic intervention from Sir David Steel in which a stunned chamber was informed that the architect was ill and would be 'stepping back' from the project. A design which, in its constantly evolving form, now bore scant resemblance to the winning entry, and had yet to rise from the ground, was not even to be overseen by its 'world-class' architect. It seemed that the construction process and final design was now up to RMJM, whose own submission to the 1998 competition had failed to make it past the first stage, though they would be paired off with Miralles at a late stage in the architectural competition. RMJM's Brian Stewart had conjured up a video-tour of a virtual parliament, and images resembling a 'Gotham City

meets Rug-rats' computer-generated futureworld appeared
in the press, but activity around the as yet unbuilt chamber
complex somehow had the eerie echo of the *Marie Celeste*.

The fact was that, vote or no vote, Holyrood continued
to be dogged by uncertainty. It was no longer clear who
the architect was, or when it would be ready. The costs
remained frighteningly indeterminate. Queensberry House,
the urban palace where the very idea of Great Britain was
dreamed up in 1707, was possibly to be demolished. The
design, layout and scale of the proposed complex had
metamorphosed into one thing, then another. In a manner
reminiscent of a cabal of medieval bishops disputing the
length of the devil's toenails, the form had moved from
boats, to rocks, then leaves, and finally towers. The public, bemused, looked on in consternation as the Scottish
executive tied itself in knots and well-briefed critics such
as Donald Gorrie and Margo MacDonald kept the pressure up.

No matter; by May 2000 MSPs were in possession of a
glossy A3 brochure and a swatch of A4 ground plans and
elevations. By mid-June the 'Stage D' presentation was
signed off, meaning there was now enough of a design
actually to start doing some real building work on the
chamber complex. There was even a strategic programme
table which indicated that the assembly building would be
handed over 'ready for loose furniture' some time around
mid-December 2002, with external and landscaping works
being completed by late June 2003 – a mere three years
behind the schedule predicted in September 1997!

There was also a 'progressing group' of MSPs. This wasn't
quite a cross-party affair: the Conservatives, perhaps wisely,
kept their distance. Ministers too seemed a mite circumspect
about getting involved. Sir David Steel's 'Corporate Body',
the parliament management committee, was still technically
the project client, though it had retired to lick its wounds,
having apparently served a useful purpose as an exculpation
mechanism for the decision which had brought the crisis
about in the first place. There was uncertainty about the

precise role of the progressing group, with some claiming that its remit was merely to be consulted and offer advice, though committee member Linda Fabiani of the SNP insisted that it would have the authority to hire, fire and make decisions.

We were off at last. Or were we? This finalised package, it seemed, was a *fait accompli* yet according to Edinburgh's City Planning Department the matter hadn't even been placed on the Planning Committee agenda, far less given approval. The design was still in flux, and even the choice of materials for its external cladding would take a further five months to determine. Enric Miralles, we had been told, had taken a back seat, so who was in charge? Not project manager Barbara Doig, a veteran of RMJM's Victoria Quay scheme, who was 'moved sideways' in May to another civil service department. RMJM's Brian Stewart had taken a lead role as a source of press information, but the fact that he was an engineer, rather than an architect, did not escape the notice of the project's critics.

Mystery also surrounded the architect's rumoured illness. While the head of the progressing group, Lewis MacDonald, insisted that Enric Miralles was working regularly on the project on his laptop, others were adamant that he was dangerously ill, with one close friend attributing some, at least, of the architect's health problems to his difficulties over Holyrood. A particularly galling moment had come, it seems, in mid-May when the contractors, Bovis Lend Lease, had reportedly assumed greater control of the project, in effect limiting the role of Miralles' office. He was said to be furious.

Enric Miralles died in his native city, Barcelona, on 3 July 2000, leaving a wife and two young children. With the death of the architect, Donald Dewar's Holyrood project was instantly stripped of its last vestige of credibility. Even so, his determination to see it through to the bitter end remained undiminished. The appeal now was to a perverse kind of logic. A still evolving building which posterity was unlikely to recognise as the work of Enric Miralles was to become his 'memorial'. The link would be preserved by keeping his widow on the team, though in what capacity it was not quite clear, since she had not been a co-entrant to the first stage of the competition. Members of Miralles' profession were not entirely convinced: to some it seemed that the real benefits, including the lion's share of fees of around £26 million, would accrue to RMJM. The profession was guarded in its comments – RMJM had already had a writ served on one architect for some critical comments – but the drift was clear. Was this a Miralles masterwork, or simply an ordinary workmanlike RMJM re-rendering of some of his ideas? Margo MacDonald suggested the best option, in the circumstances, might be to abandon the scheme altogether. She was reprimanded by Sir David Steel for making a remark in poor taste. Taste was not an issue, however, when the fax that Miralles had transmitted to RMJM the day before his operation, and a full week before David Steel's 'surprise' announcement during the debate, was posthumously released by the company to the *Herald* in an attempt to suggest that Miralles had, in any case, considered his role complete. Someone, somewhere, had decided to keep this critical information from MSPs ahead of the debate.

This was one of the grimmest moments of a project with so many negatives attached to it the wonder was it had survived at all. Holyrood had begun life as a clever compromise between Leith and Calton Hill. It was the choice that no one, including Donald Dewar, had actually wanted. Above all, it was a constitutional paradox: Scots had voted for devolution, and yet were told to accept Downing Street's choice of site. In the event fewer than half the MSPs supported it in June 1999.

If the victory secured at this second debate was meant to draw the sting from the scandal it was a forlorn hope. For one thing, at £230 million the cost overruns were of world record proportions. MSPs struggled to maintain the pretence of a capped £195 million budget but the Auditor General for Scotland was on the case. His report of September

2000 used measured language, as one might expect, but the conclusions were devastating, and gave the lie to the 'official' £195 million, which, it turned out, was based on 1998 figures, non inflation-adjusted, and conveniently excluded costs for landscaping and access totalling around £14 million. The indications were that the final cost could top £250 million. The building that nobody had asked for in the first place was now set to do serious damage to Scotland's budget.

There was no escaping the Holyrood scandal. In 1998 I had asked Donald Dewar exactly what his rationale had been in ditching the Calton Hill parliament building without any reference to democratic process and substituting it with an expensive modern alternative. The answer was predictable enough: devolution was a new process, and a new building was appropriate. End of story. Then, almost flippantly, he added, 'Of all the issues I've had to deal with as Secretary of State, this is the one I've most needed a flak jacket for.'

That metaphorical flak jacket would never be put away. Throughout his time as First Minister, according to his head of policy, Brian Fitzpatrick, Donald Dewar 'reached the black depths' as a result of 'discomfort and anxiety about the unknown hidden costs of the Holyrood project', and became exasperated with civil servants who seemed to be constantly keeping him less than fully briefed on the subject. The critical coverage that followed the Auditor General's report (run by *Private Eye* amongst others) piled on further pressure. The story refused to go away. In early October it emerged that a 'mystical' 40,000 square feet had 'come to light', which had been quietly added by the design team. The completion date, too, was threatening to collide with the next Scottish elections, while the £195 million 'capped' budget was redefined as a hoped-for target. Unattributed 'well-placed sources' referred to expected all-inclusive final costs in excess of £300 million.

Downing Street and Dover House, worried about the electoral fallout, made their views known in rumoured high-level frank exchanges. An all-Scotland repeat of Ayr in a May 2001 UK election was, naturally, a horrifying prospect. Accounts of furious outbursts in which white-faced civil servants scuttled from the First Minister's office became commonplace.

Donald Dewar, still recovering from a heart operation, was seen to be buckling under the strain. Holyrood was not his only problem. The chaos following a systems breakdown in the Scottish Qualifications Authority had also rocked the executive; but Holyrood was uniquely associated with the First Minister in the public mind, and criticism was directed at him personally. His colleagues, increasingly concerned about his deteriorating health, played down the problem, but when his car had to be driven into the forecourt of the Mound building as he walked gingerly down the steps it became obvious that all was not well.

Donald Dewar died on 11 October in an Edinburgh hospital after a stumble at his official residence, Bute House, in Charlotte Square. Scotland was stunned, and the tributes poured in from across the world. The deep sense of loss was accompanied by a foreboding that the vacuum at the centre of his devolution legacy was going to be difficult to fill. His self-deprecating style was never presidential, and he famously disowned the term 'father of the nation', but few doubted that his 'class act' would be a hard one to follow.

'I will carry the can', Donald Dewar had said, announcing his inclination to veto Calton Hill in September 1997. Just how many people had he carried this can for? What was Downing Street's role, and who were the civil servants behind the idea? Where did his fellow politicians stand on the issue? The reality is that Donald Dewar was never the sole inspiration behind the Holyrood project, however enthusiastically he advanced it in public. Nor can he be held entirely responsible for ruling out the Calton Hill parliament in the first instance. This was being carefully written out of the script long before the 1997 general election, and its demise was being aired at private meetings in the Scottish Office well in advance of the

September referendum. As it happens, a participant in one of those first key meetings was an ambitious young Westminster MP.

His name was Henry McLeish.

# 3  Designing Devolution
## Labour's Divided Self

> *Let not England forget her precedence of teaching*
> *nations how to live*
> John Milton: *The Doctrine and Discipline of Divorce*

TO APPRECIATE WHAT the symbolism of the Holyrood parliament is going to be, it helps to understand what devolution was meant to be. It is a word that eludes precise definition. It is generally thought of as a delegation of power by central government to a local or regional administration. Straightforward enough. Yet we are also told it is 'a process, not an event', which introduces an element of viscosity. There are those (invariably unionists and nationalists on their one patch of common ground) who claim it is an illusory half-state on a par with being slightly virginal.

It doesn't take a cynic to see what devolution really is, however, which is quite simply a neat constitutional device whereby the nationalist threat would, in Lord Robertson's famous words, be 'killed stone dead'. It is also a policy that carries a degree of risk: get it wrong, and Scotland might just start trundling along Tam Dalyell's 'motorway without an exit'. Get it right, and nationalism becomes an irrelevance. Getting it wrong, big-style, has been the principal characteristic of the Holyrood project to date.

Before we can appreciate what the Holyrood *v* Calton Hill *v* Leith scam was about we must consider its underlying theme: devolution itself. First, the above quotation from Milton needs qualifying. This issue is not about England's precedence at all. Rather, it concerns the power neurosis of a British government whose ruling élite, as it happens, contains many Scots who really ought to have known better.

If ever there was a government that ought to have been sensitive to the issue of how to set about locating a parliament in Edinburgh it was surely the one formed by Tony Blair in May 1997, yet it messed up spectacularly, then dumped the predictable problems on Scotland's fledgling institution before absolving itself of all responsibility.

The reasons for this high-handed approach are not difficult to find. Professor Peter Hennessy has identified the Prime Minister's style as 'Napoleonic'; an exaggeration perhaps, yet the Blair ethos is hardly consensual. He pays less heed to his National Executive Committee, his cabinet colleagues, and even parliament itself, than any of his predecessors. For the Blair regime, a key determinant of policy is presentation, and the creation of a symbolic devolved parliament is, above all, a presentational issue.

Mr Blair's current problem with Labour's Scottish dimension is nothing new. The Calton Hill veto, indeed, is simply the latest manifestation of a century-old angst. The Holyrood controversy is about more than buildings, sites, costs, or 'modernity versus heritage'. Its roots lie in Labour's ambivalent relationship with the principle of Scottish self-government. For other leaders, too – Harold Wilson, James Callaghan and John Smith in particular – the nub has been not so much one of power devolved for its own sake, as of conceding just enough devolution to satisfy the home-rule aspirations of the electorate while maintaining the Scottish bulwark vote at Westminster.

A paradox of the Blair project was that while it played down its socialist past it was adept at using historical reference points to pragmatic effect. The Labour movement was born of late eighteenth-century working-class resistance to oppressive laws, and internal discipline was a necessary *coda*. Loyalty and unity, cherished as virtues when the ruling establishment was hostile, were to become useful emotional cornerstones when the party itself became the ruling establishment. To this day, the sentimental appeal to harmony is frequently resorted to by the leadership, and it follows that any sectionalist ambition which contradicts this tenet, be it a call to grass-roots action, or a demand for devolved government, puts strain on Labour's democratic-centralist instincts.

Labour has always been an association of shades of doctrinal interest, rather than a monolith, and this frustrates the leadership's desire for vertical control. A particularly sensitive fracture has long been the one between the party in Scotland and the Labour establishment in London. From the start, Scottish socialism was fundamentally different from its English equivalent. At the first meeting of the Socialist League in 1884 a dispute arose about the rights of the Scots to set up their own organisation with its own membership lists, without reference to London's party hierarchy. 'Our executive do not see any necessity for seeking any authorisation from your executive,' thundered James Mavor, the Scottish secretary. Awareness of a separate identity was evident at the Paris Conference of the Second International, where Keir Hardie ferociously interrupted any speaker who called him English. Not surprisingly, when the Scottish Labour Party was formed in 1888 the demand for a Scottish parliament was at the top of its agenda.

Scots radicals were frequently dismissive of an English socialist-liberal tradition which favoured the ameliorative benefits of gradual reform over the hazards of agitation. Scotland's working classes in general enjoyed higher levels of literacy than those of their English counterparts thanks to post-Reformation parish education, and this enabled them to organise and communicate effectively. In essence, socialism in Scotland was more demotic than patriarchal, with its roots in literacy and elementary education. Not for nothing did the reactionary eighteenth-century Professor John Robinson of Edinburgh condemn circulating libraries as 'nurseries of sedition and impiety'.

In England, by contrast, the philanthropical middle classes were the ascendant group. Some, like William Morris, sought to live an 'ideal' socialist life (though still with servants). John Ruskin, doyen of the socialist intelligentsia, was hardly the quintessential Victorian Englishman,* but his patriarchal values reflected those of a wider metropolitan cognoscenti which assumed for itself a leading role in the movement for social reform. As individuals they may have been committed to the cause, but the ethos of these southern urban radicals, as far as many of the more gritty Scots were concerned, was corrupted by their unrepentant bourgeois habits – a foretaste, perhaps, of the Scottish old left's disdain for the backsliding Islington apparatchiks of New Labour, with their alleged love of Tuscan holidays, seared polenta and celebrity networking. England's centre-left establishment has generally reciprocated with a deep-seated anxiety about the volatility of Scots radicalism.

For New Labour, a party that seeks to present a unified and increasingly homogenised image to the voting public, devolution is a particularly awkward policy, for it is, by definition, about one group of the electorate choosing to be different from the mainstream, and if that one group can assert its own interests, why can't the others? Persuading the public that a hazy 'third way' promises a new world of social harmony is something of an achievement, but it is also a fragile consensus which only survives if the truce between society's factions can be maintained.

This truce was a desperate necessity, brokered after eighteen years in opposition, but it was also a pragmatic arrangement which recognised that you don't get elected by parading your differences on the conference floor. In the months leading up to May 1997 the Millbank machine's mission was to secure the election of a Labour government. Presentation was critical. This was a matter of an image being successfully projected, while the internal divisions of a century-old political party were airbrushed into oblivion.

* Ruskin acknowledged an indirect debt for his own intellectual development to the rector of Edinburgh's High School, Dr Alexander Adam. His father, John James Ruskin, had been a pupil there, and was friendly with the Glasgow-born stonemason's son, Thomas Hamilton, who would later design the new school building on the Calton Hill.

The brand on offer was a party with a non-pluralist programme for power.

Devolution, with its potential for discord, ultimately
threatened this veneer of unified purpose, and had to be
controlled. Edinburgh, Cardiff and civic London offered
the worrying prospect of power bases being developed
by factions of the traditional left which might challenge
the authority, and even the sovereignty, of Westminster.

In Wales, the party's internal tensions were vividly revealed
in a gladiatorial leadership contest between Downing Street's
favoured apparatchik, Alun Michael, and brooding son
of the valleys Rhodri Morgan. Michael's victory patently
stitched up courtesy of a voting system designed to out-
franchise the constituency membership, was a PR disaster
for Labour. In the election that followed there was a 30 per
cent swing to Plaid Cymru in the Rhondda, the Welsh heartland equivalent of Strathclyde. The loss of this, Labour's
second safest Westminster seat, and the failure to win control of the assembly was compounded by Rhodri Morgan's
personal success when, alone amongst Labour's candidates,
he exceeded his general election majority. Downing Street's
humiliation was complete when Morgan replaced the hapless First Secretary Alun Michael for the leadership of the
assembly, redesignating himself 'First Minister'. London
Labour MP Ken Livingstone, standing as an independent,
likewise trounced a forlorn Frank Dobson, Labour's candidate, in the contest to become mayor of London, leaving
a tarnished government open to yet more accusations of
stitch-up politics.

The Welsh and London débâcles were merely two aspects
of the fragmentary potential of party control. Labour's post-
war history is characterised by the centre's perpetual struggle to maintain control over its aberrant factions. For Tony
Blair's New Labour, forged out of the epic internal battles
of the 1980s, the politics of schism and dispute represent a
discredited past, while the harmony of all parts amounts to
a political state of grace. This became all the sweeter with
that defining moment in May 1997 when it seemed that

homogeneity had triumphed. Conformity was an article of faith for Labour's leadership. The flawed dynamic underlying the Holyrood controversy was that Westminster's diktat was entirely at odds with the decentralising trend which was the point of devolution in the first place.

In the rebranded Labour Party, pluralism coexists uneasily with the ubiquity that is now New Labour's stock-in-trade. Conferences, *pace* America's political rallies, become staged events where delegates (at least on camera) are meant to adore the leader, not heckle him. It is an approach that seems to have been vindicated by the election result, yet as events have shown it is hardly an unqualified success. To stifle opinion is to nurture resentment. It gives the unsettled fringes something to kick against.

The gut fear of devolution is by no means the exclusive prerogative of Westminster's modernisers. Its opponents have included entrenched radicals who held old-left values of international solidarity, municipal barons who had enjoyed decades of unchallenged power-broking, and the *nomenklatura* in a quango industry rooted in networking and patronage. Not so long ago many on the left regarded nationalism as pernicious, even dangerous, inviting dark comparisons with the rise of European fascism.

For today's left-wingers such as Brian Wilson and Robin Cook there is a less apocalyptic, if equally dismissive, view of devolution. It threatens the mechanism of government by providing opportunities for strife, and a political ratchet which leads inexorably to break-up of the UK. By this analysis the compelling logic of Tam Dalyell's 'motorway without an exit' on the road to independence is a self-evident truism.

The counter-argument proceeds from the belief that devolution is a device for outflanking those who seek total independence. As a package that combines the benefits of autonomy within the framework of unionism it is designed to satisfy a sense of Scots nationhood while preserving intact the structure of the British state.

Devolution is an inherited pledge which the Blair government had no choice but to concede, yet it is anathema to its innate philosophy, for it flatly contradicts the instinctive Blairite requirement to consolidate power at the top. The Prime Minister and his advisers have trimmed back the Westminster parliament by, amongst other things, lengthening the recess, shortening Prime Minister's question time, and creating the sort of second chamber that would have delighted Robert Walpole. This discernible shift of power from a legislature to an executive contradicts the fundamental principle of devolution which, by definition, is about the reduction of a centralised authority's hold on power. The pragmatic containment policy for nationalism which Blair inherited from Wilson, Callaghan and Smith only works if he can control his Scottish and Welsh party machines. If they prove troublesome, the prospect of nemesis looms.

Labour's 1997 Scottish conference demonstrated devolution's potential for releasing the radical Scots genie from London's 'command and control' bottle. Angered by proposed single parent benefit cuts, delegates tore into the party hierarchy with the sort of vitriol once reserved for the Thatcher regime, labelling them 'economically inept, morally repugnant, and spiritually bereft'. Alastair Campbell was visibly shaken. 'A fucking parish council is what they deserve, and a fucking parish council is what they'll get,' he bellowed, to the astonishment even of those in the press gallery accustomed to his tough style. Clearly a Jeffersonian temple to democracy on Calton Hill was hardly an option. To no one's surprise, the following year's Scottish conference was given a Millbank makeover.

Yet Campbell was merely voicing doubts that had troubled his party for decades. More than a century had passed since Keir Hardie had endorsed Scottish home rule. It yielded to an internationalist view of socialism between the wars, but never quite died out. Some, such as Secretary of State Tom Johnston, described themselves as patriotic Scots, and the home-rule issue still occasionally surfaced, but the trend was towards centralism. This was epitomised by the pre-war reduction of Scottish local authority powers, a measure carried through despite the opposition of Scots Labour MPs.

For the party of Attlee and Gaitskell the home-rule question was of minor significance. The big issues were post-war economic reconstruction, the new health service, and the provision of housing and education. Despite the 1½ million signatures of the Scottish Covenant for home rule, nationalism was never really regarded as a threat, and there were few appeals to 'Scottishness'. Labour politicians such as James Maxton, who had at one time subscribed to the romantic-nationalist values of Cunninghame Graham and had even been castigated by MacDiarmid for his prickly Scottish chauvinism, lost momentum when they became *habitués* of Westminster. Maxton, indeed, was latterly given to making sinister, if fanciful, links between Scottish nationalism and fascism. Labour's 1958 Scottish conference overwhelmingly opposed devolution on the grounds that Scotland's problems could 'best be solved by socialist planning on a UK scale'. Central demand management had become a core belief.

While there were some specifically Scottish initiatives taken under Labour, such as the creation of the North of Scotland Hydro Electric Board, political devolution, as such, was never a comfortable option for the party of centralised planning. Labour secretaries of state, like the provincial governors of classical Rome, had a critical role as mediators between the chieftains of the industrial and municipal Scottish left on the one hand and the Cabinet Office and Whitehall on the other. A consummate operator like the guileful Willie Ross knew how to deliver the Scottish vote to Westminster in exchange for tribute in the form of subvention, though the long-term value of projects such as Dounreay and the Invergordon smelter were questionable.

In the two decades following the last war Labour was Scotland's dominant political force. The nationalists, led by a kenspeckle assortment of characters and much derided by an unsympathetic press, were of little consequence, despite one short-lived electoral victory when SNP's Dr Robert McIntyre won a parliamentary by-election. The Tories garnered their votes from class and commercial interests, for the most part, and the Liberals from the declining rural constituencies.

Professor Henry Drucker of Edinburgh University has described the case of a Labour MP of the 1950s who, as soon as he was elected, went off on an eighteen-month overseas jaunt. On his return he was presented with a large quantity of constituency mail which he blithely threw into the bin. Drucker spoils his tale rather by suggesting it might be apocryphal, but the point is made: the Labour establishment of the time took Scotland for granted and regarded the voter with disdain. It certainly didn't want to think about devolving power, particularly since it would have undermined those bastions of authority, the large municipalities of the central belt.

Despite the complacency, Labour's hegemony was not as absolute as it seemed. In Scotland's post-war elections only one party ever breached the magical 50 per cent threshold: the Conservatives. Labour's fiefdoms gave the impression of being impregnable, however, and in most of the industrial areas the party benefited from the loyal efforts of constituency activists. This, typically, was the power base which upheld the Labour ascendancy, but by the mid-1960s the ranks were thinning, the activists getting older. Then, almost overnight, there was another force to be reckoned with. Nationalism.

When Harold Wilson was confronted with a 1967 by-election meltdown at Hamilton devolution became a big issue for Labour. Winnie Ewing's SNP victory led to the creation of the 1969 Royal Commission on the Constitution, and then to the Kilbrandon Report of 1973 which recommended the establishment of devolved assemblies for Scotland and Wales elected on the basis of proportional representation.

Devolution would come to mean different things to different people in the Labour Party, but for the hierarchy it has always been essentially a reactive policy rather than a deeply held philosophical belief. Margo MacDonald's 1973 Govan by-election victory for the SNP, a salutory re-run of the Hamilton rout, was another defining moment. Wilson, then in opposition, personally accepted devolution as a mechanism that had to be carefully calibrated to deal with the threat of nationalism. A statistician by both training and instinct, he was also enough of a pragmatist to grasp that regaining power in Westminster meant keeping the Labour-voting Scots on board, and if the price was to concede a measure of decision-making on domestic affairs, then he was prepared to pay it. He was deeply hostile to the pro-devolutionary views of intellectuals such as John Mackintosh, and ensured that the latter could never gain enough of a power base to cultivate a pro-devolutionist coterie, while at the same time he isolated those such as Tam Dalyell who claimed devolution would ultimately be unworkable. The *raison d'être* of Wilson's devolution was, patently, to derail the SNP's 'It's Scotland's oil' bandwagon.

Labour's reactive strategy came into play once more in February 1974 when the party regained power after Heath's disastrous spat with the miners. Wilson's victory was a narrow one, not helped by the fact that the SNP now had seven MPs. Reading the runes, the party did a *volte face* on its anti-devolution beliefs at a special conference in Glasgow where, ironically, it was the trade union block vote that imposed London's will on a reluctant membership. Labour had committed itself in the white paper 'Democracy and Devolution: Proposals for Scotland and Wales'. This accepted a number of Kilbrandon's key recommendations. Though still a containment strategy for nationalism, it was decisive in that it made devolution a plank of national policy.

As a means of stemming nationalism, however, it was ineffectual. At the second 1974 general election, held a few weeks after the paper's publication, the SNP increased its representation to eleven seats, a total which, if anything, understated the threat, for its percentage share was a mere six points behind Labour's. Another white paper appeared the following month: 'Our Changing Democracy: Devolution to Scotland and Wales'. This formed the basis of the Scotland Bill which became law in 1978, and which stipulated that a binding referendum on devolution should be held.

At this point Edinburgh's former Royal High School entered the lists. Labour's commitment became a physical reality in 1977 when the government's Property Services Agency was instructed to convert the main building in readiness for its role as a Scottish assembly. A design team under architect Bill Pritchard carried out a minimal scheme, creating a new public entrance and fitting out the former school assembly hall with dark green leather upholstered benches linked to a voting console. The full 'turnout' cost was estimated at £3.4 million, though since the contract was not progressed to completion less than £3 million was actually spent.

Scotland had its parliament-in-waiting, albeit no more than a focus for an aspiration with an iconographic significance rather than an actual purpose, but it was a powerful symbol. It was also the moment at which the two words 'Calton Hill' became synonymous with 'Scottish parliament'.

But devolution was still, under Callaghan, a matter of conceding as little as possible. On 25 January 1979 – Burns Day, no less – the Islington Labour MP George Cunningham successfully moved an amendment which set a minimum 40 per cent threshold of the entire electorate for the 'yes' vote. The government, mired in Winter of Discontent unpopularity, declared its support for the 'yes' campaign.

In March, despite a 33 per cent 'yes' vote to 31 per cent for 'no', the referendum failed to deliver. The Cunningham amendment had done its job, which was, expressly, to safeguard the union and undermine the surge of nationalism. In the event, however, it was to do the Labour Party little good. The following May the Conservatives under Margaret Thatcher swept into power, and devolution once more became a sideshow to the new business of UK politics: the pursuit of ideological free-market radicalism.

Yet nationalism remained the pressure valve of the Scottish protest vote. Labour's nightmare recurred in Govan in

1988 when Jim Sillars took the seat for the SNP, wiping out a 19,000 majority. The devolution dance was resumed in earnest with John Smith as choreographer, while Donald Dewar championed the cross-party Constitutional Convention and waxed lyrical about 'independence in the UK'. The policy was no longer a mere strategy for containing nationalism. It was also a wedge in the battle against Thatcherism, providing Labour with patriotic credentials to offset the Anglocentric Tories. John Smith had displayed a measure of ambivalence on aspects of Kilbrandon's report and as Michael Foot's deputy with responsibility for devolution had undermined John Mackintosh's bid to include proportional representation in the 1977 Bill. Three years earlier he had opposed devolution, arguing that it would weaken Scotland's position in the UK cabinet, but he bowed to public opinion in the mid-1980s, and campaigned vigorously for a 'Calton Hill parliament'. When the SNP turned its back on the convention in 1989 for an all-or-nothing independence policy Labour laid claim to devolution as its own initiative, albeit with support from Churches, trade unions, Liberal Democrats and even a few sympathetic Tories and business leaders.

It was a campaign that Smith conducted both inside and outside the party, and the scale of the operation was daunting. He not only had to persuade his often lukewarm Westminster colleagues that the policy was critical to Labour's prospects; he also had to convince doubters amongst the ranks of Labour's Scottish National Executive and privilege-conscious local authority barons as well as members of the Institute of Directors and the CBI Scotland, fearful of the effects of devolution on business.

When, as shadow Chancellor, John Smith was engaged in a 'prawn cocktail offensive' designed to persuade corporate Britain that Labour had given up its anti-business ways, he addressed a gathering of company chiefs in Erskine House, Edinburgh. The Scottish business community at that time was overwhelmingly hostile to devolution and Smith had come to offer reassurance. He later submitted himself to a question and answer session with the press in a side room, where I raised the thorny point of the Cunningham amendment. How could the electorate trust Labour to deliver when a decade earlier the party had sabotaged the outcome with its 40 per cent rule? Smith brushed this aside as 'old history'. Devolution was now at the heart of Labour's policy, and it would apply in the English regions, as well as Scotland and Wales.

We had a drink together afterwards and I raised a further problem: the awkward symbolism of the building on Calton Hill which, I suggested, had been tainted because of its indelible association with Labour's failed referendum. His response was forthright: 'We can't run away from it; we must confront it.' He made the point with emphasis, even raising his hand. There was no doubt, no equivocation. He was then, and has been since, accused of a certain pragmatic ambivalence over his attitude to devolution, but on this question he clearly harboured no doubts. John Smith evidently appreciated one point that Donald Dewar would later fail to grasp. The most effective way to neutralise a difficult symbol is to adopt it as your own, just as Germany's politicians have since done with the Reichstag.

An architectural symbol is a key image in any national political venture, and in some respects it is especially important where devolution is concerned, for as an exercise in shared sovereignty it comes with a critical in-built disadvantage. As a 'brand', devolution lacks the virtue of clarity and the capacity to appeal to simple patriotic emotions. It is a working compromise, and though it may go some way towards satisfying aspirations of self-determination it is also about not yielding up power from the centre. If Westminster miscalculates the degree to which power should be ceded, friction will follow, inviting those who oppose devolution to exploit its inherent flaw, which is that it is neither independence, nor unionism, but a synthetic construct lying uneasily between the two. To be an effective strategy devolution must maintain an equilibrium between those opposing forces. If it fails to do so, the mechanism is put under strain and can fail altogether.

The irony of the Holyrood scandal is that it subverts the inherent purpose of Labour's own devolution strategy. All those years of agonised calculation which were finally distilled into a working policy have been put at risk thanks to an issue that need never have arisen in the first place. If the Royal High School had assumed its parliamentary role as a functioning building, rather than an imagined 'nationalist shibboleth', the Labour Party would have saved itself a mountain of trouble. It might also have saved the Scottish taxpayer a few hundred million pounds.

The most mystifying aspect of the entire, tortuous Holyrood episode was that it simply wasn't necessary. If a few politicians and civil servants had set aside their fear of Calton Hill it is more than likely that MSPs themselves would sooner or later have gone for something new and purpose-built. This, with the benefit of hindsight, is what should have happened. So why did an administration with the largest majority in modern British history decree otherwise? A love of big-signature *leitmotiv* architecture? A neurosis about controlling the aberrant Celtic fringes? An innate belief in the superiority of its own metropolitan sense of values?

Or were Mr Blair and his colleagues simply sending us a message about the sort of devolution they had in mind? And might they, by any chance, have blown it?

# 4 The Mortgaged Ideology
## Labour Reinvents Itself

> *And he that sat upon the throne said, Behold, I make*
> *all things new*
>> Revelation of St John the Divine 21: 6

IN SEPTEMBER 1997, more than a century after home rule had first become Scottish Labour Party policy, Tony Blair's New Labour government finally delivered devolution. Within days, the word was out that this new Scotland would, at London's behest, be getting a brand-new 'signature' parliament, rather than the existing chamber-in-waiting on Calton Hill. The project was to be a monument for our times, a defining architectural gesture representing a return of self-determination after three centuries of rule from Westminster. By any objective assessment, of course, it was the antithesis of self-determination, being the outcome of a decision taken in Downing Street when the legislature in Edinburgh hadn't even been elected. Before heaping criticism on those MSPs who were subsequently foolish enough to persist with Holyrood as it careered out of control, however, it should be borne in mind that it wasn't their idea in the first place. As far as Holyrood, Calton Hill, or Leith were concerned, self-determination didn't have so much as a look-in.

The anticipated Scottish parliament building, in a very real sense, was going to be the architecture of imperialism, imposed by a central authority; but this was not the imperialism of Palmerston, of Lutyen's New Delhi, or of Nathaniel Curzon. Rather, it celebrated the triumph of the *fettuccine revolution*, an élite metropolitan programme for restyling the face of Britain. The instigators of the new imperial mandate were anything but grim-faced chiefs-of-staff huddling over maps in the War Office, or a patrician cabal discussing affairs of state over port and cigars in the Carlton Club: on the contrary, they were the casual-smart and politically influential *elegante* of such ritzy New Labour watering-holes as the River Café. A much more engaging and hedonistic group, no doubt, deploying glamour and charm rather than heavy weaponry in its mission to eliminate the barbarities of the unenlightened, but as determined as any military-colonial juggernaut in achieving its ends.

Lurking beneath the plans for Edinburgh there was some quirky New Labour psychology at work. The devolution package was very much a Labour creation, but it was one that the modernised party of Blair, Gould and Mandelson had inherited with some unease. A prevailing concern was that the autonomy of Edinburgh, Cardiff and civic London should be carefully circumscribed so that potential rifts between Westminster and the emerging legislatures could be held in check. The Prime Minister was constantly having to reassure devo-sceptics such as Jack Straw (who strongly resisted the loss of many reserved powers) while simultaneously giving a general impression that devolution was a continuing commitment which he supported with enthusiasm.

It was one thing for Mr Blair to mollify his Commons colleagues with comforting homilies about sovereignty staying with him, or the Edinburgh parliament being akin to a parish council, but quite another when these sentiments turned up in the Scottish press, where they invited accusations of London control-freakery. Given devolution's game plan it was self-evident that this was a policy package that was going to have to be delicately orchestrated if irksome problems were to be avoided.

In the event caution was to be eclipsed by hubris. The Labour landslide of May 1997 followed one of the most successful general election campaigns in British history and the result seemed to vindicate everything Prime Minister Tony Blair and his modernising inner circle stood for. The 179 majority, thirty-three more than Attlee's 1945 triumph, far exceeded even the most optimistic expectations of Labour's campaign managers. The Blairs' entry into Downing Street recalled Margaret Thatcher's 1979 début, and though we were spared the doorstep quotation from St Francis of Assisi the emotional charge was, if anything, even more intense.

Labour confidence was in hyper-drive: understandable in the circumstances, perhaps, but it tended to obscure the old truism about electoral victory being on the one hand an endorsement by the voters, and on the other a punishment of the *ancien régime*. Tony Blair, however, reminded those around him that New Labour's success had owed as much to the stasis of an enfeebled Tory Party in terminal disarray as it had to its own 'people's manifesto'. The public had basically had it with a Tory administration racked by sleaze and incompetence and led by a Pooterish Prime Minister whose reputation was at rock bottom. For the new occupants of Downing Street, simply winning the victory wasn't enough. It had to be firmly consolidated. 'We were elected as New Labour, and we shall govern as New Labour,' promised the youthful Prime Minister to his assembled admirers. The Blair project was about to begin.

Toryism, as a brand, was clearly on the wane. Margaret Thatcher, whatever her perceived shortcomings, had at least given the party a coherent image, but after her downfall the high command had failed to build on John Major's 1992 election victory with the sort of conviction-based policies that had been her stock-in-trade. What was Majorism? The comedian Rory Bremner had cruelly portrayed Major as a sad suburbanite with wooden syntax, reinforcing the general impression of a leader who couldn't control his party. Even so, the Labour hierarchy knew that a renewed Conservative Party led by an effective communicator such as Michael Portillo might be less of a walkover at the next election, or even the one after that.

While the Major regime had been in its death throes an invigorated Labour machine had been gearing up. For some years a group of party workers had taken a close interest in the computer-based wizardry of Bill Clinton's Democrats in the USA, and when the tycoon Philip Jeffrey offered to back a sophisticated new software programme based on the American model, Excalibur was born. If not quite the all-powerful Hal of Kubrick's *2001*, this new database capable of scanning 92,000 pages per second, and backed by rapid automatic indexing and rebuttal facilities, was certainly a super-intelligent beast.

A more corporatist Labour machine was also emerging, having moved from Walworth Road's pseudo-Georgian John Smith House in October 1995 to the bland Thameside 1960s fortress of Millbank Tower. Attempts to transfer Smith's name to some space such as a meeting room in the new complex were vetoed by the modernisers. Rebranding would tolerate no Old Labour memorialising. Besides, Peter Mandelson, the one-time Kinnock protégé, had been sidelined by Smith and, some suggested, had relished this opportunity to cut an Old Labour link. Millbank's expanding workforce had been given the task of winning a distinctly New Labour election, and the party had set about making non-ideological friends. Business and the media, seeing which way the wind was blowing, had deserted the Conservatives in droves.

At the heart of the Tories' problem was New Labour's rightward drift, and the lack of 'clear blue water' between their programmes. This process had had a long gestation, marked by policy shifts that had begun under Neil Kinnock's leadership. On a number of issues such as, for example, the right to buy council houses (which Labour had at first vehemently opposed) the programmes of both parties were often so similar in detail that Conservative ministers repeatedly bemoaned Labour's policy-hijacking tendencies. The image of the left was also changing, as vague concepts of fairness and social justice supplanted ideological socialism, and Armani suits replaced comradely denim.

There was an elementary rationale underlying these trends. The socio-demographic profile of Britain was changing and Labour was having to change with it. The country's industrial base had diminished during the Thatcher years, bringing a concomitant reduction in trade union membership. In his 1989 polemic *Where There is Greed* Gordon Brown had chronicled this decline. Between 1979 and 1981 alone around 1½ million manufacturing jobs had been lost, and these were mainly in traditional Labour areas. Cloth-cap Britain was disappearing, and with it the reliable voting habits of the industrial proletariat. Class realignment was distorting the old, predictable patterns of support, and new strategies were needed if the party was ever to regain power.

This industrial decline threatened to undermine Labour's heartland vote by weakening the party's natural tribal loyalties. A working man in his sixties with a council house and a lifetime in the unions behind him knew where his political interests lay, but what about his thirty-year-old mortgage-paying daughter who was more likely to be employed in the non-unionised service sector? The working class was no longer Labour's clearly identifiable new model army, willing and eager to do service. Younger anti-Tory Scots, in particular, seemed dangerously prone to switching allegiance to the nationalists.

In 1980s Britain as a whole the once innate working-class distrust of the Conservatives had ceased to guarantee support for Labour. A third of socio-economic group DE voters (unskilled manual workers and those on state benefits) had supported Margaret Thatcher in 1979, for example. Even in the post-industrial heartlands voting habits were being transformed, and the traditional dogmas of socialism seemed outdated. Labour's strategists soon worked out that the party, to be made electable, would have to be weaned off its dependency on a declining 'tribal' constituency and extend its appeal to a wider band of the electorate.

The answer, it seemed, was fundamentally to reposition the party by repudiating its primary role as the champion of the poor and oppressed, and forge a 'new politics' in which material success was viewed as a positive virtue. Labour, distancing itself gradually from a society of failure associated with sink estates and deprivation, latched on to the positive buzz of the aspirational ethos of the modernist tendency. In essence, the aim was to woo the confidence and allay the fears of the middle classes. The battleground for supremacy became Mondeo-driving middle England. New Labour was, in essence, the old party apparatus bowdlerised of its disputatious past. It was now a revamped production which had something for everyone, and offended no one, other than narrow interest groups such as the hunting lobby and street beggars.

Former party insider Derek Draper has claimed that a defining moment was the 1994 style coup of Campbell, Mandelson and Gould in which the conference backdrop with the inoffensive slogan 'A Fresh Start for Britain' was dismantled and replaced by another proclaiming the birth of an altogether different creed: New Labour.

The party's traditionalist old guard disapproved of these trends, but their complaints were ignored. Some, such as Tony Benn, would stick around, where others, such as Arthur Scargill, would flounce out (to the undisguised glee of the leadership). Nor was it simply the left that was concerned. Roy Hattersley, a Gaitskellite centre-rightist who had himself been at the forefront of Labour's 1960s modernisation drive as a young Sheffield councillor, was unhelpfully critical of the Blair project.

Despite the sniping from the sidelines, the rise of New Labour was unstoppable. Soft-left top-rankers such as Cook, Beckett and Brown bowed to the inevitable and remained on-message. John Prescott was kept on board for reasons not unrelated to Lyndon Johnson's adage about it being better to have a maverick inside your tent, while his old left rhetoric usefully concealed his modernising proclivities (it was Prescott, reputedly, who persuaded Blair to continue with the Dome). Neil Kinnock, who had first brought Peter Mandelson to prominence in Labour's red roses bid to soften the party image after the 'grotesque chaos' of the Militant years, was positively ecstatic. 'Je suis nouveau

Labour,' he proclaimed at a party bash in London's Royal Lancaster Hotel.

On the face of it the 1997 result seemed to justify the change. In 1979 almost two-thirds of social class group AB had voted Tory. In 1997 it was just over a third. The switch amongst C1 (white collar) voters was equally dramatic. Over half had voted Tory in 1979, but barely a quarter did in 1997; indeed Labour itself was within a whisker of capturing half of this group. Meanwhile, the working class had stayed on board, probably because, as spin-guru Philip Gould famously said, they had 'nowhere else to go'. The new alchemy seemed foolproof, even if the Scots and the Welsh weren't always willing to underwrite this particular thesis.

In reinventing itself as a party acceptable to the middle class, New Labour had one crucial difficulty to confront. At a cursory glance, much of its underlying political philosophy resembled that of its opponents. Despite issuing a pledge card and mouthing neologisms like 'inclusiveness', its message came across as a rehash of compassionate conservatism, and sometimes – as when Jack Straw laid into 'pan-handlers and squeegee merchants' – even the compassion seemed in short supply.

Labour's spectacular victory did not disguise the fact that, in the long term, a reconstructed Tory Party could set about making up this lost middle ground, where voter loyalties might yet prove ephemeral. The party strategists were naturally aware of this, and even in the aftermath of victory were determined to keep up a campaigning momentum. Eighteen years in opposition had sharpened Labour's appetite for power; it had also developed an acute appreciation of the benefits of pre-emptive tactical planning. The party had grown accustomed to being on a war footing, while the Tories had given the impression of succumbing to sleaze and complacency. To obviate the potential threat of middle-class disenchantment the Labour brand had to maintain its popular appeal by cultivating a 'feel-good' image which was more about lifestyle than politics. The aim was to connect with the way people felt and behaved, then identify and empathise with the things that interested them in a general sense. At times the effects were eccentric; for example, the Prime Minister intervened over 'The Weatherhead One', when *Coronation Street*'s Deirdre was wrongly imprisoned. For the most part, however, it was a product-placement drive. Labour was the brand, and the brand had to be associated with up-beat glamour wherever possible.

It was a matter of conveying an image of a government with an out-of-the-office interest in laddish bonhomie. Interviews were peppered with football metaphors. Pop impresario Alan McGee, who had donated £50,000 to the party's election fund, was invited to a Number 10 bash with Noel and Meg Gallacher and Simply Red's Mick Hucknall. Elton John did a gig for Mo Mowlam and a roomful of suits in Stormont Castle. The PM chose a Fender Stratocaster as his object of the twentieth century for inclusion in the Museum of Scotland's collection. There was now an exciting new area of government policy. It was called, unofficially, Cool Britannia.

As a marketing device, Cool Britannia neatly filled the vacuum left by socialism, the discarded brand which had been locked in the closet. Something had to take socialism's place so that an increasingly bland product could be adequately differentiated from its equally bland rivals. Whatever it was, that 'something' had to *look* radical, though it didn't have to *be* radical. It was enough that it should merely capture the *zeitgeist* of a new, forward-looking Britain without actually committing the party to anything as fearsome as a left-wing political agenda. Core beliefs enshrined in Clause 4 were jettisoned. The people's flag of deepest red became *passé* and a fresh anthem – Things Can Only Get Better – was struck up. *The Ragged Trousered Philanthropists* gave way to *The River Café Cookbook* on the coffee tables of the fashionable left.

Happily, the new faith even had its own shorter catechism in *Britain TM, Renewing our Identity* by 23-year-old Mark Leonard. Published by Labour's favourite think-tank,

Demos, this amounted to a homespun litany of handy hints for updating the style ethos of dowdy old Britain. The author, though from Camden by origin, was largely raised in Brussels where his father, Fabian veteran Dick Leonard, was a successful apparatchik bureaucrat. This may explain Leonard junior's preoccupation with the state of departure lounges, railway stations and other points of entry to the UK, the majority of which, no doubt, would have benefited from a revamp.

Leonard's underlying intent, however, was to take the mission a step further than a Carol Smillie makeover. Basically, Britain was handicapped by tradition and needed a strict dose of modernisation to catch up with the rest of the world, and this meant creating lots of glitzy 'signature' buildings. The problem with Leonard's radical new take on our imagined national malaise was that it was neither radical, nor new. The veteran modernists Eric Mendelssohn and Walter Gropius had travelled the world (even lecturing in Edinburgh) with the self-same message seventy years earlier. The Festival of Britain had been launched in similar vein. Worst of all, the catastrophic destruction of much of inner-city Britain in the 1960s was predicated on the same fallacy, and there was a spooky linguistic similarity with the 'New Britain' visions of such 1960s urban clearance gods as Newcastle's T. Dan Smith, Glasgow's David Gibson and Sheffield's Lewis Womersley.

In a sense, Leonard's 'modernist' thesis was itself a hoary old piece of heritage. Its renewalist message offered a continuation of the laissez-faire recklessness that had typified Nicholas Ridley's style as Mrs Thatcher's environment minister, an incumbency so disastrous that he was moved across to Trade and Industry in 1989. Ridley had at least had an excuse; his political views had been formed in a post-war climate in which reconstruction and renewal were the norm.

For Mark Leonard and his contemporaries a different set of standards should have applied. The profligacy of mass building might do wonders for the *zeitgeist*, but it squanders energy and aggravates global warming. Retaining the heritage, on the other hand, is a responsible use of resources. Leonard's critique, in short, ignored the need for progressive sustainable development practices which are the complete opposite of the renewalist excesses of image-driven acolytes of rebranding like himself.

Cool Britannia was not so much a policy as a policy surrogate in a vapid political landscape, a tepid echo of Harold Wilson's 'White Heat of Technology' wheeze without the benefits of the latter's industrial investment strategy. The word *cool* itself was quaintly old-fashioned, and dated back even further than Miles Davis' *Birth of Cool* recorded more than half a century ago. It is a term redolent of the music of Black America, the backslang of Kerouac's beat generation, and Viv Stanshall's Bonzo Dog Doo Dah Band. Millbank's rebranders had discovered a past, not a future.

A little froth with the dream factory in Downing Street was one thing, but when Cool Britannia went seriously architectural its hazards became all too evident. A coterie including several leading developers, entrepreneurs and architects with New Labour leanings was soon paying court to this government entranced with the Private Finance Initiative and awash in lottery takings. The developer Robert Bourne pledged a substantial sum to party funds; James Palumbo, owner of the Ministry of Sound nightclub and son of the high-rolling property developer, Lord Palumbo, had lent a chauffeur-driven limo to Labour's election campaign; while Stuart Lipton, an astute and highly successful London developer, became particularly intimate with the inner workings of the 'court of King Tony'.

Lipton's links with the Labour establishment had begun almost twenty years earlier when he had become interested in the potential of a rundown area on the south bank of the Thames near the old Bankside power station. This had already attracted the attention of several architects and developers, and at one time the Heron Corporation, headed by the controversial Gerald Ronson, had a proposal for the tallest hotel block in Europe. After the oil crisis and property slump of the early 1970s Heron reassessed the plans and sought to expand them, claiming extra office space would be essential to make them viable. The local residents of the area around Coin Street, behind the landmark Oxo Tower, set up an action group to fight the scheme, but Heron persisted, joining forces with Commercial Properties, a company headed by Lord Vestey.

A public inquiry began in 1979, during which Heron pulled out, leaving the way open for Lipton's company, Greycoat London Estates, to combine with Vestey's Commercial Properties, the new company being Greycoat Commercial Estates. Richard Rogers was on board to provide a strong 'signature' for a third-of-a mile-long riverside scheme in which passing reference was made in the glossy presentation to the high-value investment component of one million square feet of office space.

Enter Greycoat's solicitor, Garry Hart, of the London law practice Herbert Smith. He and his lawyer wife Valerie were close friends of Tony Blair and Cherie Booth, to the extent that he later became godfather to one of the Blair children. Hart, suggests one source, rang Tony Blair and asked if he could recommend a top-flight QC to represent his clients. He was given the name of Blair's own boss, Derry Irvine.

By the time of the second Coin Street inquiry the core *dramatis personae* of Labour's embryonic modernising wing were becoming well acquainted, though there was one notable exception. Peter Mandelson, as vice-chairman of the local planning authority, had given his initial support to the Coin Street residents. The developers were to lose the inquiry, and Derry Irvine and his junior, 'Young Blair' would go on to help Neil Kinnock sort out his hard left, but an élite group, which was later joined by Mandelson, was now in place, and the synergy was positively buzzing.

One of rebranding's most effective proselytisers was Richard Rogers, whose brother Peter was Lipton's business partner. He had famously co-designed the eye-catching Beaubourg in the historic Marais district of Paris in the 1960s. An Archigram-influenced monument to the President of the Fifth Republic, Georges Pompidou, it was produced in association with the Italian architect and fellow 'bad boy' (Rogers' words) Renzo Piano.

Rogers represented all that was bold and dynamic in modern British architecture. He had a following, he had wealth, and he had influence. His daughter-in-law, Lucy Musgrave, would later take charge of the Architecture Foundation, while Stuart Lipton, who had first come to public notice as a high-octane Ferrari-driving speculator in the Thatcher years, was to be appointed chairman of the Commission for Architecture and the Built Environment (CABE), which went on to replace England's Royal Fine Art Commission in August 1999.

Lipton was identified as a suitably qualified 'Architecture Tsar', and certainly his track record suggested that he appreciated the value of good design, particularly where this provided planning leverage. He had joined forces with the property financier Godfrey Bradman of the Rosehaugh Group (and also joint chairman of Victoria Quay Limited, of which more later) to build the Broadgate Complex around London's Liverpool Street Station in the 1980s. By 1989 Lipton's one-third share in the property company, Stanhope Securities, was worth £100 million, a cushion of wealth which, a decade later, enabled him to turn down the £30,000 salary that went with the two-day-a-week CABE job.

The symbiosis within this powerful London network was potent. Lipton, the ambitious multi-millionaire developer, shared an interest in art with Irvine, the ambitious QC and builder's son whose taste for opulence would become legendary. There was also no shortage of ambition in Irvine's chambers. Besides Tony Blair and Cherie Booth there was Blair's flatmate Charlie Falconer who, as a schoolboy at Glenalmond, had once announced, Heseltine-like, that being Prime Minister was part of his future life plan.

Since no one was taking minutes on the social circuit, which took in the dining room of Irvine's Kilburn house, or the River Café, the modish restaurant run by Rogers' wife Kate, or the smart Islington and Holland Park residences of the subfusc New Labour élite, the precise influences behind the formulation of policy are presumably lost to history, but there can be little doubt that by the time Labour was in power this rich London clique was setting the tone for much, if not all, of the party's rebranding agenda.

Even so, it would be a mistake to stereotype it as a tight-knit body of plutocrats and Medici wanabees. The big players in Labour's smart new 'modernising tendency' were mostly wealthy, or, like Philip Gould, had rich partners, but many were not. Peter Mandelson, Labour's self-styled 'ambassador to the rich and famous', had glittering aspirations but lacked the matching funds. He had also inherited the rebranding gene from his grandfather, Herbert Morrison (responsible for, amongst other things, the 1951 Festival of Britain and the destruction of Rennie's Waterloo Bridge).

Others in the modernising mould, but with none of Mandelson's appetite for *la dolce vita*, included Chris Smith, who became culture minister. This was a key appointment in the Cool Britannia game plan. Smith lived modestly, had a certain bookish charm (he had written a doctorate on Wordsworth), and enjoyed such wholesome pastimes as hillwalking. Unlike Peter Mandelson, he had never been particularly interested in concealing his sexuality, and his candour in this respect was appreciated by his adversaries and friends, as well as his electorate.

But Smith also had an agenda for his ministry, which was itself a rebrand of a rebrand. Under Norman St John-Stevas the portfolio title had been the Office of Arts and Libraries, then along came David Mellor, and it was redesignated the Department of National Heritage, or, in Mellorspeak, the 'Ministry of Fun'. Chris Smith decided to make another change, and two months after the election the new stationery was emblazoned with the words: Department of Culture, Media and Sport.

Under the guise of 'inclusiveness' and 'accessibility' Smith set about reforming the cultural component of his brief with quiet determination. Critics, including a number in his own party, were soon drawing dire conclusions about a 'dumbing-down' mentality. Some discerned a drift to the lowest common denominator. There were few surprises when the Royal Opera House in Covent Garden fell out of favour, or when broadcasting, which stayed firmly with London as a reserved power under devolution legislation, was stacked with New Labour sympathisers. Historic buildings became positively *passé*. The new ministry was to 'look forward, promoting the best of Cool Britannia', claimed Derek Draper approvingly, adding, 'At long last the deification of heritage is history.'

Smith's demotion of heritage included a perceived element of 'toff-bashing', as far as many of his critics were concerned. He turned down an invitation to address an annual general meeting of the Historic Houses Association, sending instead his junior, Alan Howarth, who left the assembled owners of old, and often crumbling, buildings with the distinct impression that they were relics of privilege out of tune with the New Britain.

The inference that those who were for old buildings were somehow allied with the 'forces of conservatism' was fairly rich coming as it did from a junior minister who, not so many years before, had defected from John Major's ranks. The new government line also contradicted its 'inclusiveness' mantra, since half the point of the Historic Houses Association is to encourage the public to experience buildings and collections which had previously been the closed domain of the privileged. While it may be ideologically unsound actually to *be* a Duke of Devonshire or an Earl of Leicester in the rebranded Britain, no one could seriously take issue with the vital contribution that great houses such as Chatsworth and Holkham make to the fragile rural economies of Derbyshire and Norfolk. In Scotland, which few visit for a beach tan or its club scene, historic buildings, by any objective standard, play an even more vital role in the tourist economy. Traquair, one of the most successful and imaginatively run, is even lived in by a prospective Labour parliamentary candidate, Catherine Maxwell-Stuart, whose excellent home-produced real-ale range includes a 1997 Blair's Brew.

The irony of the anti-heritage line was that the party once inspired by Ruskin and Morris was historically not always averse to the built patrimony. Attlee commissioned a historic buildings report from Sir Ernest Gowers and his Chancellor Hugh Dalton set aside £50 million in the National Land Fund with a view to restoring some of the country's more important examples. It would be a conservative, Enoch Powell, who was to pillage all but £10 million of this heritage treasure-chest a decade later.

The anti-heritage posture of New Labour's modernisers was a neat conjuring trick, and a disingenuous one at that. It hinted at a breaking away from privilege, yet New Labour and privilege were inextricably linked. The people's party worked out of Millbank Tower, ate in Granita's or the Atlantic Grill, and de-stressed itself in Tuscany. It consorted with every rich businessman* who would give it the time of day, and networked furiously to secure contributions from almost any source that would provide a counterweight to its financial dependence on the unions and constituencies. American-style fund-raising bashes offered paying corporate bosses valuable 'face-time' with ministers over the *tranche de saumon au thym sauvage*. Tycoons such as Geoffrey Robinson were encouraged to trawl their City contacts for private-sector partnership investments. An invaluable 'networker', he also became Paymaster General and Treasury minister in charge of the Private Finance Initiative. Michael Levy, whose wealth owed much to the success of rock star Alvin Stardust, amongst others, is said to have engineered contributions of around £2 million into Labour's pre-election trust-fund treasure-chest, and was rewarded with a peerage for his 'services to charity' three months after the victory. Bob Ayling, the former civil servant who rose, under Thatcher, to become head of British

---

* And women too – the more rich and glamorous the better. Anita Roddick, Stella McCartney, Helena Bonham-Carter, Vivienne Westwood and J. K. Rowling were all wooed, to greater or lesser effect.

Airways, and was noted for his robust attitude to the unions, became 'a model New Labourite'.

As far as the architectural rebranding of Britain was concerned the developers' writ was the one that counted. In the global economy, it was argued, central London in particular simply had to give in to mega-scale office developments. Flash and cash were back. Norman Foster, another of Labour's court architects (who, like Rogers, was given a peerage), proposed building a massive 'world-class' commercial office block at the heart of Godfrey Bradman's 150-acre Elephant and Castle scheme. It was necessary, apparently, to build big and build high to dissuade merging corporate institutions from taking off for Paris or Frankfurt in a world made up of time zones, rather than countries, though quite how a company like Price Waterhouse Cooper (in line for a mega Thames-side building with space for 8,000 employees) could have recruited a qualified English-speaking staff in Europe was never fully explained. In an act of solidarity with the *leitmotiv* brigade John Prescott decided that the listed Baltic Exchange building should be demolished, rather than restored, after being partially damaged in an IRA attack. A Norman Foster 'erotic gherkin' was pencilled in to rise over the site.

We were, in spirit, back in the sixties, albeit with a quality of architecture rather better than the dreary grid-glazed monoliths of the old Seifert design style. Britain was now at something called the 'cutting edge', and had an international profile to keep up. Even the builders had raised their horizons. Bovis Lend Lease, principal contractors on the Holyrood site, had shown its mettle in Kuala Lumpur where it had erected Cesar Pelli's 88-storey Petronas Towers which were, *pro tem*, the world's tallest buildings. Duly impressed, the Sellar Property Group began talks with them about the proposed construction of a Renzo Piano-designed 'tallest block in Europe' at Southwark, while Foster and Partners made efforts to top the Petronas by two storeys with their proposed Millennium Tower. Macho-priapic was back in fashion.

The disapproval of heritage values even penetrated the inner sanctum. There was talk of the 'Prime Minister's closest advisers' making plans to leave Downing Street for new purpose-built offices; Numbers 10 and 11, which had just had £1 million lavished on them, would become a museum, claimed *The Times*. New Labour, New Britain meant new buildings, usually with the specious adjective 'world-class' applied. You didn't need to dig too deep for the disconcerting Nietzschean subtext.

'New' was an inexact term. The hand-me-down relatively new was acceptable, at a push, provided it had an appropriate buzz, and could be brought into service as a modernist marker. Canary Wharf was amongst the first. Selected as the venue for the European Ministers' Summit, it was a symbol of unfettered Thatcherism and a bizarre choice for Labour's Cool Britannia gesture, being fairly low on the Britannia quotient. Designed by the Argentinian architect Cesar Pelli and backed by Canadians, Olympia & York's thrusting skyline-breaker had been a financial dud until a Tory government had helped it out. This choice of venue particularly infuriated Ben Elton, who was scathing about the Prime Minister trying to upstage the French with 'a couple of Habitat sofas' in an indignant denunciation of Cool Britannia.

The whiff of the 1960s was unmistakable, but the language was more subtle as its impact was softened by a socio-speak in which 'regeneration' became the euphemism for the blitz 'n' build comprehensive development fad of Richard Crossman's era. The collapse of Ronan Point, which had done so much to discredit high-rise housing, and the Mansion House carbuncle-debunking speech by the Prince of Wales, were now distant memories. The promotional style was soft-focus persuasive, rather than sixties prescriptive, and, as it happens, some genuinely good architecture was appearing alongside the developers' gruesome techno-wurlitzers.

Architectural rebranders were now much more adept at self-promotion. Richard Rogers, a master of lucrative 'wow' mega-structures such as the Millennium Dome and the Lloyd's Building, could also promote quasi-holistic solutions for urban brown-site housing as head of the government's 1998 Urban Taskforce (though Deborah Orr of the *Independent* thought the main beneficiary would be urban yuppiedom). Godfrey Bradman, in addition to being a shrewd money-making renewalist, was also a supporter of the Green movement and had a proactive interest in freedom of information issues, which rather set him apart from Lord Irvine, who had, according to one minister, 'effectively buried' freedom of information by expunging it from Labour's first Queen's speech. Stuart Lipton's taste could be measured and responsible, despite his tough reputation as a businessman in search of a profit. Even so, entrusting the care of the built environment to individuals such as CABE's Stuart Lipton who made their fortunes from large-scale urban redevelopment was arguably on a par with giving the fox the key to the chicken shed. We had come a long way from the dilettante era of that urbane and scholarly old-style patrician, Norman St John-Stevas, Lipton's predecessor at the (now rebranded) Royal Fine Art Commission. The guardianship of the built environment had been handed over to multi-millionaire property speculators, bullish architects and *leitmotiv*-obsessed image-packagers.

Nor were those most closely associated with the Blair project necessarily rebranding absolutists in their own drawing rooms. The Lord Chancellor, a man with an eye for a good Sickert, provoked outrage when he ordered £300 a roll Pugin-designed wallpaper for his official residence, before selecting choice pictures from the National Galleries of Scotland.* Celebrated New Labourites Geoffrey Robinson and Ken and Barbara Follet employed the anti-modernist

---

* *Josephine and the Fortune Teller* was a particularly august choice
  for the man who has compared himself to Cardinal Wolsey.
  It illustrates the episode in which the rise of Napoleon's
  future empress was predicted. Perhaps a little extra piquancy
  was afforded by the fact that the artist, Wilkie, was an
  ancestor of Tam Dalyell's!

founder of the Victorian Society, Roderick Gradidge, as an architect on their respective houses, and even Peter Mandelson, high priest of the *fettuccine revolution*, had a soft spot for traditional imagery, it would seem, when he allowed Snowdon to snap him in front of a baroque portrait of a periwigged youth in the house which Robinson had helped him to buy.

When it came to a personal endorsement of cutting-edged modernism, indeed, Labour's rebranding tendency seemed most at home in the timid Victorian stock brick terraces of Islington and the wedding-cake stucco of Notting Hill and Holland Park. It was the distinctly Old Labour Bob Marshall-Andrews, a tireless critic of the Blair project, who had actually commissioned an uncompromising modern design for his own home which would merit inclusion in any top ten list of late twentieth-century British houses.

The rebranding formula was essentially about high-profile signature buildings as sexy status symbols in an international market-place. Frank Ghery's brilliant titanium-clad Guggenheim was doing great things for post-industrial Bilbao, and it was assumed that a dose of the same medicine would be good for the 'New Britain'. We were at the crossing point of two mindsets. On the one hand, the swinging clergyman who gets rid of the old pews and the old hymns in some misguided drive to make his church 'more relevant and exciting' to young people; and on the other, Nicolae Ceausescu, whose obsessive monument-building and heritage destruction was a crass attempt to glorify his image as the *Übermensch* of the people's Romania.

Edinburgh and Cardiff were constituent parts of this rebranding strategy, but the great paradigm was to be the Millennium Dome, a Heseltine brainwave inspired by his imagined success with Liverpool's Garden Festival (which produced no lasting benefits). The Dome was a supreme gesture of false confidence which, on close inspection, belied the inherent frailty of modern Britain in an American-dominated world which buys its consumer goods from the

Far East. For Westminster, now haemorrhaging its decision-making functions to Brussels, Scotland and Wales, the Dome was a reassuring comfort. It was meant to be a replay not just of the 1951 Festival of Britain, masterminded by Mandelson's grandfather, but also of the 1851 Great Exhibition.

A glance at history shows how ludicrous both comparisons were. In the mid-nineteenth century Britain was a world power. A network of railways and major advances in technology had transformed the national economy. The social order may have been far from perfect, with poverty rife in the pollution-blighted industrial cities, but there was a shared belief in progress at almost every level of society. The 1851 exhibition proved so popular that the accumulated cash surplus was enough to fund the building of museums in South Kensington, Edinburgh and Dublin.

Comparison with the Festival of Britain was equally fatuous. Six years had been spent fighting Hitler, and six more in a post-war austerity in which consumer goods continued to be rationed. An exhausted nation was picking itself up off its knees, and desperately needed a tonic. The Skylon and the 'Dome of Discovery' provided it.

The Millennium Dome was the crude manifestation of a New Labour in-house culture which venerated presentation and brand promotion much as old Labour had venerated egalitarianism and wealth redistribution. Cool Britannia was an article of faith amongst the group that Clare Short described as the people in the shadows. The Downing Street policy unit, inspired by the success of Clinton's brilliant *spinmeister* George Stephanopoulos, included several advisers who believed that cultural rebranding should entail a thorough purging of old precepts, and there was little to stop them. Given the new administration's similarity to the classic Hobbesian model of hierarchical rule which concentrates power at the top, and resists such tiresome inconveniences as parliamentary accountability, the management team had a level of privileged access to the Prime Minister which few MPs could ever approach, and was well placed to direct policy-making in its search for a *zeitgeist*. As Tom Nairn noted, a hint of Old Vienna, with the pompous substance of its decaying imperialism thinly screened by the gilded *fin-de-siècle* style of Klimt and art nouveau linear arabesque, lay heavy on the air. The Dome, however glitzy it looked, was essentially a re-run of the more bombastic triumphalist extravaganzas of Franz Joseph's favoured architect, Otto Wagner.

If the principle of parliamentary accountability had been trimmed by Margaret Thatcher it was to be deftly topped and tailed in Tony Blair's Britain by the new boys on the Downing Street block. The Prime Minister even displayed an aversion to the House of Commons itself. Question time was truncated, announcements flagged up in advance by Campbell's press office, and cabinet meetings became executive planning sessions in which the presentation of policy, rather than its creation, was the primary consideration. The cabinet, according to Derek Draper, was now 'more of a sounding board than a decision-making forum'. Ministerial statements were meticulously cleared and a rebuttal strategy laid in place to counter criticisms. Good headlines were cultivated like rare orchids, and in a party that had grown used to taking one tabloid hammering after another throughout the 1970s and 1980s this was no doubt a cause for satisfaction. There was even scope for manipulation. Journalists who were over-critical might find themselves frozen out of the information network, or given a 'bollocking' for being unhelpful. Jo Revill of the London *Evening Standard* was summarily informed, after one off-message article, that if her paper 'was going to kick the shit out of us' there would be a strict rationing of advance briefings. Radio 4's satirical slot, *Week Ending*, vanished from the airwaves. Its format was said to be outmoded and it was replaced by dull sports chat, but it was widely known that Peter Mandelson, in particular, had taken exception to the 'Prince of Darkness' role he'd been assigned.

Rebranding's praetorian guard in Downing Street and

Millbank was a formidable force headed by the triumvirate of Mandelson, Campbell and Gould, while Irvine continued his role as Prime Minister's mentor. Director of Policy Matthew Taylor, son of media-friendly sociology professor Laurie Taylor, was the in-house intellectual who had framed much of the 1997 manifesto. David Miliband, son of the Marxist philosopher Ralph Miliband, headed the policy unit. Pat McFadden, a graduate of Edinburgh University, was a consummate speech-writer with a fixer's way of dealing with Old Labour dissent in the ranks. Geoff Mulgan, founder of Demos, was another policy unit boffin, as was root-and-branch modernist James Purnell, whose remit, disturbingly, included heritage. Peter Hyman, a former researcher to Donald Dewar, was a modernising evangelist firmly in the Mandelson and Gould 'magic circle'. Derek Draper, another Mandelson henchman, would later boast that there were seventeen people who counted in government, and he had access to them all.

The moderniser's priority was to control press coverage, and the function of the theoretically neutral civil service spokesman rapidly gave way to that of the party spin-doctor charged with putting a New Labour gloss on the flow of information. Civil service staff who had worked under the Conservatives were suspected of being tainted and moved aside. In Scotland, Scottish Office director of communications Liz Drummond took early retirement. The long-term relationships and, in many cases, mutual respect which Scottish journalists and civil service press and information staff had developed were thrown overboard as the tough-talking Campbell style came north. The Prime Minister himself took a hard-man line with Scotland's political journalists when he described them collectively as a 'bunch of unreconstructed wankers'.

At the court of King Tony the manner was robust, the purpose clear. There was another election to be won a few years down the line, and an election after that. Any deviation from prescribed New Labour orthodoxy was strictly off-limits. The ghosts of elections past still haunted the darker recesses of party folk memory. The broad church of disparate interest groups, conference spats and fiery leftist rhetoric had finally been exorcised. The triumph of New Labour was the triumph of 'third way' political management, passionless, homogenised, style-infatuated, and geared, above all, to the retention of power.

So how did Donald Dewar, with his Old Labour past and his disdain for shallow style statements, fit into this New Labour Cool Britannia dreamscape of signature buildings and cutting-edge modernism?

# 5 Monumental Folly
*Building by Decree*

> *A vast and sublime idea*
> James Boswell, on the Colosseum

A VISIT TO Monastir, in Tunisia, is a strange experience.
The birthplace of 'father of the nation', Habib Bourguiba, it
was systematically rebuilt after independence in 1955. The
old centre, cleared of its inhabitants, was demolished and
replaced by a twee folksy-modern colonnaded inner core. It
recalls some small town in Normandy which, after wartime
devastation, has attempted to recapture its lost character in
a municipalised rebuilding programme – a brave attempt,
if not quite the real thing.

But Monastir was more than a town-planning scheme. It
is dominated by the mighty Bourguiba Mausoleum, with its
gilded cupola and twin minarets, as well as the Presidential
Palace and Bourguiba Mosque. To add to the general air of
unreality, it has also been a popular film location, thanks to
a combination of low labour costs and decent weather. The
cult that most British visitors would identify with is not the
one built around Bourguiba, however, but that of Monty
Python, for *The Life of Brian* was filmed here. It seems to
be customary to leave the film sets to rot in the North
African breeze, providing an edge of gimcrack surrealism
to Monastir's toytown ambience.

Bourguiba was no Ceausescu, and, as autocrats go, he
was benign and socially progressive, but he shared with
the Romanian tyrant a wish to perpetuate his memory in a
panoply of magnificent buildings. This syndrome is hardly
unusual, though some are more accomplished than others.
Thomas Jefferson, Catherine the Great, François Mitterrand,

Pope Julius II and the Emperor Hadrian were all convincing exponents of the idea that national greatness can be materially expressed in buildings. Others 'stretched the envelope' a little too far. Ludwig of Bavaria, arguably, was indulging his own whimsy, as was Emperor Bokassa of the impoverished Central African Republic when he decided to build Africa's most over-the-top cathedral.

In this respect the Scottish parliament building follows international form. It was never meant to be just a big meeting hall for politicians. It was conceived of as a monument, and as with any monument we should stand back and consider two things. First, its intended 'monumentalising' purpose, and, second, its success in fulfilling that purpose.

The individual most closely associated with Holyrood has, from the start, been Donald Dewar, who in September 1997 offered to 'carry the can' for his decision to look at sites other than Calton Hill. This was, of course, no solo initiative. Sir Robin Butler, as cabinet secretary at the time, was doubtless aware that a single minister's pronouncement on any one issue represents the thrust of government policy and, under the doctrine of collective responsibility, all such decisions are taken on a joint basis, and ultimately authorised by the Prime Minister. It is also important to remember that ministers act on the basis of the advice proffered by civil servants.

Even so, Donald Dewar was clearly taken with the idea of becoming the *de facto* patron of a grand edifice that would in some way celebrate the 'New Scotland' and his part in its creation. This introduces a number of conflicting elements into any consideration of the facts, for it was well known that Donald Dewar subscribed to the old-fashioned Presbyterian values that eschew gestures of self-glorification. When, shortly after his death, the *Daily Record* asked its readers to contribute to a statue there was an outcry from several of his friends who suggested that a statue 'was the last thing Donald would have wanted'. He reputedly loathed having a fuss made of him, and winced at the title 'father of the nation'. So why was a man known and admired for his lack of pretension so taken up with the need to raise his own monument?

Part of the answer is, of course, that the point of the exercise was about *disposing* of a monument – the Callaghan government 'shibboleth' on the hill – and that Holyrood was the ultimate outcome of an attempt to create a perceived Leith downgrade which went wrong. Donald Dewar was reining in a symbol, as much as creating one, and it could be suggested that the iconoclasm involved outweighed the hubris. But that doesn't explain the determination to see Holyrood through to the bitter end.

Could it be that Donald Dewar's Holyrood project was an act of homage to the triumph of a New Labour government which had, after all, brought devolution into being? This seems unlikely, given the Old Labour credentials of this senior politician who had entered parliament under Harold Wilson and had little rapport with the Millbank set. Donald Dewar's view of the Blair project was largely one of pragmatic accommodation. 'He could live with New Labour, but he wasn't a New Labourite,' wrote Jimmy Reid in the *Herald*. 'He was too much his own man for that.' And the ultimate irony of Holyrood was that this was a monument that Donald Dewar didn't actually need, since he already had a perfectly good one. It was called devolution.

Throughout the Holyrood débâcle of soaring costs, changing plans, public dismay, presentational own-goals and negative press publicity, there were many who questioned Donald Dewar's determination to press on with a project that was clearly doing his own party more harm than good. This included senior figures in the Labour high command, and MPs such as George Galloway who, at one point, even suggested the First Minister should consider resigning. So why did he persist?

In his *Independent* obituary of Donald Dewar the MP Tam Dalyell offered some telling insights into the character of the man who, more than any other, made the Scottish parliament a reality. Dalyell was criticised for his alleged lack of respect for a leader who, at that point, was being widely eulogised. Some felt that it was matter of settling old scores; after all, the member for West Lothian had been a long-time opponent of devolution, and he had also fallen foul of a Scottish Labour Party Glasgow University clique which had done him few favours in the course of his own political career.

But Tam Dalyell is nothing if not scrupulously honest, and the pen-portrait of his old party colleague seemed to identify a critical missing piece in the Holyrood jigsaw. Dewar, he claimed, was 'a driven, scheming, interesting, unusual politician' rather than a 'nice' one, and certainly those who worked with him would probably not dissent from this, though it has been said that he could be over-protective to those around him, often to his own detriment. Dalyell's most incisive comment, however, maintained that Donald Dewar's passion for devolution arose from a personal tragedy which had affected his outlook on life in general, and British politics in particular.

Donald Dewar, the only son of a Glasgow consultant, Alasdair Dewar, and his wife Mary, had a childhood blighted by parental illness. At the age of five he was sent to a prep school at Bonchester Bridge, in a remote area of Roxburghshire, but returned to Glasgow to attend Moss Park Primary and Glasgow Academy. He then entered Glasgow University Law Faculty, where he formed close friendships in a group that included John Smith and Derry Irvine. In 1964 he married a fine arts graduate, Alison McNair, and two years later won the once rock-solid Tory seat of Aberdeen South. In the Commons he soon demonstrated his skill as a performer with a rigorous intellect, and was taken on by Anthony Crosland, President of the Board of Trade, as PPS.

A brilliant career seemed assured, as did a rewarding family life. Then things began to go wrong. In the 1970 election he lost his seat to the right-wing Conservative, Iain Sproat, a man whose values he found deeply offensive.

For Donald Dewar, who had a genuine belief in social justice, that was bad enough; but worse was to come. As he prepared to leave London with a view to resuming his work as a lawyer in Glasgow, his wife announced that she would be staying to live with his old friend from university days, Derry Irvine.

'It is not hard to imagine the impact of this bombshell,' wrote Tam Dalyell, 'let alone on someone with such a vulnerable childhood. His friends were appalled at the cruelty. From that moment I believe Donald Dewar harboured a deep resentment against London. Here he was, having to start his life again as a solicitor in Scotland – seeing his son and daughter, to whom he was devoted, being brought up in the Irvine household. His attitude was very human. And if I mention these personal and delicate matters it is because they are central to Dewar's political credo of removing power from London to Scotland.'

Tam Dalyell was certainly not making this up, for Donald Dewar had never concealed his deep dislike of the English capital. 'London is a closed book to me,' he once said. 'I just work and camp there. I have the mark of Scotland on me.' He returned to Glasgow on his own, to be with friends who cared deeply for him. He would not be neglected; on the contrary, as a witty and intelligent unattached man he had a wide circle of women admirers, while as an adept political operator he had a loyal following amongst the predominantly male bastions of the west of Scotland Labour establishment.

Even so, the life Donald Dewar was leading in Glasgow, while it may have left little time for solitary reflection, was in stark contrast to the glittering life which his ex-wife (they divorced in 1973) was leading with the rapidly ascending Derry Irvine in London. Irvine would even be created shadow Lord Chancellor and recommended for an honour by Donald Dewar's friend, confidant and political soulmate, John Smith. Dewar, meanwhile, had contested and won the seat of Garscadden in a landmark 1978 by-election which had checked the progress of the SNP. The Labour government was in its last year, however, and the prospect of high office receded as successive Conservative governments left

Labour in the lurch. 'Independence in the UK' became his rallying cry as, with John Smith, Campbell Christie, James Boyack and others, he cut the devolution template that would become a 1997 manifesto commitment.

Labour's victory brought the opportunity Donald Dewar had been waiting for, and the Scotland Bill was prepared for its passage through parliament. First of all, however, its detailed proposals had to be negotiated through the upper ranks of the Labour Party.

This was by no means a straightforward process, particularly since, given the size of Labour's majority, there were those who inclined to the view that the new government could enjoy a certain latitude in the matter of devolution, and that it wouldn't be necessary to concede too much to the Scots and the Welsh after all. Schedule five of the Bill, all seventeen pages of it, was finally hammered out in the DSWR cabinet committee on devolution to which the Prime Minister had appointed none other than his old boss, Derry Irvine, as chairman.

Schedule five listed the reserved powers which was, in effect, a general guarantee of sovereignty for Westminster over a wide range of issues such as power generation, data protection, broadcasting, drugs, financial markets, oil and coal extraction, and abortion. Devo-sceptics such as Jack Straw, Robin Cook and Brian Wilson doubtless took some persuading, but Donald Dewar, as Secretary of State for Scotland and the former chairman of the Select Committee on Scottish Affairs, had the authoritative voice. He stressed the vital importance of maintaining the credibility of a constitutional reform which, to be meaningful at all, would have to be provided with powers rather greater than those of an old regional municipality. Blair's 'parish council' faux pas was to demonstrate the potential hazards of appearing disingenuous as far as devolution was concerned. The weaker the Scotland Act looked, the more the SNP would try to undermine it, and since the Scotland Act's elementary purpose was to undermine the SNP, it naturally followed that it had to be convincing.

The parliament building, too, had to be a serious and upfront affair. The old Callaghan building on Calton Hill, with its embarrassing associations, was deemed unfit for the new experiment in democracy. Devolution had to be seen as a 'big event', and it was suggested a new home, designed by a highly rated international architect, would showcase it most effectively. 'This was Donald's thing,' said one minister (adding that he himself had seen 'nothing wrong with Calton Hill'). Others spoke out against the proposal to ditch the old High School. Even Tam Dalyell advised him, both publicly and privately, to abandon the Holyrood project on the gounds that the cost alone could prove ruinous for Labour's future prospects.

Since cabinet proceedings are secret, and Donald Dewar is no longer here to enlighten us, it is impossible to know precisely what the official 'not Calton Hill' agenda actually was, but it is certainly the case that it was agreed at the highest level in London that a new signature building would, in due course, house Scotland's parliament. It may have been 'Donald's thing', but it was Downing Street's decision.

It has been suggested more than once that Donald Dewar had his own compelling personal motive for seeing the project through. One well-informed view runs as follows. If the old friend who had betrayed him all those years ago, now the Lord Chancellor of England, could serenely present himself as a patron of the arts in his lavishly appointed quarters in Westminster, could hold court in the splendid high-Victorian opulence of the House of Lords, and could even select choice paintings from Scotland's galleries, why should not he, Donald Dewar, create a little palatial splendour of his own in Edinburgh? This observation may be unkind; it may even be untrue; but it is at least tenable. And if true, it explains a great deal.

Donald Dewar was not a man for self-aggrandisement. He was cultured, knowledgeable, and appreciated fine things, such as antiquarian books and the paintings of the Scottish Colourists. He believed in connecting with people of all ages, and at all levels of society. His lifestyle was anything but hedonistic. He was as happy to 'stoke up' in his local supermarket café or Indian restaurant as he was to dine at Babbity Bowsters or Malmaison. The values that mattered to him were cerebral ones, and though he clearly gained immense satisfaction from a job well done (particularly the Scotland Act) the outward trappings of success were of little consequence. When he died he was at the high watermark of an honourable political career. Honours, as such, eluded him, though no doubt if he'd really wanted a title he would have been given one. To be called 'Donald' by elderly ladies in Drumchapel and passers-by in the Lawnmarket was, for him, better than any title. It was plain to see that being one of 'Jock Tamson's bairns' meant a great deal to Donald Dewar.

It is an uncomfortable thought that Holyrood, with its problems, delays, cost overruns and grim publicity, will be for ever associated with him. Holyrood is the issue that, more than any other, blighted Donald Dewar's time as First Minister and brought him 'to the black depths of despair'. It exposed the flaws in his character: obstinacy, a prescriptive approach to decision-making, a tendency to engage in intrigue. This is not the Donald Dewar most Scots would care to remember: better the committed democrat with a genuine belief in social advancement. Holyrood, whatever its architectural merits, will be a reproachful legacy, reminding us of a man who, like Shakespeare's Coriolanus, was overtaken by folly at his moment of supreme triumph.

Even so, in a century's time Scottish schoolchildren will know the name of Donald Dewar, the 'father of the nation'. And who then will remember the Lord Chancellor of England, Alexander Andrew Mackay Irvine?

# 6  New Labour, New Britain
## *The Evolution of Rebranding*

> *He so improved the city that he justly boasted he had
> found it brick, and left it marble*
> Suetonius of Augustus Caesar *c.* AD 120

SINCE THE CULT of the new is probably as old as mankind,
a brief archaeological interlude is perhaps in order. After
all, far from being an exciting symbol of some imagined
new age, the Holyrood project is actually part of an ancient
tradition of politically motivated public building extravaganzas and formulaic planning.

The background to the project itself is well known. Two
weeks and four days after the declaration of the Scottish referendum result Donald Dewar announced that he was minded
to build a new Scottish parliament. Though he maintained he
was keeping an open mind, there was no mistaking where
the Secretary of State was coming from. The neoclassical
'New Parliament House' on Edinburgh's Calton Hill was
finally being written out of the script. Those who thought
rule by diktat had gone out of fashion with Mrs Thatcher
were suddenly aware that prescriptive decision-making was
still in vogue with the Westminster establishment.

A report in the following day's *Scotsman*, quoting a 'well-
placed government source', fixed on a giveaway phrase. The
choice, it seemed, was between 'modernity and heritage',
and Mr Dewar had revealed that he was excited by the idea
of a modern building on the waterfront at Leith.

Since the *Scotsman* article was written by Peter MacMahon,*

* MacMahon could in fact be an objective and incisive analyst,
  as shown in his *Scotsman* article of 1 July 1998 headlined
  'How Labour lost the plot'.

who would later become the equivalent of Alastair Campbell in 'team McLeish', it can be assumed that the spin was as reliable as spin ever can be, yet it somehow seemed at odds with the character of a Secretary of State renowned for his love of history and the arts. Donald Dewar, the pragmatic Scots lawyer known for his self-effacing dry wit, seemed an unlikely champion for a blustering grand project.

Something didn't quite gel. As previously mentioned, of all politicians, Donald Dewar was the least prone to style makeovers. For advisers such as journalist Lorraine Davidson, attempts to sharpen up his dress sense were an uphill struggle. Nor did he much care about the look of his cars. One of his strengths, indeed, was this anti-style persona. A cautious lawyer with the soul of a scholar, he disdained 'flim-flam'. Even adversaries admired his old-fashioned values, and voters were reassured by the down-beat manner, a welcome antidote to the Rolex and Armani set in Granita's.

The underlying theme was, naturally, Millbank's modern-ising agenda. Donald Dewar, despite a prickly relationship with the Mandelson faction, was taking the faith north. New Labour was dominated by synthetic iconoclasts who disparaged tradition in all its forms, whether old-fashioned constituency-based activism, or old buildings. In the new lexicon, 'modern' was in, 'heritage' out. The four legs good, two legs bad logic of Orwell's *Animal Farm* reigned supreme, as did much of *1984*'s doublethink.

This neat classification gave rise to an official demonology in which those speaking up for 'tradition' were branded anti-modernist, off-message and out of touch, while those evangelising for the new orthodoxy were supposedly lead-ing a mission to create a forward-looking 'inclusive' Britain of tomorrow. Just as advertising creatives appreciate the first-perception value of brand image, so New Labour, in selling itself as a product, set about upping its appeal by closing the shutters on the Old Britain.

At times, the spinners went overboard, as when they laid into 'the forces of conservatism'. For a party developing problems with the word socialism, led by a man who came close to portraying himself as the heir-apparent of the Thatcher legacy, this was an interesting display of mind acrobatics.

The 'New Britain for Old' message, like the lampseller in *Aladdin*, was not all that it seemed to be. Indeed, Scotland's parliament project was not about 'modernity versus heritage' at all, for the very simple reason that it would have been perfectly possible to build a spectacular modern building on any one of a number of sites on, or around, Calton Hill. It was, patently, nothing less than a glib subterfuge designed to avoid the former Royal High School while lubricating the synergy between corporate interests which might expect to do well out of the move to Leith and those Sir Humphreys who, after a century of serene, unperturbed and unaccountable administrative rule, wished to maintain a discreet distance between themselves and the people's representatives.

The modernisation on offer had little to do with the 'participatory democracy' that New Labour allegedly subscribed to. There had been no attempt whatever to find out what the Scottish public, in general, felt about a move from Calton Hill, for the simple reason that the vast majority of them would have seen little sense in it and dismissed it as a ridiculous waste of money. The party of focus groups which wooed us with morality-affirming words like 'empowerment' had absolutely no intention of empowering anyone on this issue. On the contrary, the rejection of Calton Hill, the scuppered attempt to relocate the parliament in Leith, and the emergence of Holyrood had all the characteristics of a 1960s-style prescriptive planning fix.

In general, New Labour was putting it about that it had somehow come up with a cutting-edge socio-political agenda that would 'modernise' the nation. It wasn't altogether easy to determine precisely what this philosophy was. Tony Blair had intoned its basic precepts in October 1994, shortly after becoming party leader. 'Our Party. New Labour. Our Mission. New Britain. New Britain. New Labour.

New Britain. New Britain.' The abolition of the verb, it seemed, was axiomatic. Likewise, the continuation of the Conservative government's plan for a mega-signature Millennium Dome designed to capture the spirit of this imagined New Britain.

As a rhetorical device, the stirring appeal to supplant the established order with something purporting to be more up to date has a long and variable pedigree. Step back half a century, and hear the echo. 'The voice of Time cries out to Man: Advance,' proclaimed Robert Bruce in the preamble to his horrific 1945 plan for the clearance and reconstruction of Glasgow, to be considered in due course. At that time even a genteel academic such as Sir John Summerson damned traditional styles as 'architectural Toryism' in *The New Ground-work of Architecture*, insisting vacuously that 'the architecture of today must be – not of a class, but of the community itself'.

This 'New Britain' soundbite has ancient roots. 'We must act anew; we must build anew,' declared Abraham Lincoln in his Congressional address. This was a meaningful sentiment in a nation riven by war. In the 1860s America really was being transformed. Its hinterland was being intersected by railroads, its cities absorbed waves of immigrants. By comparison, late twentieth-century Britain was hardly on an expansionary roll. Indeed, with the loss of Hong Kong, the influence of Brussels, our slide in world economic league tables, and the emergence of devolution, it seemed to be rapidly downsizing. So what *zeitgeist*, one wonders, were Millbank's rebranders actually celebrating?

Public architecture can be the authentic expression of the values of a society establishing or consolidating its identity, or a culturally invigorating means of improving the image of a city in post-industrial transition, or a promotional tool for a company which seeks to associate success with a talismanic built icon. There are many fine modern examples, from the Seagram Tower to Ghery's Bilbao Guggenheim.

But architecture can also be a fig-leaf for a society that has failed to define itself, or is suffering from the stresses of decline. Is it any accident that the most bombastic buildings of Vienna were put up in the twilight years of the Hapsburg Empire?

The intriguing thing about modernism (and its nervous alter ego, post-modernism) is its antiquity. Most of the world's great buildings were once statements of a coming age. We need only imagine the impact that Inigo Jones' Banqueting Hall, or Wren's St Paul's, first had on the inhabitants of London to appreciate this fact. New Labour's *bête noire*, the Royal High School on Calton Hill, was itself a startlingly modern building in its day, even though its Doric style evoked an ancient Athenian Socratic academy.

So where does modernism begin? For the Regency 'modernism' of Hamilton's Royal High School, 3000 BC is a fair starting point. Of all the architectural orders, the Doric is particularly ancient, the oldest known example being the proto-Doric colonnade by Zoser's pyramid at Saqqara. It is possible that the style evolved for largely practical reasons. The right-angled corners of upright shafts were obviously vulnerable, but if the column had eight faces, rather than four, the risk of damage was minimised, the freightage load reduced, and more light allowed into the walkway.

It seems that the ancient Egyptian architect Imhotep, as the Richard Rogers of his era, had technical problem-solving skills as sophisticated as any around today. His Saqqara stepped pyramid is, in a sense, the world's first great modern building.

Leaving Egypt aside, architectural rebranding in Britain got into its stride with the Normans and attained its apogee with the flowering of Gothic in the centuries before the Reformation, at which point Henry VIII, partly to regularise his marital problems, removed not only the patronage of the Catholic Church, but many of its buildings as well. Scotland's iconoclasts were not far behind. The reconstituted clergy no longer enjoyed the near-monopoly previously taken for granted, and the industry began to meet the growing demand for secular buildings.

Protestantism, with its didactic inclinations, brought a

new view of architecture's purpose. In *Utopia* Sir Thomas More described his ideal earthly paradise, a Tudor foretaste of a 1960s council estate: 'He that knows one of their towns knows them all, they are so like one another.' More's vision betrayed a fixation with social control disguised as philanthropy with which many modernists would have empathised.

Curiously, modern architecture as we understand it in contemporary Scotland has a direct link with the eighteenth-century agrarian revolution when 'systemisation' of crops and livestock was an obsessive pursuit for many of the gentry. Crop rotation, animal husbandry, land enclosure and the publication of transactions that described new methods were to change the landscapes of Britain within a few generations.

The improvement mentality of landowners such as Gilbert Elliott of Minto, who introduced commercial potato farming to Scotland, rippled outwards as the parallels between model farms and model towns became evident. In 1752 Elliott turned his attention from rural potatoes to urban populations in his 'Proposals for certain Public Works', the blueprint for Edinburgh's Georgian New Town.

Another landowner with a *penchant* for civic planning and social reorganisation was Sir John Sinclair of Ulbster, who shared his ideas with George Washington, amongst others. Just as a farmer might study methods of increasing crop yields, so Sinclair analysed 'the quantum of happiness' in human populations, gathering data on a parish-by-parish basis in his *Statistical Accounts*.

The rise of the capitalist economies during the industrial revolution brought other influences to bear, not the least of which was the concentration of large populations in rapidly expanding cities. As urban overcrowding increased, prescriptive interventions became necessary. It wasn't simply a matter of social conscience, though undoubtedly the writings of Dickens and Mayhew affected liberal middle-class opinion.

It was often a matter of expediency. When operatives

were being ravaged by cholera, factory output fell. For manufacturers, Sinclair's 'quantum of happiness' was now a social regulator, rather than a noble end in itself. The ideal community of Rousseau's *Social Contract* was mostly forgotten, though a handful of non-conformist industrialists and Quaker manufacturers made honest efforts to improve the quality of life of their workforces.

The pragmatic transfer of empirical logic from agrarian cultivation to an industrial context became a reality at New Lanark, where Robert Owen conducted the social experiments which brought him into the left's pantheon as 'father of the co-operative movement'. Tellingly, Owen is not only venerated on the liberal left. He is also admired in corporate Japan as an industrialist with consummate organisational skills.

New Lanark may be a long way from Holyrood, but they have this in common: both were devised for political ends. In *A New View of Society* Owen extolled the benefits of good housing and elementary education, and at New Lanark his theories were applied. His approach was entirely prescriptive. Unlike Jeremy Bentham, a New Lanark shareholder, he had little interest in questions of individual liberty, viewing social improvement as a way of avoiding, rather than advancing, fundamental change. Owen, a paternal conservative who feared agitation, wrote of the 1820 radical uprising: 'Already are the seeds of revolution sown – and quickly must produce a sanguinary harvest, unless the condition of the lower orders is considerably ameliorated.'

New Lanark's top-down reforms required a workforce that accepted improvement on the philanthropist's terms. An 'Institute for the Formation of Character' dominated a utopian community in which workers were expected to be docile and grateful in their happiness. For the reforming libertarian George Canning, Owenism, with its 'quadrangled paradises', was 'inimical to individuality'.

Owen was positively benign, however, compared to many of the 'prescriptives' who were to follow. In an age increasingly obsessed with classification a scientific-rationalist view of the world ruled, offering the prospect of reductive solutions to even the most intractable social problems. Prescriptive panaceas of every description appeared, from the ultra-successful phrenology fad of the Edinburgh Combe brothers, to the dialectical materialism of Marx and Engels.

At the end of the nineteenth century technology and the international manifestos of the revolutionary left collided to produce the early Modern Movement. The underlying imperative was a purging of the 'decadence' that had gone before, which was not in itself such a radical idea. After all, Ruskin had once railed against the supposed aridity of the neoclassicism of his father's city, Edinburgh. For him, as a socialist romantic, the antidote to classicism lay in a past of imagined aesthetic spontaneity. The Gothic celebrated artisan dignity, whereas the repeated forms of classicism simply demeaned the creative vision of the workman.

The driving force of the Modern Movement was the European avant-garde, and unlike Ruskin its primary aim was to reject the past altogether. Italy's Emilio Marinetti, whose Futurist manifesto of 1909 extolled the 'dynamism' of the machine age, even tried to persuade Mussolini to allow him to demolish the perfect Ruskinian city of Venice.

In Germany, the Nietzschean view of a Teutonic destiny profoundly influenced architecture. Bruno Taut, author of such books as *The Dissolution of Cities*, proclaimed his revolutionary creed through the expressionist group the Glass Chain, while the Austrian Adolf Loos declared ornament to be a crime in his famous polemical essay of 1908. Taut's disciple, Walter Gropius, published the Bauhaus manifesto in 1919: 'The new structures of the future . . . will one day rise toward heaven from the hands of a million workers like the crystal symbols of a new faith.' The aim of the Bauhaus was 'corporate planning of comprehensive Utopian designs . . . communal and cultic'.

In 1925 Le Corbusier, in similar vein, proposed replacing the centre of Paris with eighteen giant skyscrapers. Three years later the Modern Movement went evangelical when the Congrès Internationaux d'Architecture Moderne set the agenda for a new world, declaring, 'it is only from the present that our architectural work should be derived'.

The 'International Style', the product of a generation of slogans, manifestos and declarations of intent, was the final synthesis which was unveiled in New York's Museum of Modern Art in 1932. Architecture was reduced to a 'single body of discipline' in which an anti-historicist and anti-ornamental rectilinear code was compulsory. The new faith had already arrived in Britain. A pupil of the Constructivist Alexander Rodchenko, Berthold Lubetkin, who had designed the Soviet Pavilion for the 1929 Strasbourg Exhibition, was working on his London Zoo penguin pool and his Highgate flats, with their Corbusian roof terraces. The future had arrived.

Hindsight allows us to judge modernism's messianic theorists with scepticism, however brilliant some of their architecture. In post-war Britain their influence was profound and often pernicious. They were, after all, assuming an almost mystical role for their profession at a time of cultural and economic uncertainty. Architects and planners became the self-selected healers of shattered cities, socially benign alchemists who believed they could raise a scientific paradise over the ruins of chaos and disorder.

The contention that the ills of society could be resolved by large-scale planning blueprints must have had a seductive appeal to the rising generation of architects and planners such as Robert Bruce, whose 1945 proposal for a reinvented Glasgow was uncompromisingly absolutist. Le Corbusier had attempted much the same in 1922 with his 'Plan for a City of Three Million inhabitants'. Glasgow's purifying renewal was frustrated initially as the council built standard tenements on peripheral estates, but then the breakthrough came. A council delegation visited Le Corbusier's Unité d'Habitation in Marseilles in 1954 and returned with a taste for municipal modernism.

'The skyline of Glasgow will become a more attactive one to me because of the likely vision of multi-storey houses rising by the thousand,' said the corporation's convener of housing, Bailie David Gibson. 'The prospect will be thrilling . . .' Gibson was one of a breed of 'housing crusader' and his Edinburgh counterpart, Pat Rogan, was no less apocalyptic. He watched with delight as whole streets of city tenements were pulverised, and fought unsuccessfully to build multi-storey council housing at Holyrood. The socialist dream of housing for the masses was also, as it happens, a bonanza for Scotland's building barons, and the money would occasionally eclipse the selfless idealism, as in Dundee, where corruption was commonplace.

Gibson and Rogan were not operating in isolation. They were, in effect, the facilitators of the low-quality end of the global Modern Movement. An elemental force was at work, at the core of which lay a blind belief in the superior benefits of modernism.

In 1950s and 1960s Britain 'modern' was a relative term, however. For many councils it meant cheap housing, quickly built; for others, it had quasi-religious connotations. The husband and wife team of Peter and Alison Smithson took the reverential view. To them modernism, if not quite the machine-dream metropolis of Fritz Lang reborn as a technical reality, was at least a kind of revealed truth.

Their guru was Ludwig Mies van der Rohe, a modernist with roots in the neoclassical revivalism of Bismarck's Germany who, after discovering Expressionism, devised a scheme for Berlin's Alexanderplatz that anticipated much of the city-centre brutalism of the 1960s. Mies succeeded Gropius as director of the Bauhaus until it was suppressed by the Nazis in 1933. As a professor of architecture in Chigaco he was to find his perfect métier in a city of wealthy clients who were prepared to adopt him as a visionary style mentor.

The Smithsons, enraptured, wrote of his buildings as if they were the monuments of an ancient civilisation – 'If 860 Lakeside Drive is the Parthenon of his steel phase, Crown Hall is his Ephesus' – and, as with many cultists, they were not so much influenced as taken over. 'My own debt to Mies is so great that it is difficult for me to disentangle what I hold as my own thoughts, so often have they been the result of insights received from him.'

Unfortunately, reinterpreting Mies' spectacular Seagram building or the stylish bronze and glass apartment blocks he designed for the prosperous citizens of Chigaco as low-budget local authority housing and schools in Britain was an impossible task. Writing of the Smithsons' Hunstanton Secondary Modern School in 1984, when it was just over thirty years old, Martin Pawley claimed: 'It is in a class of its own for glazing failure, heat loss, acoustic reverberation, and maintenance.' The plain prose of the critic is in stark contrast to the tortured syntax which the Smithsons deployed in talking up the Miesian cause: 'an architecture that can awaken a sun, nature, climate, aspect-prospect consciousness . . . makes the necessary base connection on which the collective design impulse depends . . . for the machine-supported present-day cities only a live, cool, highly controlled, rather impersonal language can deepen that base.'

The anti-heritage line was another Smithson speciality long before *wunderkind* Mark Leonard and Cool Britannia had even been thought of. The Smithsons, like many of modernism's propagandists, were blatantly élitist in their kitsch credo of 'scientific socialism', yet they could assume a class warrior's loathing of anything that they themselves considered élitist. In *To Embrace the Machine* withering scorn was poured on the 'Waugh/Maugham/Green[sic]/Duff Cooper stigmata of uselessness – their not-worth-holding attitudes to life – such an atmosphere is still the malady of culture; the slithery enemy of true change – the cool of the seventies is more stood off, with reason replacing snobbery, both the conceit of snobbishness and freewheeling of historic revival'.

The calm dignity of the past, in other words, was an affront to the Smithsons' purifying mission to create an ordered, sterile world for the masses. Theirs was an intellectual position betraying a snobbishness far more virulent than anything Waugh or Greene would ever have contemplated. Yet even as late as the mid-1970s this waffle was regarded as a form of received wisdom by many of those seeking to solve the 'problem' of the cities by breaking up communities and smashing down homes.

It was, of course, supremacist nonsense recalling the megalomania of Le Corbusier and the Nietzschean excesses of Bruno Taut. Where the prescriptive paternalism of nineteenth-century reformers such as Owen was primarily a matter of creating contented small-scale communities, the mega-visionaries of inter-war Europe dreamed of reshaping the built environment on a gargantuan scale to effect the reprogramming of humankind.

'Scientific socialism' in architecture was rarely either scientific or socialist. Indeed its precepts often provided useful iconic associations for the right-wing dictators of the day. Mussolini, for example, commissioned Terragni's all-glass Casa del Fascio as a purifying symbol of his creed. The 'socialism' tag can be applied promiscuously. To Le Corbusier, Henry Ford was a 'primitive socialist'. Certainly the Ford Corporation, through its 'Sociological Department', applied intrusive, Soviet-like controls over the personal lives of employees. For modernists such as Le Corbusier, Ford's attempts to create a new kind of worker geared to the innovations of industrial technology were laudable and progressive; such dehumanised specimens, after all, would have made model citizens in the habitation zone of a bleak Le Corbusier towerscape.

In the hard new world of the architectural future democracy was an irrelevance. Le Corbusier viewed his ideal City for Three Million as a managerial ghetto, a Cité d'Affaires, where only the favoured bureaucratic élite would live, while lesser mortals would be banished to the industrial linear cities of the 'Four Routes'. With each cross-axial tower identical in height, and thus anti-competitive, it was the prescriptive vision par excellence, a demagogue's attempt to construct a world stripped of historical decadence and individualism. A hardy bacillus, it survived in the city planning departments of post-war Britain, though the rhetoric became less strident, stressing the attractions of fast-build technology on a low budget, rather than reinventing the species. But the underlying ethos remained that of a visionary package in a well-ordered local authority paradise.

The germ incubates still, in the shallow, anti-heritage, New Britain message needlessly concocted by the New Labour machine. Gibson, Rogan and their ilk may have been destructive and unsavoury, but the very least that can be said for them was that they were providing social housing for working people. Le Corbusier and Mies may have been aesthetic tyrants, but in their day cities across Europe had been devastated, and were going to have to be built anyway. And at least fantasists like Taut and Marinetti had some sort of mad, passionate commitment.

# 7 Scotching the Symbol
## *A Shibboleth Too Far*

*There's a scheme for you! The Parthenon of Edinburgh – the Westminster Abbey of Scotland – the National Acropolis. The scene hallowed by the ashes of Hume, Burns, Playfair*

Henry, Lord Cockburn, 1835

THERE IS AN intriguing subplot to the former High School's rejection, and it concerns a political pathology that projects the idea of power through the manipulation of image and iconography. New Labour's determination to create its own gleaming symbol for Scotland was conjoined with an underlying fear of the historic symbol with its awkward Old Labour links. The neoclassical school was a potent emblem, and it was not to the liking of a section of the party hierarchy. By actually looking like a parliament building along standard Jeffersonian lines it posed an implicit challenge to the pragmatic concept of devolution as a mechanism for containing nationalism. By tradition, the wider Calton Hill precinct was nothing less than a contrived statement of Scottish nationhood, though given the Hanoverian-unionist context of Lord Cockburn's time this was imagery safely subsumed within the ascendant authority of the British nation-state.

So why did a New Labour faction nurse a negative obsession bordering on paranoia about something as innocuous as an old school on a hill? Of the few official reasons advanced for 'New Parliament House' being ruled out in 1997, two were particularly eye-catching. One played on the inherent mutual *schadenfreude* to which Glasgow and Edinburgh politicians are so often prone. Killing off Calton Hill, it was suggested in all seriousness, was a 'poke in the eye for the Edinburgh establishment'.

This pronouncement, dismal as it was to those who had hoped that the emerging political climate would overcome traditional Glasgow-Edinburgh animosities, was by no means representative of Glasgow opinion. Glasgow council, indeed, was firmly opposed to the move to Leith, and Glasgow in due course would be hung out to dry over the issue of the temporary parliament chamber's location, as we shall see.

This was, if anything, more about an enmity between the politically active middle-class coteries of both cities, a schism often apparent in the Scottish legal profession – 'We'll have none of your Glasgow High Court hectoring here, sir,' was a reprimand addressed by an Edinburgh judge to a young Glasgow advocate – and, in Scotland as elsewhere, politics and the law are closely connected. According to one Labour Party source Calton Hill was 'a bit too close to the New Club for comfort'* for some of Labour's Glasgow University *alumni.*

Another notorious expression which gained currency was the peculiar label 'nationalist shibboleth'. This was widely attributed to the devo-sceptical Minister for Scotland, Brian Wilson (by Labour MSPs, amongst others). However when I mentioned this in a *Herald* article Mr Wilson responded with a curt denial and an elliptical suggestion that he had, in fact, supported Calton Hill at the outset.

It was perfectly possible, of course, that this issue had entered Labour's gruelling internal 'turf war', and that certain interests in Scotland were attempting to exculpate

* For those unfamiliar with the social habits of Edinburgh's *haute bourgeoisie* the New Club is the city's most élite gathering place. It was foolishly rebranded in 1966 when the stunning 1834 Renaissance palazzo designed by William Burn and David Bryce was demolished and replaced with a dreary grey block by Alan Reiach. Anti-heritage sentiment was alive and well long before New Labour got in on the act!

Donald Dewar by implying that others, including Brian Wilson, had promoted the 'rubbishing' of Calton Hill. The choreography of blame, after all, is a necessary aspect of news management; by January 2001 I was even being assured by one senior MSP that Holyrood was 'all Mandelson's doing'.

It has been said that 'nationalist shibboleth' was Donald Dewar's own phrase, applied after a visit to the former Royal High School where he had been less than enamoured of a bronze plaque commemorating the radical nationalist Wendy Wood. This, it so happens, had been fixed on an interior wall on the instructions of Edinburgh council's Labour-controlled Women's Committee as part of a programme to celebrate 'Women of Achievement'. A further point is that Wood herself occupies an uneasy place in nationalism's litany, and her plaque was as likely to upset the SNP as please them. She was the sort of fey maverick today's sober-suited nationalists would rather forget, a soap-box orator with an invective style which ensured that the cause was kept marginalised throughout the 1950s and 1960s. Some even had her down as an *agent provocateur* planted by the security services.*

Whatever the details, there can be little doubt that Calton Hill's historically evolved role as an icon of nationhood influenced New Labour's perception of it. Yet what, exactly, was this concept of 'nationhood' which seems to have niggled a government which, given the size of its Westminster majority, should have felt as secure as any in history? Nationhood is a difficult term to define, being riven with subjective overtones which present us with no single meaning. Even the most convinced unionists are prepared to

* An elderly Wendy Wood, resplendent in quasi-military Lovat green, would often gather up available young people after her splenetic Sunday harangues on Edinburgh's Mound and invite them for tea to her house in Howard Place. I was part of such a group on one occasion. She regaled us with stories of the South African wars where she claimed that as a five-year-old she'd been taught to shoot from the back of a covered wagon. The consensus was that she was highly entertaining, but also highly eccentric.

concede that the concept is a valid one in so far as the experience of being a Scot is qualitatively different from that of being otherwise. A nation is not so much a geographical unit of administration as a psychological construct founded on the idea of shared interests and perceptions. A bus driver in Shettleston, a Black Isle farmer and a stockbroker in Longniddry may have nothing in common with each other, yet they can subscribe emotionally to the idea of a place called Scotland with a distinctive culture and history which they all feel part of.

It can be argued that this common bond is almost absurdly abstract, yet no one could deny its strength. Indeed, it is the abstraction that endows nationhood with its elemental secular-mystical dimension. We don't know what it is precisely, but we do know that it's pretty powerful, and those who mess about with it do so at their peril.

The touchstones of a nation are its symbols and its heroes. Vilify these, and dignity is offended. The political neurosis associated with Scottish national identity is by no means limited to the Labour Party, an interesting case in point being that of Tory Scottish Secretary Michael Forsyth and his assertion that William Wallace was 'a loser'. Mr Forsyth made this ill-advised remark after the première of *Braveheart* and there was widespread public outrage. Plainly, being skewered alive in public was a bad career move for Wallace on a purely personal level, but in terms of securing a place in the national pantheon it conferred the martyr's crown and guaranteed immortality. The popular rejoinder to Mr Forsyth's put-down, predictably, was that judged by the same criteria Jesus, too, was a loser – a neat way of indicating that Wallace is the warrior Christ of Scottish popular imagination. It didn't much matter that Michael Forsyth was making his pronouncement in the context of a film epic that bore little resemblance to known historical fact. In criticising Scotland's paramount heroic folk symbol he had quite simply blasphemed, and in doing so had insulted national sentiment.

To give the man his due, he did try to make amends.

Having knocked one symbol, he took steps to reinstate another when he persuaded the Queen to send Scotland's ancient relic of kingship, the Stone of Destiny, back to Scotland. It is believed that this harmless ruse was dreamed up by his speech-writer and adviser, the journalist Gerald Warner, a historically minded Tory of the old school with monarchical leanings. Whatever the truth of the matter, Forsyth's adversaries had it down as a bit of a ploy; he had gaffed over Wallace, an election was in the offing, and this was an opportunity to showcase his Scottish credentials.

A ceremonial re-entry of the stone was staged at the Borders town of Coldstream, a few miles north of Flodden Field, scene of the 1513 battle which proved particularly critical in the annals of Anglo-Scottish grievance and mutual suspicion. Ian Hamilton, who as a student in 1951 had been involved in the sensational removal of the stone from Westminster Abbey, had scented the whiff of political opportunism and turned down an invitation to attend. As the convoy came to a halt on Smeaton's Border Bridge special effects were provided by two swans flying overhead and a ray of sunshine breaking through the November cloud to the strains of 'Highland Cathedral'. A large crowd lined the road between the bridge and the town, where a podium had been raised for the benefit of Michael Forsyth and his opposite number, George Robertson.

On the slightly iffy pretext that my nine-year-old son might benefit from witnessing this event, we went along and looked on as the affable Mr Forsyth marched around glad-handing the lieges. It was a good show, but in the end what I was to find particularly memorable was not the competent stage-management, the sentimental political speeches, the pipes and drums, nor even the sun's providential intervention, but the fact that as the sealed army Land-Rover carrying the stone drove past there were grown men standing on the kerbside with tears in their eyes.

Scotsmen crying in public? Absolutely – and clearly they were not part of any organised political faction. Deep in private thought, they had the look of retired shepherds or

tradesmen. They were all certainly old enough to remember
the romantic episode of Christmas 1951 when Ian Hamilton
and his fellow students had last brought the stone to Scotland under rather different circumstances. For these very
ordinary elderly men this was obviously a powerful and
extraordinary experience. An old stone in the back of a
Land-Rover, of itself, has no great significance; but as a
symbol, as a repository of an ancient national sentiment,
it meant something to them which was enough to bring
forth a very un-Scottish emotional response. As a gesture,
it may have failed to save Mr Forsyth's Stirling seat, but it
certainly did not lack profundity.

This episode on Coldstream Bridge, like the shenani-
gans over Calton Hill, exposed a raw nerve in Scotland's
political establishment, whether of the left, or the right.
Potent symbolism, it would seem, is a bit of a worry.
Nor are these isolated instances. The most blatant case
of shibboleth-phobia occurred a century and a half ago
when Stirling council decided to commission a Wallace
monument for the town, and the distinguished artist Joseph
Noel Paton submitted a design for a massive statue of a
chained lion locked in struggle with a typhon. This was
initially approved of, but then, after some thought (or,
more likely, a quiet word with higher authorities) it was
rejected on the grounds that it might offend English visitors. The present mock-medieval spiky tower was raised
instead.

Given the ingrained problem of symbolism for Scotland's
ruling establishment, it's perhaps to be expected that the old
Royal High School, one of the finest neoclassical buildings
in Britain and the glorious centrepiece of a perfect urban
acropolis, was a bit of a frightener for the politically timid.
After all, for two centuries Calton Hill, a volcanic rem-
nant in the heart of Edinburgh, had assumed the role of
a Valhalla, being covered with Robert Louis Stevenson's
'field of monuments'. The hill was generally seen, one way
or another, as the embodiment of the Scottish soul. For
the historian Rosaline Masson, writing in 1904, the 'most

mystically beautiful' view of Edinburgh was that seen from its Calton Hill acropolis by night.

The Holyrood parliament, ultimately, will be a monument to the rejection of this *zeitgeist*, for its origins are rooted in a singular act of political iconoclasm. Jonathan Glancey of the *Guardian* summed up the Holyrood site's ethos succinctly when, in February 1998, he described it as a representation of 'the lie that Scotland is to govern itself'. But it also represents something else: the proprietorial assumption of a political élite seeking to perpetuate itself through large-scale building projects.

In a democracy, of course, it could be deemed unwise to pursue self-aggrandisement through a lavish programme of palace building, since the voters might take it amiss, so a different kind of self-promoting vehicle is required. With Emperor Vespasian's Colosseum as an exemplar, it can be seen that the way to the people's hearts lies in the dispensation of 'gifts' of unsurpassed architectural magnificence for general cultural and recreational use.

It doesn't always work (qv. Millennium Dome) and inevitably cynics will point out that the generosity involved is being underwritten by public revenues, but even so the general effect is of a benign and enlightened authority seeking to improve the lives of the population as a whole.

Besides, an incoming government formed by a party that has been out of office for two decades is subject to the same simple temptations as the family that, after years of saving, has finally bought a house. Like most creatures with a territorial consciousness, we value gestures of ownership. Out goes the old kitchen, the faded curtains, the worn carpets. Weekends are spent buying wallpaper, paint, fabrics and flatpack furniture. The resulting show of taste defines us socially, and provides the satisfaction to be gained from creating a new environment in our personal space. New governments, like new house-owners keen to renovate the front lounge, find the urge to spruce up the national image irresistible, an added consideration being that the verdict of history might, several generations down the line, be better disposed if our descendants can judge us by a legacy of splendid buildings for which, theoretically, they will be immensely grateful.

As discussed earlier, there is something of this at Holyrood, which was, after all, a rebranding government's bid to mark out its territory. Devolution was to be defined by a 'world-class' building bestowed by a political authority eager to demonstrate its belief in change. The problem was that this was Scotland's personal space, and the neighbours were fixing it for us. Nor was it a cause for celebration when it emerged that Scottish taxpayers would be footing the entire bill.

Symbols can arouse resentment as well as admiration. They can be dysfunctional and counter-productive, as opposed to confident and affirmative. They can demonstrate ineptitude and deceit, or sophistication and creativity. Holyrood's tragedy is that it is characterised by the negative attributes, rather than the positive ones. In other words, it has ended up being precisely the sort of symbol Scotland's fledgling political institution didn't need, and we are all, one way or another, paying a high price for it.

The initial act of folly, of course, was the banal and erroneous assumption that Thomas Hamilton's 1829 masterpiece on Calton Hill was a 'nationalist shibboleth', when, in reality, it was the opposite: the quintessential Hanoverian-unionist ideal expressed through the medium of a Periclean depiction of architectural harmony.

Calton Hill was a near-perfect reflection of the 'settled will'. Unlike Dublin's Post Office, or Boston's Beacon Hill, it had never been the rallying point for an armed insurrection. Perhaps the most dramatic event to occur there was a brief occupation by a handful of nationalists who were quickly removed, a low-key invasion which resulted in a £100 fine for SNP's Jim Sillars. For many nationalists, indeed, Calton Hill was an unsuitable symbol. Even after the 1997 referendum George Adams of the SNP's youth wing spoke out against the Callaghan government's 'New Parliament

House' and urged a takeover of the original Parliament Hall in Edinburgh's Old Town.

The Holyrood débâcle, in short, was the outcome of a false perception. The 'nationalist shibboleth' was no such thing. True, there had been a vigil held there during John Major's premiership, when the prospects for devolution had seemed particularly bleak, but this had been a strictly non-partisan affair, without party-political banners or badges. There was also a pro-devolution event which consisted of a few thousand people linking arms around the site. Nationalists had taken part in both instances, but so too had Labour activists, Greens, Liberal Democrats and even Conservatives. Their shared aim, in any case, was to provide a show of support for Labour's devolution policy under both John Smith and Tony Blair. As soon as Labour were in office the vigil struck camp and consigned itself to the history books.

As far as Labour was concerned, the symbolism of Calton Hill called forth a twinge of conscience and a flush of embarrassment. The truth that dared not speak its name, not even as much as whisper, was that Calton Hill was a shibboleth all right, but it wasn't a nationalist one. This was the Labour Party's own devolutionary heart of darkness, the scene associated with a political fix which, for some, amounted to a cynical act of betrayal. There may be a plaque to Wendy Wood fixed to the wall, but there is another, more pervasive, spirit that still lurks there.

It is that of George Cunningham, the Labour MP for Islington, who obligingly fronted the amendment that scuppered the outcome of the Callaghan government's 1979 devolution referendum. For Labour, it would seem that the fundamental problem of Calton Hill was the party's own sense of guilt.

Towers of Perception
*The Mythic Architect*

> *When Alexander the Great intended to build a city for*
> *his glory Dinocrates, the architect, came to him . . .*
> Niccolo Machiavelli: *Discourses*

GOD WAS AN architect, or so it would seem from Blake's engraved frontispiece to *Europe* of a bearded figure with dividers. Jesus too, claims the Reverend Gordon Strachan of Edinburgh, a lecturer in architecture. In *Jesus, the Master Builder*, Strachan suggests that Christ worked on the Graeco-Roman theatre at Sepphoris, near Nazareth, and even visited Britain to check out the Druids' sacred geometry.

Architects, divine or not, occupy a special niche in the social hierarchy. They have George Bush senior's 'vision thing', implying an affinity with far-seeing mystics of old. If successful, they become celebrities with expensive PR, guaranteeing even greater fame and fortune. Sir Keith Joseph, in his contentious 'socio-economic scale' of the 1960s, had them in the top group, some way above politicians, though this possibly owed something to his construction Industry link. Bovis was the family firm.

These matters are of interest here if only because of the immense deference shown, for the most part, to the conceptual vision of the late Enric Miralles. The Holyrood site was clearly problematic in terms of restricted space, historic context and its accessibility, and the quality of the proposed architecture was its only selling point, so it had to be talked up furiously. There were some glitches. Miralles was dubbed 'El Collapso' by an unsympathetic critic when it emerged that the roof of a sports hall in Aragon had failed. He responded robustly, insisting that it was not his fault. The contractor had simply misread the plans. It was also suggested at one point that he was not actually registered to operate as an architect in the UK, though in the event that turned out to be a minor technicality.

Enric Miralles certainly had an engaging personality and an inventive approach to design. He was adored by his students and fêted not just in his home town of Barcelona, but around the world. His buildings mostly worked well and looked good, though getting through the construction process and holding down costs could be difficult. Bart Joziasse, the project manager for Utrecht Town Hall's renovation, says that although there were budget problems with that particular Miralles scheme, the end product was popular with both staff and public, and 'Enric was great to work with'.

The problem with questioning the work of modern architects, litigation apart, is that the critic appears anti-progressive and philistine. It engenders the sort of fear that, say, pooh-poohing a Turner Prize-winner might arouse, and who wants to appear anti-art, even if the art in question is an unmade bed? There are many reasons why architects enjoy high status, the obvious one being that we can't escape them. No one has to read Proust, or listen to Bach cantatas, or look at Poussin's paintings, or see a Brecht play, but we are all confronted by buildings. Even a hermit in a home-made clay-biggin in the hills of Sutherland has to get out occasionally, perhaps to catch a glimpse of the turrets of Dunrobin or Golspie primary school.

Architecture, to a greater or lesser extent, is in the business of faith. It isn't simply a matter of selling a 'vision' to a planning committee, but something much more abstruse and deep-seated. Western culture has largely given up on organised religion, yet people, for the most part, have certainly not given up on the need to look up to something greater than themselves, and architecture has all the right qualities. It combines tough technical ingenuity with abstract thought, creativity and an assumed understanding of the needs of society. The practitioners in this engineer-artist caste have the power to heal, or at least make us feel much better by providing clean, new, comfortable buildings. They are signifiers of progress for whole populations, and indeed the world

– look at Bilbao, Seattle, Sydney, Vancouver, Singapore.

Considering new architecture as 'a good thing' is, for some, almost a form of religious observance, the more so since the heretical Prince of Wales reminded us about how horrendous the 1960s were for Britain's cities. At that fateful hour the profession rose up to defend itself. The fightback was tenacious. Royal Institute of British Architects President Maxwell Hutchinson led the counter-charge, with heavyweight support from other interests, including the estate-agent turned developer who is now Tony Blair's 'Architecture Tsar'. It was interesting, at the time, to hear the cream of the profession 'welcome' the prince's contribution to the debate on carbuncle architecture, when what they really wanted to tell him was to get his tanks off their lawn so that they could just carry on building and earning. The profession had to work hard to regain its dignity. It learned the gentle arts of planning gain and consultation (helped by PR budgets which no amenity group or mere individual could hope to equal, of course). With Cool Britannia came the heady joy of rehabilitation. Architects could once more issue wise pronouncements, and even Prince Charles, with minor reservations such as the Millennium 'blancmange', became generally supportive.

It helped, of course, that the general standard of building design had improved markedly during the 1980s and 1990s, and that modernism gave up most of its sinister brute tendencies. Next to the tired, grey-streaked concrete hulks of the 1960s the new generation of buildings looked positively glamorous. Try comparing Edinburgh's impressive Saltire Court with the nearby ageing government office block of Argyle House, for example. It helped even more that many in the profession became genuinely community-conscious and cast off the aloofness and superiority of the Smithsons' generation. Architecture is no longer the one-dish menu of the 1960s, with the occasional garnish in the form of a restored tower house from niche practitioners such as Ian Lindsay and Robert Hurd. Architecture has become diverse and often beautiful.

The architect super-hero returned to redeem our world,

after a brief interlude of abasement which, in some ways, was ill-deserved, for the Prince of Wales could not, for constitutional reasons, attack the real culprits of civic annihilation, namely the politicians who let it happen and occupied some of the worst buildings. But it should not be forgotten that architecture is a profession which, at the top end, knows how to sell itself better than almost any other. Visual presentation, after all, is what the business is all about, which provides an instant advantage over doctors and lawyers. Then there are the famous historical precedents. Sir Basil Spence, without batting an eyelid, could compare himself to Sir Christopher Wren. Others modestly assume the mantle of Bramante in the sense that, like him, they work at a drawing board. Even modernism enjoys a comforting afterglow from its long and glorious past.

Money also provides much excellent leverage. Given the total market value of a city-centre commercial development, what's a few thousand spent on glossy brochures, journalists' lunches, video-promos, helicopter trips and a swish presentation or two for the councillors and planners in a smart hotel? The Scottish Parliament Project even has its own £250,000 custom-built deluxe big hut to present its case, though without the benefit of the one feature that might have been useful: a viewing platform. Naturally, it's all perfectly legitimate. The objectors to mega-schemes, meanwhile, maybe scrape up enough to hold a few meetings in a draughty church hall.

The big practices discovered spin around the time that Peter Mandelson discovered red roses. Keeping the press on-side is vitally important, or, even better, one can *be* the press. Stuart Lipton being interviewed by Maxwell Hutchinson in *Architectural Design* was, as puffs go, a truly baroque exercise in adulation. We learn from Hutchinson, for example, that 'Lipton is an enigma' who, as a property developer 'breaks the mould of fast talking, quick dealing, shallow greed, and ambition' and that he is 'shockingly quiet-spoken, thoughtful and attentive'. Of course, when one is worth somewhere between £80 million and

£120 million one can presumably break any mould one chooses. 'In the Lipton catalogue of mine we include heroism – courage – often to withstand public criticism,' continues Hutchinson ecstatically. It is, however, refreshing to know that 'this country's architectural impresario par excellence' is a man of relatively simple tastes with 'no country house, no yacht, no racehorses'.

It would be incorrect to describe Sir Stuart as an architect super-hero, since he isn't actually an architect. He merely employs them. And when all's said and done he has an eye for quality, and he knows its value, which certainly places him in a different league from the bureaucrat patrons of the 1960s who were largely obsessed with low-cost mega-builds, the uglier the better.

The all-time definitive example of the manic architectural super-hero has to be Howard Roark, who, thankfully (given what he was up to) didn't exist, as such, being a fictional invention from the fevered imagination of Ayn Rand, a right-wing Russo-American novelist of the 1940s. *The Fountainhead* was made into a movie by King Vidor, with Gary Cooper in the lead role. The essence of the film was the favourite American theme of the man of destiny battling against the odds, which caught the mood of the era of McCarthyite witch-hunts when it paid to stay off the blacklist by celebrating rugged individuals who refuse to be put down by dark forces.

*The Fountainhead*, with its underlying anti-communist dynamic, rode along on the somewhat paradoxical thesis that soaring high-rise tower blocks of the purest unadulterated geometry were in some way representative of assertive individualism. Ms Rand was on shaky ground here, given all the pamphleteering about 'scientific socialism' which preoccupied so many of the early modernists. Mies van der Rohe, indeed, had even designed a monument to Rosa Luxembourg and other heroes of the Marxist-Leninist cause before finding his way to America, and a lucrative line in luxury apartments on Lakeside Drive for the freewheeling Chicago smart set.

Roark went on to excel himself by dynamiting one of his own buildings when it went a bit off-spec during construction. The epic courtroom drama which saw this champion of the architectural New World Order in the dock featured an outburst in which he stated his credo; he was fighting, above all, for the sacred 'right of the ego'.

As an example of characterisation Roark was, even by the often low B-movie standards of 1940s Hollywood, unreal to the point of absurdity. Yet something of his spirit was abroad in post-war Scotland, with its 'housing crusaders' in the mould of Gibson, Rogan and Bruce. In *Our Fathers* Andrew O'Hagan describes a fictional Glasgow architect, Hugh Bawm, who had set his course by the very same principles that Roark was espousing: 'We must make ourselves all over again – what are we here for if not for progress.' Bawm was in the vanguard of an all-embracing socialist cause: the rehousing of the masses. This had been no part of Ayn Rand's agenda, yet the end result was nevertheless a fulfilment of Roark's 'master of the universe' vision of a purged world brought to fruition on Red Road and Royston Hill.

In the circumstances, Scots naturally tend to be more than a little wary of the supposed benefits of Cool Britannia rebranding. We have been here before. In the 1960s prescriptive reprogrammers of a land with an architectural tradition rooted in Robert Adam and Charles Rennie Mackintosh decided the past wasn't good enough and set about wrecking it, providing, instead, tower-block deserts with endemic social problems and crippling long-term maintenance costs. Talk of a 'New Scotland' doesn't particularly inspire widespread confidence, given such folk memories.

It is often suggested that part of the problem in the 1960s was that many of the system-built high-rise blocks put up then were not, in fact, the work of creative architects, but consisted of factory-made components put up by low-skilled labour squads under the supervision of engineers and technicians. However it's also the case that many were architect-designed, even by the top-drawer practices of Sir Basil Spence and Sir Robert Matthew, amongst others.

Widespread doubts about mass renewal, and in particular the social effects of destroying and dispersing communities, were already being directed at planners and architects when a low point was reached thanks to John Poulson, whose association with the corrupt Scottish Office civil servant, George Pottinger, was exposed by *Private Eye* in 1972. The Poulson affair also had political repercussions, particularly in the north-east of England, where several Labour councillors were investigated for corruption, in particular 'Mr Newcastle', or T. Dan Smith, who was one of a number imprisoned. While no one holding high office in government was implicated directly in any Poulson-related criminal activities, the scandal embarrassed housing minister Richard Crossman, for one, who had been eulogistic in his praise of Smith. In the United States, bellowed Crossman, a man of T. Dan Smith's energy and vision would have been the confidant of presidents.

The Poulson approach to architecture also came under scrutiny. Essentially it was an in-and-out process of creating wealth, rather than creating buildings of any quality. According to one contemporary he 'couldn't even design a brick shithouse'.

As the life-denying 1960s look began to descend into tackiness and the technical flaws became apparent, the old comprehensive development approach fell out of favour, and a new phenomenon, community architecture, began to make an appearance. A rising generation of architects, planners and politicians sought development solutions that, today, would be called sustainable. Even the RIBA experienced a palace coup as Rod Hackney, doyen of the community architecture movement, took up the presidency.

The new philosophy was disarmingly simple. Instead of driving entire populations out to suburban housing estates Highland clearance-style, the idea was to decant them locally, improve their homes to a tolerable standard, then put them back in, releasing the 'decant' flat for a tenant on the housing list. Owner-occupiers and landlords could also apply for improvement grants.

The change in thinking came just in time to prevent Edinburgh going the same way as Glasgow. Eighteenth-century George Square had been lost in the 1960s, despite a lively campaign to save it. The final blow had been delivered by the Secretary of State's adviser on conservation, Robert Matthew, who was also professor of architecture at that same university that intended to rebuild the square as a modernist high-rise campus. When Matthew later picked up the commission to design one of the replacement buildings on the cleared site there were mutters of disapproval, as well as disappointment. Matthew, founder of RMJM, which is now steering the Holyrood project, had been an inspirational force behind the conservation of Edinburgh New Town, and was largely thought of as a 'good guy'.

The destruction of George Square was instrumental in changing attitudes to the 1963 plan for redeveloping the entire Southside area which had been drawn up jointly by the university, Edinburgh corporation and a private developer, Ravenseft. This entailed a wholesale blitzing of literally thousands of houses, the majority historic tenements.

In 1972 a revised Town and Country Planning (Scotland) Act brought statutory protection of listed buildings into force, and a degree of public participation in the planning process. The city's first Labour Lord Provost, Jack Kane, represented the Craigmillar Ward, and knew at first hand the social problems that resulted when populations were moved en masse from familiar neighbourhoods to bleak peripheral estates. Craigmillar was a particularly stark example. It had even horrified the instinctive renewalist Herbert Morrison, Peter Mandelson's grandfather, who had condemned its 'barrack block' appearance during an early visit.

Kane had no second thoughts about supporting the emerging conservation lobby in the city's Southside and Old Town, and he took many of Labour's younger activists along with him, though many of the old guard retained the

attitudes of Pat Rogan, as did the city's Director of Building
Control, Ron Cooper, who was relatively profligate in his
use of 'Section 13' dangerous buildings notices.

Discontent was also stirring in the university. John Llewelyn
of the philosophy department and Duncan MacMillan of
fine arts became the core of a small group of dissenters
which was later expanded to include a number of local
residents like myself, the housing specialist Peter Pharoah
and Oliver Barratt, who would later become secretary of the
Cockburn Association.

The resulting Southside Association was initially an ad
hoc group of individuals rather than a credible movement.
I gravitated into becoming chairman, and we put on an
exhibition in a flat in a Georgian block in West Nicolson
Street which was due to be demolished, and which we had
taken to a public inquiry. This block had housed the studios
of the artists Sir David Wilkie and Alexander Runciman,
which gave the campaign a useful added edge.

Public support was overwhelming, and although the
association lost the public inquiry the proposed demolition
was put off, and eventually the street was rehabilitated. Two
individuals had taken a particular interest in the case. Robin
Cook, then recently elected MP for Central Edinburgh, and
the university's high-profile student rector Gordon Brown.
Both were opposed to the continuation of the 1963 Comprehensive Development Area proposals, and Brown went
so far as to set up a 'Rector's Working Party on Planning'
with a view to reassessing and reforming the university's
expansionary ambitions. It was decided that the Edinburgh
University Student Publications Board would publish a
book, *The Forgotten Southside*, with contributions from those
of us who were by now committed opponents of the 1963
proposals.

The book sold out, and Brown and his planning working
party resolved to repeat the exercise with *The Unmaking of
Edinburgh*, which extended the boundaries to include other
threatened areas, such as the Old Town and Fountainbridge.
Robin Cook, as well as being the local MP, had been

chairman of the council's housing committee, and had a formidable detailed knowledge of housing legislation. His contribution was a well-considered vindication of the Southside
Association's proposals for the retention of the existing
community within the existing housing stock. He also made
a point which, however distantly, gives an echo to the
current Holyrood affair. The former Tory council, he wrote,
had more or less given away 'most of Fountainbridge for
one of Europe's largest brewery complexes'.

It is worth pausing for a moment's reflection here. The
beneficiary of this alleged largesse was Scottish Brewers,
later to become Scottish & Newcastle Breweries, owners
of the site which, in December 1997, would become an
'eleventh-hour entrant' to Donald Dewar's list of options for
the parliament building. Planners, developers, councillors
and amenity bodies had been discussing this 'eleventh-hour
entrant' for around a quarter of a century. It even featured
as 'Canongate Square' in a glossy 1989 Old Town Plan.

The involvement of both Robin Cook and Gordon Brown
in the campaign to save the historic core of Edinburgh helped
to ensure success. The EUSPB books, though largely planned
in the Meadow Bar on a *samizdat* budget, had involved a
range of talent and interests, including Dejan Sudjic, now
an architectural writer, the journalist George Rosie, and even
the society photographer Broderick Haldane. Eventually the
1963 proposals were dropped, the Southside and Old Town
declared conservation areas, and the blight lifted. Brown,
then a 'Red Book' radical, shared with Cook a genuine
passion for a community-led approach to the planning
and regeneration of inner cities. The idea of building an
overscaled public building on a site formerly proposed for
housing would, at that time, have been anathema to both.

When, on 8 December 1997, Donald Dewar brought
Holyrood on board and pronounced it a 'smashing site'
my own first reaction was that this decision would damage
Edinburgh and also damage the Labour Party; neither
prospect seemed particularly desirable, as far as I was
concerned. It also seemed unlikely that an industrial site

which still had a complex of old buildings on it could be cleared, detoxified, excavated and provided with a 'world-class' parliament building, all for the sum of £40 million, as mentioned in the white paper.

I decided to make a few inquiries and rang one of Scotland's leading commercial land development specialists. He had already been thinking about the matter. 'You can multiply that figure by six,' he insisted. I rang a structural engineer who had worked on several large-scale building projects in Britain and abroad. 'At least £200 million,' I was told. From an architect: 'Between £100 million and £150 million for site clearance, design and construction, but then there's the problem of the constraints of the site and its hopeless location. It might take another £50 million to sort all that out.'

This was, potentially, the fast track to disaster; both electorally, for the Labour Party, and physically, for the medieval core of a UNESCO World Heritage Site. On the day Dewar's choice was made public I wrote a two-page letter to Robin Cook who was, by then, foreign secretary, suggesting that a scheme which purported to symbolise devolution, yet which was being tied up in London before devolution had come into effect, was merely going to became a propaganda gift for the nationalists, thus undermining the whole point of Labour's devolution scheme. There was also the inevitable cost trajectory. Clearly the electorate weren't going to be too pleased if the £40 million building they hadn't asked for in the first place ended up costing £200 million or more. I received a polite, but brief, reply. My comments had been noted.

As to what individual members of the cabinet thought or said on this issue, we can only guess, or wait for the memoirs. One member of Blair's first cabinet has spoken of concern about the cost implications, particularly in July 1997, when Irvine's £650,000 refurbishment of his Westminster quarters was attracting negative press coverage. By that point Donald Dewar had already made it clear in Downing Street that he wished to dump the Royal High

School, despite the fact that it was simultaneously being run in pre-referendum literature by name. Blair, who had publicly stressed the need for his ministers to limit the 'trappings of power', was said to be uneasy about the plan.

Cardiff City Hall, too, was in the process of being vetoed in favour of a 'big signature' Richard Rogers assembly building. Even Rogers seemed concerned about possible repercussions (saying, 'I'll have to watch my backside,' according to *Private Eye*), while London was in line for a Norman Foster 'egg' for its new mayoral assembly building near Tower Bridge. Meanwhile, agriculture minister Jack Cunningham was pressing ahead with a £2 million office refit at a time of crisis in the farming industry, which didn't play too well in the prints, particularly since his alderman father had been imprisoned along with T. Dan Smith in the 1970s, and the right-wing press were given to unearthing this fact from time to time. Labour's image as the squeaky-clean alternative to the sleaze-ridden Tories was beginning to look less than convincing.

Gordon Brown's views on Donald Dewar's extravagant Cool Britannia aspirations would be especially interesting. His reputation as the son-of-the-manse 'iron Chancellor', after all, owed a great deal to his preoccupation with strict spending controls. As a student rector in the 1970s Brown had also been a dedicated proponent of the 'cities are for people' school of planning, and had championed the cause of community involvement, even locking horns with the principal, Sir Michael Swann, over the matter of the composition of the university court, then very much the domain of the great and the good.* Brown, the consummate

---

* Brown even nominated my aunt, Helen Crummy, to the University Court on the basis that she was an ordinary housewife who had set up a pioneering community-based arts festival in Craigmillar and strongly believed in extending educational opportunities to children from deprived backgrounds, as he himself did. The nomination was blocked, but years later the same university was to confer an honorary doctorate on her in recognition of her community services.

political operator, was rumoured to be exerting influence through his girlfriend, Margarita, a Romanian princess and god-daughter of the Duke of Edinburgh, the university Chancellor – an interesting *modus operandi* for a radical-left student, and one since substantiated in Paul Routledge's biography of the Chancellor.

Gordon Brown, as much as Donald Dewar, had been devolution's *meistersinger*. He had campaigned vociferously for an assembly in the late 1970s, opposing the anti-devolution stance of his former ally, Robin Cook. In the lead-up to the 1979 referendum Brown had delivered a rousing speech in Edinburgh on the merits of devolution, as he saw them, chief amongst them the need to end 'the culture of closed files and secrecy' which had led, in his view, 'to the Poulson and Pottinger affairs'. Yet barely two decades later he was a central figure, with Donald Dewar and devolution minister Henry McLeish, in bringing devolution to fruition in a 'New Scotland' which was being burdened with the cost of a Cool Britannia signature building of a scale, and in a context, that was as damaging as anything that had been inflicted on the Southside thirty years earlier. Worse still, the Byzantine manipulation involved in getting the scheme through in the teeth of public opposition recalled, if anything, the very 'culture of closed files and secrecy' that he had railed against in the late 1970s. It is an extraordinary turnabout, even if it was motivated by respect for his friend and mentor, Donald Dewar, who obviously wanted to leave his mark architecturally, as well as politically.

The awkward truth about Holyrood can never be hidden by architecture. The thinking behind it was morally flawed from the outset. An architect with an international reputation and a 'signature' style was needed to distract public opinion away from the scandal of Calton Hill's rejection. The 'upturned boats' commission which Enric Miralles had called the opportunity of his lifetime became stranded in the murky waters of stitch-up politics, personal ambition and deceit.

To Enric Miralles' cost, and to Donald Dewar's despair,

the Cool Britannia vision was revealed for what it was: a cynical and prescriptive window-dressing exercise which fooled no one, and was set to cripple the Scottish budget. The 'New Scotland'? Even the tacky, discredited 1960s didn't have problems on this scale.

The winner of numerous design awards, Enric Miralles himself admitted to me in December 1998 that a terrible truth was beginning to dawn on him. Holyrood was a 'near-impossible' challenge. 'What have I got myself into? I'm in the middle of something I don't understand,' he confided to a colleague a few weeks before his death.

He was right. No architectural reputation in the world would have been big enough to redeem it. The architect super-hero can only achieve so much.

# 9 Athens Reconvened
## *Setting the Temple on the Hill*

*How could I describe it? When God in Heaven takes up*
*panorama painting you can expect something terrific*
Felix Mendelssohn, 1829, on the view to Calton
Hill and the Forth Estuary from Arthur's Seat four
weeks after the opening of Thomas Hamilton's
High School

AS I WRITE this, we cannot yet judge the parliament building
we are going to get at Holyrood. All we can hope for is that
it fulfils the three requirements of the Sale of Goods Act.
Namely, it should be as described, fit for the purpose, and
of merchantable quality. It's the least we should expect for
£300 million.

On the other hand, we can certainly give consideration
to the parliament we were denied, since it already exists.
The monuments and buildings of Calton Hill were deliberately composed over a period of a century and a half as
components in an idealised urban landscape representing
the nationhood of Scotland. Friedrich von Schelling's dictum about architecture being frozen music certainly applies
to Calton Hill. Indeed, some element of this music may even
have found its way into Mendelssohn's consciousness, for
the day referred to in the opening quotation was, he wrote,
the very day he thought up the first bars of the theme of
his Scottish Symphony.

So what was it exactly that New Labour's iconoclasts
objected to in the symbolism and associations of Calton
Hill? A protean terror, perhaps, of its true significance as
a national icon? The hill's character is not, and never has
been, the result of mere municipal pride. Lord Cockburn

was distinctly relieved that it was unsullied by monuments to local dignitaries. Its purpose, for him, was to celebrate the entire Scottish nation, a role still recognised in the late 1920s, when Edinburgh's Lord Provost, Sir Thomas Whitson, described it as 'Scotland's Whitehall', and understood by the author and statesman John Buchan who bridled at the thought of Scots being 'like the Jews of the Dispersion, a potent force everywhere on the globe, but with no Jerusalem'.

The emblematic character of Calton Hill represents Scotland, the nation, and its will to maintain an identity. It is a potent symbol, fulfilling Thomas Jefferson's idealistic view of how an emergent democracy should house itself. The Doric façade of Thomas Hamilton's Royal High School even fits Jefferson's description of the Capitol in Washington: 'the first temple dedicated to the sovereignty of the people, embellishing with Athenian taste the course of a nation looking far beyond the range of Athenian destinies'.*

Calton Hill is the architectural set piece of Enlightenment Scotland, and its origins are rooted in a national apotheosis. In the middle of the eighteenth century the country reached a watershed. From being a wretched post-medieval state on the fringes of northern Europe prone to famine and religious strife, impoverished by the Darien disaster, and subsumed against the popular will into a union with its larger neighbour, it had struggled with some success to maintain its distinct identity against odds that were often overwhelming.

The final reckoning had come in 1746, with the crushing of the Jacobites. The Hanoverian ascendancy was now beyond contention, and the Scots, accepting the inevitable, concentrated their efforts elsewhere. Put another way, the nation embarked on a rebranding drive, though this was one with serious meaning and purpose.

The outward sign of the Scottish intellectual revolution was the gradual transformation of the built environment,

* Thomas Jefferson to Benjamin Latrobe, 1812.

both rural and urban. Edinburgh, a walled medieval city that clung to its rocky citadel like something out of *The Decameron*, spilled out of its congested centre in 1757 when Lady Nicolson's Parks, which lay to the south of the 1513 Flodden Wall, were offered for development. There was a frenetic uptake and much high-rolling speculation by, amongst others, the architect William Adam, whose son Robert returned from his grand tour a year later, his head filled with ideas about a 'corrected style' of classicism which he'd perfected in the company of the French artist Louis Clérisseau and the Italian engraver Giambattista Piranesi. His aim was 'a kind of revolution' in national architecture.

The starting point was the development of the Southside, and until the destruction of the 1970s the move from burgh vernacularism to neoclassicism – the world's first truly 'international' style – could be read like a book in each decade of building, culminating in the unified palace front elevations of the late Georgian period. The know-how gained in the Southside was employed to spectacular effect in the construction of the grid-plan Edinburgh New Town designed by James Craig.

The New Town was the epitome of Hanoverian-unionism: Thistle Street and Rose Street were amongst the first built, and the names of many that followed, such as Union Street, Pitt Street and Hanover Street, advertised the political creed. Craig's uncle, the poet James Thomson, had even written the words to 'Rule Britannia'.

During the development of the first phase of the New Town Calton Hill was cut off from Craig's grid-plan by a ravine, but the monumental landscape value of the site was recognised by Robert Adam in 1778 when his Hume mausoleum, based on that of the Emperor Theodoric at Ravenna, was built on the southern slope of the hill. This was the beginning of the hill's role as the repository of the national *zeitgeist*. Adam went on to design the city's Bridewell Prison (1795) where St Andrew's House now stands.

More monumentalising followed. In 1807 the architect

Robert Burn designed a monument to Nelson as a 100-foot-high version of the admiral's upturned telescope. By the time William Henry Playfair's Greek-cross observatory was finished in 1818 the idea of Calton Hill as a unified expression of a national identity was taking shape.

Its role as the pantheon of the nation's honour was fully realised in 1822 with the bridging of the ravine by the engineer Robert Stevenson, the construction of Elliot's Waterloo Place, and the beginnings of a scheme to replicate the Parthenon on the crest of the hill as a monument to the fallen of the French wars. To Lord Cockburn, the effect of Waterloo Place, framed towards Princes Street by Archibald Elliot's twin Ionic porticos of golden Hailes stone, was 'like a curtain going up on a theatre'.

Elliot's processional boulevard was certainly architectural drama of the highest order. Like Nash's London equivalent, it was ostensibly a celebration of victory over Napoleon, but in reality it was the triumphal culmination of Edinburgh's civic transformation. This was a moment of apotheosis, when the Scottish capital could count itself amongst the world's great modern cities, a moment that the exiled Jacobite, the Earl of Mar, had yearned for a century earlier when, admiring the glory of the Place Vendôme in Paris, he'd regretted that no such vision seemed possible in his own impoverished country.

It was the moment, too, when the Calton Hill became the symbol of Scotland's growing vitality and confidence. The most far-reaching attempt to satisfy this role as an outdoor pantheon imbued with a powerful *genius loci* was the attempt to build Charles Robert Cockerell's replica of the Parthenon as a temple shrine to the fallen of the French wars.

Cockerell, son-in-law of the Scottish engineer John Rennie, was a fastidious scholar who had measured and recorded the Greek original. Trained by his father (who had also taught Jefferson's architect, Benjamin Latrobe), he had gone on to work in the office of the classicist Sir Robert Smirke. Cockerell was appointed principal architect in 1823, with

William Henry Playfair as his associate. The promoters of the National Monument set a target of £42,000, but in the event raised less than half that amount. By 1829 when the scheme was abandoned only twelve columns and their architrave had been built. Scotland would never get its 'Westminster Abbey' on the hill.

That same year, however, it would have another triumph to celebrate: the opening of Thomas Hamilton's sublime marriage of structure and landscape, the new city High School.

Thomas Hamilton was a remarkable man, and typical of that new breed that was beginning to define the nation in its buildings. The son of a stonemason, he was born in Glasgow in 1784. His family later moved to Edinburgh, where he was enrolled in the city High School in Infirmary Street, opposite the university.

Hamilton left to train as a stonemason in his father's workshops, much as William Adam, 'bred a mason', had done a century earlier. The combination of hands-on experience and a knowledge of classics and 'high art' was far from unusual in Scotland at that time, giving many architects a practical understanding of materials, as well as a familiarity with the more refined principles of design.

By 1817 Hamilton was practising as an architect on his own account, and within three years he would demonstrate an advanced appreciation of classical precedents in his competition-winning scheme for a memorial to Robert Burns in Ayr based on the Athenian Choragic monument of Lysicrates. A political radical, he regarded the association with Burns honour enough for the commission, and refused to accept a fee.

In June 1825, when he was invited to design a Calton Hill replacement for his old school, Hamilton was already a successful architect with a considerable body of work behind him. Competition amongst Scotland's Regency architects was fierce and he was hard-working and ambitious. One contemporary described him as 'mild-mannered', but his bitter rival, William Henry Playfair, marked him down as 'a man full of intrigue and vulgar taste' – a bit rich, perhaps, coming from someone whose own career had been feather-bedded by nepotism, particularly since Hamilton's chaste neo-Greek style was fundamentally a reaction against 'vulgar taste'.

Whatever the means, Hamilton secured the job of designing a new High School, and set about making the most of the challenge. Since it was assumed that the National Monument would be completed, he treated the design as an integral element of a wider landscape-based composition, using the Doric model of the Propylaea on the Acropolis. Like ancient Athens, Edinburgh's topography suited the Periclean ideal of man-made forms harmonising with their natural setting, and Hamilton massed his building accordingly.

The interplay between site and design followed the precepts of the architectural theorist William Stark, who believed that urban design should respond to nature by recognising contours and incorporating creatively designed landscapes, rather than imposing rectilinear street patterns on the ground. True to this view that a building should harmonise with its surroundings, Hamilton seized his opportunity to exploit the setting with a variation on the Temple of Theseus. Looking at the result – and we should perhaps try to imagine it as Mendelssohn saw it, a gleaming jewel of pale stone beneath an azure sky – it's curious to reflect that at the time this exceptional site had had its opponents.

Few disputed that the old High School building in Infirmary Street was no longer fit for its purpose, but there had been widespread support for finding a new location in the Southside, and preferably one near the university. Middle-class Edinburgh's centre of gravity had moved to the New Town, however, and there was pressure to build the new school to the north of Princes Street, where the independently constituted Edinburgh Academy (to the great annoyance of Edinburgh's magistrates) was being built. At a public meeting in July 1824 it was announced that the school would be in St Andrew Square, on the site where the Excise House stood. In the 1820s, as now, sites could be hotly disputed. According to one contemporary diarist the majority were in favour of the school remaining in the Southside 'but all things considered their determination will throw little weight into the scale'. Fate intervened, however, when the Royal Bank bought the St Andrew Square building (its present headquarters) in March 1825, forcing the council to look elsewhere.

By June the council had fixed on the south flank of Calton Hill. It was an imaginative compromise, being outside the main axis of the New Town, yet close enough for convenience, while it looked towards the Old Town and the Southside. Relations between the council and the Academy's trustees were prickly, and while the rumour that Playfair's St Stephen's Church had been built to spoil the view towards the Academy probably merits a 'not proven' verdict, it was certainly intended that the High School should outshine William Burn's 1822 design for the rival establishment.

Despite misgivings about the cost of excavating the Calton Hill bedrock, it was expected that Thomas Hamilton would create a building of supreme quality on a par with anything in Britain, and this is precisely what he set about doing. The foundation ceremony of 28 July 1825, presided over by Lord Glenorchy, was held 'in the presence of an immense multitude'. It was anticipated that the £18,000 costs would be raised by the sale of the old school building and by public subscription.

Given the nature of the site, it is not surprising that technical problems affected both schedule and budget. By September 1826 the foundations for the main block were still being excavated, though building work had begun on the west wing. By December, when the King boosted subscriptions with a £500 cheque, both wings were complete to the first storey. A year later the first storey of the main block was up, but the council were fretting about the prospect of a permanent £500 per annum burden on the city rates. By June 1828 this crisis had been resolved, but another loomed:

the contractor's business failed. The shell of the school was complete; it lacked only a roof and its main colonnade, both scheduled for completion by October. Refinancing and the appointment of a new contractor, however, resulted in a delay of eight months.

On 25 June 1829 the Lord Provost led a procession of magistrates, bailies, high constables, professors, clergy, schoolmasters, former pupils, the band of the 17th Lancers and 700 boys from the old school to Hamilton's glorious Athenian lyceum of pale Craigleith stone which now dominated the southern slopes of Scotland's Valhalla. It was behind schedule, it was over budget, but it was a masterpiece: 'one of the two finest buildings in the kingdom' according to the Glasgow architect Alexander 'Greek' Thomson.

Calton Hill is an unfolding story, the final chapter of which should have been its emergence as Scotland's seat of political power – the practical endorsement of its aesthetic and emblematic *raison d'être*. Its development over the century and a half witnessed the birth of the modern democratic ideal not just in Scotland itself, but throughout the wider world. Hamilton's Royal High School represented a phase in the creation of more than just a sublime urban landscape. Calton Hill was already symbol for the nation, an image that was becoming known throughout the world.

A true appreciation of the meaning of the whole can be readily gleaned from a consideration of its various elements. As already mentioned, the earliest monument on the hill was that of David Hume the philospher and historian who, with Voltaire and Rousseau, provided the intellectual framework for the modern rationalist world-view of mankind. Nearby, in the North Canongate churchyard by Lower Calton, was the grave of Adam Smith, the founder of modern economics. On the top of the hill was Cockerell's great unfinished parthenon, and the Nelson Monument. The other prominent monument on the hill was William Henry Playfair's 1826 memorial to his uncle, Professor John Playfair, which was added to his 1818 Observatory.

By the end of 1830 Thomas Hamilton's second Choragic

Athenian temple to Robert Burns was nearing completion opposite his school, and Playfair's equally Athenian response to it, the Dugald Stewart monument, was being built on the hill. William Stark's ambitious plan of 1812 for a classical urban extension linking the eastern New Town with Leith was also under way. Ultimately its promise was unfulfilled, but the completion of Doric Regent Terrace, the quarter-mile-long palace block of Royal Terrace, a variant of Rome's Piazza del Populi at Leopold Place, and the fragment of an 'Oval' at Hillside Crescent provided a glimpse of a master plan which offered, amongst other wonders, a 'Mall' where the tenements of Easter Road now stand on a par with the Champs-Elysées in Paris.

Edinburgh's civic aspirations crashed ignominiously in 1833 when the city was declared bankrupt and commissioners were called in to sort out the mess. The Augustan dream, which had spanned two generations and had gained the city an international reputation, had finally come to an end, but on Calton Hill the story was far from over.

If we move on a generation, to the time when Alexander Graham Bell was a pupil at the school, perhaps, we discover a setting that has been transformed into Scotland's out-door pantheon. The Martyrs' Memorial, a ninety-foot-high obelisque alongside Hume's mausoleum in the old Calton cemetery, is perhaps the single most evocative memorial in Stevenson's Calton Hill 'field of monuments'. It proclaims the core principle of universal democracy, and reminds us that in Scotland political reform was achieved at great personal cost to those who championed it. Designed, again, by Thomas Hamilton, its founding ceremony in 1844 was followed by a procession of 400 members of the 'Complete Suffrage Association' dressed in black who assembled before the High Court where the notorious Lord Braxfield had sentenced the Glasgow advocate, Thomas Muir, to fourteen years' transportation. Muir's crime was that he had been a co-founder in 1792 of the Edinburgh Society of the Friends of the People, an electoral reform society dedicated to the extension of the franchise. He had also visited Paris in 1793 where he had formed a friendship with the Anglo-American political theorist Thomas Paine. The severity of the sentence is reputed to have inspired Robert Burns to write the words of 'Scots Wha Hae'.

If there is any one place where New Labour's rebranders should reproach themselves for the folly of abandoning Calton Hill it is in front of this simple, dignified memorial which still has the power to move us. Around its base are words taken from Muir's own impassioned defence: 'I have devoted myself to the cause of the people. It is a good cause. It shall ultimately prevail. It shall finally triumph.'

After a successful American attempt to rescue him carried out on the express orders of George Washington, Thomas Muir returned to continental Europe where he died at the age of thirty-three. His four fellow martyrs fared little better, with only one, Maurice Margarot, returning to Britain to die penniless at the age of seventy. The others were the Pennsylvania lawyer Joseph Gerrald, the minister of Dundee Unitarian Church Thomas Palmer, and a clergyman-farmer from Fife, William Skirving.

If the martyrs' obelisque represents the democratic ideal at its most poignant, the nearby emancipation monument expands the theme with its overt reference to the abolition of slavery. The 15-foot-high monument is ostensibly the burial place of five Scottish soldiers who fought for the Union side in the US Civil War (1861–5), the plot having been gifted by the city to US consul-general Wallace Bruce, after he had been shocked to discover the widow of a Scottish Union soldier living in poverty in Galashiels. In reality, however, it is Scotland's Lincoln Memorial, the first in Europe raised to honour the assassinated President. The life-sized statue of Lincoln and a slave raising his hand in gratitude by the New York sculptor George Bissell was unveiled in August 1893 'as an object lesson to all Scotsmen' to imitate 'a great statesman who stood up for liberty'. The sentiment of this inaugural speech is preserved in the inscribed quotation from Lincoln on the granite plinth: 'To preserve the jewel of liberty in the framework of freedom'.

With this, we get a glimpse of the true significance of Calton Hill and its surrounding area. It is, in essence, a homage to the power of individuals to change society, rather than a celebration of triumphalism sanctioned by an imperialist establishment. Lord Cockburn approved of the lack of memorials to mere local dignitaries; more remarkable, perhaps, is the fact that the only head of state celebrated on Scotland's national acropolis is the President of a foreign republic.

A walk around Calton Hill is revealing. Military triumph is acknowledged in the Nelson Monument and Steell's 1848 equestrian statue of Wellington. Waterloo Place nominally celebrates victory over Napoleon, much as Nash's London equivalent does. Otherwise the tributes are to academics, scientists, literary figures, artists, political radicals and musicians. John Playfair, Dugald Stewart, Robert Burns, Walter Scott, Arthur Conan Doyle, the one-time international singing stars John Wilson, David Kennedy and John Templeton, the artist David Allan. The photographer Robert Adamson set up his studio in Rock House in 1843, where, together with the artist D. O. Hill he went on to establish the most famous partnership in the history of photography. The civil engineer and lighthouse designer Robert Stevenson established his world-renowned family business at nearby Baxter's Place. Most appropriate of all, the grave of the architect Thomas Hamilton, who largely created Calton Hill as we know it today, is only a few feet away from his martyrs' obelisque.

It would be no exaggeration to say that Calton Hill is Scotland's democratic intellect writ large, and when Scots went out in large numbers to vote for devolution in September 1997 the 'parliament in Edinburgh' referred to on the ballot paper conjured up the image of the former Royal High School bequeathed to the Blair government by John Smith. What better place for a parliament, after all, than Scotland's national Valhalla, an acropolis resonating with the symbolic democratic virtues of Periclean Athens?

# 10 Genius Loci
## Political Positioning

*A city that is set on an hill cannot be hid*
Matthew 5: 14

FIRST, A STATEMENT of the obvious. Every building in the world is bound up in its context. It occupies a space on the land, has surroundings, is viewed from other vantage points, and looks out towards an external geography in a spatial dialogue which can be harmonious, neutral, or discordant.

The placing of a building matters for several reasons. It can be in the wrong place simply because the activities it generates are disruptive to both the ambience and the physical infrastructure of its setting. If it isn't well accessed, yet imposes high levels of invasive use on neighbouring streets, it can degrade the wider urban environment. The adverse results of the misuse of a block of land don't simply stop at the boundary, but impinge on the area around it, with potentially catastrophic planning repercussions. Judged by these purely practical criteria, the Holyrood project is a disaster.

Then there are the more arcane reasons concerning the placing of a building which could be loosely classified as emotional or spiritual. Here, too, Holyrood could be in trouble. These esoteric considerations may carry little weight with modern practical-minded Scots, ever the heirs to that bracing mix of demystifying Protestant logic and the didactic rationalism of the Enlightenment. Our engineers and architects are more likely to concern themselves with the computer modelling of stresses or the anticipated life-cycle of particular types of material, or the connective functions of spaces within a building than they are to worry about feng shui and similar exotic practices.

Even so, consideration of what could be termed the 'spiritual value' of the site could teach us something. After all, nations are often deemed to have some indeterminate entity called a soul, and what else is a parliament but a place where the guardians of that very same soul are charged with its protection? And if the placing of the building arises out of a dysfunctional set of self-serving circumstances, which happen to suit the aims of a particular élite group rather than the wider interest, we are obviously heading for trouble.

The ancient Chinese practice of feng shui, though outlawed after the communist revolution as a blasphemy against 'scientific atheism', has survived to become the best known application of the notion that a building and its users can be affected by the non-material qualities of a location. It doesn't take a practitioner of strange beliefs, of course, to recognise the unsuitability of the Holyrood site; a competent town planner could spot its failings immediately. Indeed, the Scottish Office's own transport and environmental assessment of January 1998 by Scott Wilson Kirkpatrick concluded unequivocally that the Calton Hill site was much more practical than any other on offer, Holyrood included. Naturally, since this didn't fit the agenda, these findings were binned.

The Holyrood site is also constitutionally unsound, since it doesn't do to have an elected legislature sharing a name with the monarch's official residence, particularly since the former has assumed the name mistakenly, as we know. Both institutions, while functioning with a degree of interdependence, should be seen to be separate. MSPs are not courtiers, and since the seventeenth century the monarchy has had a carefully circumscribed relationship with the legislature. Fuzzing the edges between them is not advised.

Some journalists didn't think it too clever, either, to build a parliament on an old brewery plot (hardly the cachet we need in Scotland) which was at the city entry point known as the Watergate. As if all this wasn't bad enough for a start, it then seems positively perverse to push through your project against the advice of experts and the opinion of the public that elected you (and can also vote you out), and to keep going from crisis to disaster as everything that possibly can go wrong does just that. Short of the deity writing it out on the sky, it would seem that the signs that Holyrood is a bad location for our parliament are unmistakable. The parliament's corporate body predictably didn't call in a feng shui expert to sound out the location, but *Scotland on Sunday* did, and his conclusion was less than encouraging. As far as I'm aware he didn't repeat the exercise on Calton Hill, a site bearing an uncanny resemblance to a plate in the Reverend Ernest Eitel's 1878 study, *Feng Shui, The Science of Sacred Landscape in Old China*.

Other cultures take a less material approach than ours to the choosing of sites for significant buildings. The Babylonians began a trend that was taken up by the Hittites, Greeks, Etruscans and Romans: hepatoscopy. Not for the squeamish, this involved gruesome animal sacrifice and poking around in entrails, particularly the liver, and was considered essential to the placing of a settlement. It didn't always work (Pompeii being an example) but, given its long-term popularity, it obviously satisfied some superstitious need for security.

Elsewhere, the mystical arts of site selection were similarly presented as forms of divinely inspired science. Hindu writings of the sixth century refer to *silpa-sastra*, or the knowledge of dwelling, and there was even a manual, the *Manasara*, which gave specific instruction about the location and nature of buildings according to their uses.

A mystical concern with the correct placing of buildings and settlements is more or less universal, and the notion of the hill, or sacred mountain, as a focus of power within the settlement certainly predates the recorded history of mankind. If the terrain lacked the necessary features, the sacred mountain could be man-made, as at the Ziggurat of Ur (3000 BC). The focus of the hill as a seat of rule was essentially practical. An elevated site was defensible. Its occupants could look out over their domain, and be looked up to by those around. Hills could also hold religious significance, being either closer to the gods or, in the case of Olympus, the habitation of the gods themselves. A tour of the world's sacred peaks would be a lengthy affair, involving visits to every continental land-mass with the possible exception of Antarctica. Many are still revered as places of pilgrimage, and even mere historic sites, such as Dunadd, Argyllshire's ancient Dalriadan capital, or the twin mounds of Jelling, in Denmark, can retain a potent, brooding atmosphere.

Choosing sites is a process that is often associated with supernatural intervention. Romulus founded his eternal city after a flight of vultures led him to seven hills by banks of the Tiber in 752 BC. Professor Witold Rybczynski has described how a Nabdam farmer in north Ghana, after taking advice on a proposed building from his shaman, will slaughter a chicken on the chosen site. If it expires beak upwards, he will call his relatives together and they will begin work. The approval of the family and the community is part of the process – an atavistic form of consultation, perhaps. We may scoff at the notion of such primitive rites, and we'd become seriously worried if our politicians took up the practice, yet it is far from pointless. With this wider spiritual investment the building involved embodies the social and religious values of a community. Its creation is, to some extent, a shared experience, validated by accepted ritual.

In western culture the supreme exemplar of the sacred hill is the Athenian Acropolis, the first instance in recorded history of a site manifesting the will of 'the people', rather than the authority of a ruling order or priesthood. It was a case of a superior Olympian ideal of a divine mountain yielding to a human-centred view of a world in which order arose from the actions and intentions of the wider populace. 'The Zeus of Olympia is aristocratic; kings stand in his pediments,' wrote the architectural scholar Vincent Scully. 'The Athena of Periclean Athens is democratic; the people of Athens crowd into her frieze.' Edinburgh's own acropolis, Calton Hill, can thus trace its spiritual genesis back almost 2,500 years to the cradle of democracy itself.

Even as Scotland entered its age of reason the belief in a mystical interaction between a building and its setting persisted. If anything, more thought was given to the matter as classicism, based on the form of the sacred temple, supplanted the earlier vernacular building styles. As co-designer (with William Adam) of a modern version of the perfect Plinian villa at Mavisbank, near Lasswade, Sir John Clerk of Penicuik went to great lengths to illustrate this hypothesis by integrating the design of both the landscape and the building to create the ultimate contemplative and scholarly environment. He even wrote a poem on the subject, *The Country Seat*, in which he expounded his views on the significance of location. In part it was a matter of security: isolated coastal sites, for example, were to be avoided because of the hazards of 'piratick ambuscade'. Above all, however, it was a question of establishing an aesthetic and spiritual harmony, and communing with the natural, if classically well-ordered, world around.

The sense that a building should have divine approval is evident in the ceremonials traditionally performed at the inauguration of new constructions. Cardinals, provosts, aristocrats and masonic grand masters have been trundled out for centuries to officiate over the laying of foundation stones, royals and celebrities unveil plaques, workmen assemble to mark 'topping-out', all of which suggests that even in an increasingly secular society such as ours the idea of the sacred in public architecture is not altogether defunct. The opening ritual of the Scottish parliament itself on 1 July 1999 was nothing less than a consecration, even if it was a sense of shared national values, rather than a divine liturgy that dominated proceedings.

The site of a parliament is much more important than its design. When it was proposed that a parliament should be built at Leith, tucked in amongst the massive bulk of RMJM's Victoria Quay block, the planned Ocean Terminal retail and leisure complex, and some trendy flats instantly rebranded as 'consular residences', much was made of comparable waterside ventures, like the new Saxony parliament building in Dresden. No mention was made of the fact that this was in the very heart of Dresden, a substantially rebranded city as a result of wartime destruction, rather than for shallow style-based reasons.

The waterfront suggestion failed to convince, but it was run while the brewery site was being 'confidentially' acquired, and the public kept in the dark. With Holyrood, Leith's critics were meant to be won over by the intellectually vacuous mantra about a 'new building for the new Scotland' at a 'smashing' location when, in fact, we were being presented with a disingenuous compromise.

In a modern democracy a parliament building, by its nature, is an outward expression of national sentiment and an icon of patriotism. The wrong building in the wrong place, imposed by diktat and built at a cost that impacts severely on public revenues, and motivated by some gut fear of the symbolic potency of the one it was created to displace, has little chance of becoming a revered national icon.

The intention was to avoid not just Calton Hill's Old Labour associations, but to hide on low ground, to neutralise the power of the symbol. The assertion that the debate has been about 'modernity versus heritage' is itself a lie. There was no shortage of opportunity around Calton Hill for a modern architectural statement. For Jonathan Glancey it provided an opportunity to wipe out the 1960s brutalism of New St Andrew's House and the St James' Centre. A local company, TransArc, even produced a plan showing how this might be achieved. A consortium, Euroscope, put together proposals based on Waterloo Place as a 'Parade of the Regions'. The scheme by the city's development arm, EDI scheme was a detailed and costed appraisal which included both modern and adapted existing buildings. Enric Miralles could even, if asked, have produced a design for Greenside Place, on the north flank of the hill, with its orientation encompassing a sense of the nation beyond Edinburgh's boundaries.

The 'new building for a new Scotland' spin is proving to be a weak defence of the project that was meant to be New Labour's dowry in the marriage called Great Britain.

Could it yet be cited in the divorce?

# 11 The Acropolis Besieged
## *A Battle Won*

> *What experience and history teach is this. That people and governments never have learned anything from history, or acted on principles deduced from it*
>                          Georg Wilhelm Hegel

THERE IS AN intriguing precedent for the Holyrood debate, and to find it we need go no further than the finest twentieth-century building on Calton Hill. Around seventy years ago, a controversy was raging over the proposed replacement of the old Calton Jail after its occupants had been removed to the suburbs of Saughton, where Britain's first modern prison was built in 1925.

The city's Calton Jail had long been one of the more anomalous features on the hill. In itself, it was an architecturally distinguished structure built to a design of Robert Adam's, with later sympathetic additions by the architect of Waterloo Place, Archibald Elliot. A vast, battlemented fortress on its own rocky outcrop, it was frequently mistaken for Edinburgh Castle by visiting tourists. In its day it had represented a more progressive scale of social values than its predecessor, the old Tolbooth, a grim place of such barbaric confinement that the custom of spitting on the granite-patterned 'Heart of Midlothian' marking its site on the High Street remains popular with many Edinburghers, whether or not they appreciate the symbolism.

The Calton Jail encapsulated, in its way, some vestige of the Enlightenment belief that, given proper guidance, anti-social behaviour was amenable to improvement. Just as its first architect developed a 'corrected style' of architecture, so the institution sought to correct the morals of its inmates with a reformed penal code. Edinburgh's attitude to having such a building set amongst its other architectural jewels seems to have been relatively relaxed. Robert Louis Stevenson even evinced delight in one of his descriptions of the hill with sheep grazing on its heights, the future lawyers and doctors of the city scrambling around in the High School playground, and the women prisoners exercising 'like a string of nuns' in the jail yard.

After the First World War Edinburgh's soot-black prison fortress was no longer thought a fitting ornament, or for that matter a humane place of detention, and it was decided to knock it down. It wasn't all lost. The Governor's House and some of the groundworks survived, and many years ago a retired stonemason in the Southside told me that he'd served his apprenticeship working sandstone salvaged from the demolition. The material was reused in a number of essay-piece council housing projects in the city centre designed in the vernacular style by the then city architect Ebenezer MacRae – an example of 'best-practice' recycling long before our politicians began paying lip-service to policies of environmental sustainability.

With the Calton site cleared, a new purpose quickly presented itself, and its rationale – as with our present parliament building – was essentially political. The Scottish Office, established in 1885 with a somewhat diffident Duke of Richmond and Gordon as first Scottish Secretary, had long been poorly housed in Edinburgh. Its high command was headquartered in Dover House in London, and the secretary, when in Scotland, was billeted in a borrowed office near St Giles. The Health Board, continually growing in size, was making do in Victorian offices on Princes Street (a setting, according to the King's and Lord Treasurer's Remembrancer, that was much too grand). The Board of Agriculture was in former stockbrokers' premises above a tobacconist's in Queen Street. Other departments were accommodated on a similar ad hoc basis around town.

At Westminster there was a degree of ambivalence to

Scottish issues which frequently irritated home-based politicians of all parties. Scottish grass-roots politics had a
tendency to volatility which understandably worried central
government. Emotionally charged disputes over land settlement and industrial agitation in the Clydeside shipyards,
amongst other things, were beyond the comprehension of
most Westminster MPs. The disproportionate losses of the
Scottish regiments during the First World War served to
sharpen grievances against a London establishment that frequently ignored business referred to them by Scottish Office
departments; and when the same establishment reduced the
powers of Scotland's local authorities there was even more
resentment.

Then, as now, the sensitivities of the Scots produced
presentational problems for a central establishment that
often had little appreciation of the issues involved. Then,
as now, a well-engineered mollifying gesture was called
for. In 1926 the post of Secretary of State was accorded full
ministerial status. London's man in Scotland, a fully fledged
member of the cabinet, became, in theory, Scotland's man in
London.

But something more was needed. The bureaucrats' makeshift accommodation was less than satisfactory, and the
Calton Hill site presented an opportunity to reorganise and
consolidate the Scottish civil service. This was a prospect
that, naturally enough, pleased the mandarins, but it had a
valuable incidental benefit. A new, fully integrated complex
would demonstrate that the government was addressing the
Scottish interest.

Unfortunately in the late 1920s, as in the late 1990s, the
political pathology at Westminster ruled against Scotland
having any significant say in its own building. Even the site
was in dispute, the city insisting that since the Calton Jail
had been built and paid for by the city it was in municipal
ownership, the government insisting that since responsibility for the prison service had passed to the state it was a
national asset. Just as this problem was being ironed out (in
the government's favour, of course) another appeared when

the Office of Works in London announced that Edinburgh would be getting a standard-issue low-budget office block on its acropolis.

The Lord Provost, Lord Dean of Guild, and city councillors were presented with the plans in confidence for formal approval, though they seem to have elicited the opposite response. Details were leaked to the *Scotsman* which reproduced them in full under the banner headline: 'THE CALTON HILL SITE CONTROVERSY. *THE SCOTSMAN* AND THE OFFICE OF WORKS'.

The battle was joined. Across the political spectrum opinion rebelled against this perceived insult to the shrine of nationhood. The ripples even reached Glasgow and played to the benefit of the author and Scottish nationalist Compton Mackenzie in his successful bid to become rector of the university in 1932. In the same year another novelist, John Buchan, who was MP for the Scottish universities, raised the issue in the House of Commons. Buchan may have been a member of the Conservative establishment, but he was also an outspoken Scottish patriot and an astute politician who could see that all the advantages gained by conceding an upgraded Scottish administration would be lost if the civil servants imposed their own building. It was a perceptive observation which, had it been remembered seventy years later, might have saved the Blair government a great deal of trouble.

In a passionate speech Buchan denounced the high-handedness of the Office of Works and demanded 'an outward and visible sign of Scottish nationhood' on the hill. Other voices chimed in. Lady Frances Balfour declared that the Office of Works was barely capable of finding Edinburgh on the map, far less designing a building for one of its most prominent sites. The proposed elevations were variously compared to a Dundee jam factory and a Kirkcaldy linoleum works; public opinion was outraged. The eighth Duke of Atholl and his famous 'Red Duchess' set up a national committee and a public meeting held in October 1929 in the Usher Hall was packed to capacity. The

Duke of Montrose, later to become honorary president of the Scottish National Party, was also incensed.

The objectors had the support of architects throughout Britain, since the Office of Works' position was seen not just as a slight for Scotland, but as an expression of contempt towards the profession. The Marquis of Londonderry raised hackles at an Architecture Club dinner in London when he voiced the official view that it was up to the civil service to design its own buildings. Interpreting this as an attack on his profession, Sir Reginald Blomfield fulminated against 'the inordinate appetite of bureaucracies – a standing menace in the modern state which should be closely watched and firmly resisted'. In Scotland, Sir Robert Lorimer, who had entertained hopes of gaining the commission, disdainfully referred to the Office of Works as 'outsiders' lacking in aesthetic sensitivity, while the elderly architect George Washington Browne let rip against the the official design: 'The monotonous application of the same sterile theme . . . displays a lack of imagination hardly believable even in a public department.'

The civil servants remained implacable, no doubt convinced that since they had designed a perfectly acceptable prison at Saughton they could summon up a decent office block on Calton Hill. By 1930 resistance to the bureaucrats' scheme was gaining momentum. Eleven organisations, including the Royal Incorporation of Architects in Scotland, the Royal Scottish Academy, the Faculty of Advocates, and the National Council of Women, sent a unanimous resolution to Prime Minister Ramsay MacDonald, demanding a review. He responded by inviting them to his home in Lossiemouth for further discussions.

The Office of Works persisted in its obstinacy, stating indignantly that architects had no business meddling in such matters. The RIAS responded with gloves off, denouncing this as an 'unwarranted declaration of war on the profession' leaving it with 'no alternative but to accept the challenge'. The Office of Works, it thundered, was meant to be 'the servant of the public, not its master'. Downing Street was furious. 'The controversy which has been worked up in this instance is unique in its recklessness,' protested Ramsay MacDonald.

But even he had to concede defeat when a letter arrived from the Honourable Gerald Chichester, assistant secretary to Queen Mary. Though the style was discreet the meaning was clear. 'Their majesties, as you know, take a great interest in the city of Edinburgh, and they do hope that something noble and worthy of this site may be built.'

Prime Ministers may defy public opinion, but a disagreement with the monarch is another matter. By royal command, albeit a gentle one, Scotland's Valhalla was saved. There would be no jam factory. The Office of Works was trumped, but it would extract revenge, of sorts, in 1937 when it disallowed a ball in the Palace of Holyroodhouse for George VI's coronation.

Too many eightsome reels, it seemed, might damage the fabric of the building.

Nationhood Visible
*Scotland's Palace of Administration*

> *In place of the conception of the Power State, we are*
> *led to that of the Welfare State*
>
> Archbishop Temple, 1941

ST ANDREW'S HOUSE is both eloquent and grandiloquent, a hint of muscular Edwardian bombast leavened by a vibrant spirit of modernism. For the people of Scotland in an otherwise bleak decade it must have been a glorious evocation of a new and more hopeful age, though it had barely opened its doors when war with Germany was declared.

The *tabula rasa* was the rocky eminence of the demolished jail, one of the finest sites in the world, according to Sir Rowand Anderson, a Ruskinian Gothicist who had naturally been dismissive of the 'toy castle' style of the Adam and Elliot Bridewell which outlasted him by some five years. After an architectural competition organised jointly by the government, the Royal Fine Art Commission and the Royal Incorporation of Architects in Scotland, the Paisley-born architect Thomas S. Tait of John Burnet, Tait & Lorne was chosen from a final shortlist of three. Tait, a stonemason's son like Hamilton, already had an established reputation having worked in America and Australia (on the piers of Sydney Harbour Bridge) as well as the London landmarks Unilever House and the Daily Telegraph Building.

Thomas Tait's Scottish Office is undoubtedly the most outstanding inter-war public building in Scotland in terms of both scale and architectural virtuosity. Designed in a style that has been variously termed 'International Modern' and 'American Beaux-Arts', it was a masterly paradigm of power and a brilliant exploitation of the potential of its site. Its formal north elevation, offset from the line of Elliot's processional Waterloo Place viaduct, came into view almost unannounced, the majestic bulk of its façade being experienced close by in the passing, rather than at a distance. It is an elevation that exudes authority in both its mass and in its detail.

From our point in history it is a building that seems uncomfortably triumphalist, with its massive bronze doors and its wonderfully sculpted emblems of authority. Seen through the dark glass of subsequent experience it is redolent not so much of democracy as of its opposite. For the landscape architect John Byrom, who carried out a survey of Calton Hill in the early 1980s, it carried a 'hint of Mussolini's blackshirts'. The writer and artist Ian Hamilton Finlay has offered his own ironic interpretation in a drawing which shows it with an eagle and swastika above its parapet. Unhappy attributes for those of us who can only see it through the filter of the last war, and the cold war that followed, giving rise to the common solecism of judging a building by the subsequent twists of history.

Thomas Tait, deprived of such hindsight, almost certainly thought of the entrance front as a suitably dignified expression of power in the service of progress. Nor would he have been troubled by Buchan's exhortation for a building that would be 'an outward and visible sign of Scottish nationhood'. Its contemporary counterpoints were buildings charged with noble ideals: Nenot's classicised League of Nations Building in Geneva, for example, or the Royal Institute of British Architecture, and the BBC Headquarters, both in London.

This was, inevitably, a building loaded with meaning, and it was of its time, unashamedly evoking a sense of Scottish national destiny within the context of Britain's imperialist world role which, for the majority, seemed yet undiminished. It also added a new dimension to the eclectic architecture of Calton Hill; no longer was it simply a Hapsburg-like collection of monuments at the end of a processional route, affirming an abstract national pride.

St Andrew's House had a purpose. This was where the governing of Scotland took place, if only as a relay station for the real business in Westminster. It was a working environment for thousands of civil servants dealing with Scotland's health, housing and industries. It was also a genuine symbol for a new kind of aspirational Scotland.

Tait was an intuitive modernist with an advanced interest in the possibilities offered by new materials and technologies, but with St Andrew's House he also demonstrated an understanding of the value of historicism. The 'Balmerino Walnut' planted by Mary, Queen of Scots, became panelling for the Secretary of State's private office. The style may have been art-deco minimalist, but this was the fabric of history literally built in, a subtle reminder to the room's occupants that they were components in a centuries-long process of governance and administration, rather than supreme authorities in their own right.

Different Secretaries of State would react to it in different ways. Willie Ross, the nae-nonsense prescriptive dominie, was to abandon it for the arid brutalism of 1960s New St Andrew's House, which survives as his monument. Malcolm Rifkind, with his advocate's *penchant* for precedent and historic rulings, was delighted to move back in. Donald Dewar, too, was happy to stick with its opulence. Were there ever moments, one wonders, when the powerful occupants of this room were aware of its talismanic significance?

The walnut-panelled inner sanctum was not, of course, for the edification of the average voter. For them, Tait designed a north elevation that evoked a sombre sense of Scotland's national destiny within the British imperialist context. It was unashamedly the architecture of power. For Edinburgh's Lord Provost, Sir Thomas Whitson, its principal virtue was that it was power transplanted, the culmination of a vision that had begun with the creation of Waterloo Place a century earlier. With this 'Scottish Whitehall' a meaningful dimension was added to the monumental grandeur of the nation's acropolis.

This was a new experience for Scots who, since the

sixteenth century, had watched executive power draining away. The defeat at Flodden, the execution of Mary Stuart, the removal of the court to London, the Darien disaster, the loss of a parliament, the rout at Culloden, the anglicisation of the Victorian gentry, had all contributed to the sapping of national self-esteem. At times this grim litany had threatened to expunge Scotland's separate sense of identity, and the term 'North Britain' was adopted by those who deemed the idea of a nation within a nation anachronistic. But somehow, with a little help from the vernacularism of Burns and the myth-making of Scott, the national character survived.

Politically, however, it was a national character that was unrequited. Various home rule proposals had come to nothing, including one in which it was suggested Cockerell's National Monument could become a national parliament. Politicians, once in office, paid scant attention to the issue of self-determination, unless, courtesy of a nationalist upswing, it seemed expedient to do so.

In the circumstances, the symbolic value of St Andrew's House should not be underrated. This was the grandest government building since Robert Adam's Register House of 1774. Other prestigious projects had been completed – Hamilton's High School being one, Glasgow's Ludwigian Council Chambers another – but these had been home-grown initiatives. For the first time in a century and a half an administrative building sanctioned and funded by Westminster was taking shape.

The massing of the main elevation of St Andrew's House celebrated this recovered sense of purpose with an assertive aesthetic vigour. This was Scottish administration's own palace, its soaring monumentalism conferring legitimacy on the process of governance with unrestrained *chutzpah*. Tait's modernism yielded to a classical deployment of features recalling Adam's ideal of 'movement and variety'. The entrance block with its symmetrical pavilions was reassuringly derived from orthodox architectural idioms. In the 1930s our civil servants preferred their monumentalism in traditional quasi-neoclassical disguise.

1. Germ of a shibboleth? The Calton Hill vigil; *courtesy of Marion Ralls.*

2. Robert Adamson: Thomas Hamilton's Royal High School, 1843, calotype. One of the earliest Scottish outdoor photographs. *Reproduced by permission of the National Galleries of Scotland.*

3. Campaigning for a 'Yes-Yes' vote in the 1997 Devolution referendum: Jim Wallace, Sean Connery, Donald Dewar and Alex Salmond at 'New Parliament House' on the Calton Hill. *Reproduced by permission of Scotsman Publications Ltd.*

4. Holyrood architectural competition selection panel: (from left) Robert Gordon, Donald Dewar, Kirsty Wark, John Gibbons, Joan Connor and Professor Andy MacMillan; *courtesy of Spindrift.*

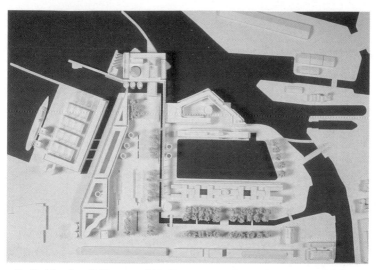

5. Leith feasibility study: Benson & Forsyth, January 1998.
*Reproduced by permission of RCAHMS/SPCB*

6. Calton Hill feasibility study: Page & Park. January 1998.
*Reproduced by permission of RCAHMS/SPCB*

7. Holyrood feasibility study: RMJM, January 1998. *Reproduced by permission of RCAHMS/SPCB*

8. Enric Miralles, Brian Stewart, MD, RMJM, and Mick Duncan, architect, RMJM, in the garden of Queensberry House. *Scotsman Publications Ltd.*

9. Scottish Parliament architectural competition: the winning entry by Miralles-Tagliabue/RMJM. *Reproduced by permission of RCAHMS/SPCB*

10. Tony Blair arrives at the Scottish Parliament with First Minister Donald Dewar and Presiding Officer Sir David Steel. *Scotsman Publications Ltd*.

11. Donald Dewar and Henry McLeish visiting the temporary parliament chamber on the Mound designed by Simpson & Brown, architects. *Scotsman Publications Ltd.*

12. The Dynamic Duo: Margo MacDonald and Donald Gorrie. *Scotsman Publications Ltd.*

13. Holyrood and the Calton Hill from Salisbury Crags. *Scotsman Publications Ltd.*

The Regent Road frontage was 'big-statement' architecture, but it was also part of a contextual range which took in Waterloo Place, the castellated former residence of the jail governor, and the Doric façade of the Royal High School, an architectural panoply which gained much from the serpentine curve of the roadway. The buildings were not set alongside each other, but revealed themselves individually, and magnificently, as a sequence of separate visual experiences, each appearing almost by stealth with the progression from or to Princes Street.

The fact that both the school and the Scottish Office were set back from the street meant that they could impress without intimidating, an effect heightened by more distant discoveries. Pass the façade of St Andrew's House and suddenly you are in a romantic landscape, with the Canongate Kirk, the roofs of Old Edinburgh, the atavistic form of Arthur's Seat, and the rose-red stone of Salisbury Crags; look north, and you have the Claudian idyll of Calton Hill itself. Lord Cockburn's description of Waterloo Place – 'like a curtain going up on a theatre' – was now even more apposite, and Thomas Tait's palace was a brilliant and triumphant crescendo.

Viewed from the south, the composition was altogether more contemporary, with a hint of landlocked ocean liner redolent of the style epithets of the jazz age. Being Edinburgh, the flourishes were restrained and the building materials traditional, but the design had an airy, uplifting flavour of coastal resort chic. If the north front was a concession to bowler-hatted imperial gravitas, its southern face was an *à la mode* swing towards the bright young things of Miss Jean Brodie's era, lifting sooty, stony Auld Reekie out of its gloom.

With the building of St Andrew's House, the quasi-mystical role of Calton Hill as the Scottish Valhalla was given glorious practical endorsement. The hill, no longer a focus for mere sentimental indulgence, a fading reminder of ancient glories, an empty echo of the redundant splendour of a post-Hapsburg dream, had become a place where power was exercised and a new kind of democratic future might be forged, albeit in conjunction with the interests of the unified British state. Above all, it signified a willingness, however grudging, on Westminster's part to address the specific Scottish interest.

The functions of the Scottish Office were not particularly glamorous – the administration of agriculture and fisheries, health and education were hardly the high arts of statecraft – but Tait's new seat of power represented a genuine palliative measure, rather than a placebo concession. It was Scotland's building, designed by Scotland's architect. If its north face looked back towards an imperial golden age, its south looked to a future of welfare and progressive idealism in a more hopeful Scotland.

It was also about resolving political tension, and in its genesis there are still lessons to be learned about the changing relationship between Scotland and England, and the role of such building projects in expressing, and even defining, these changes. It's a pity that some of those who work in the place today didn't reflect on this before they concocted Holyrood.

# 13 Bohemian Edinburgh Brutalised
## *A Battle Lost*

> *'A square of ancient handsome houses now for the most part decayed from their high estate'*
> Robert Louis Stevenson: *Dr Jekyll and Mr Hyde*

QUARTER OF A century separates Thomas Tait's eloquent monumentalism from the aesthetically impoverished grey hulk of its eponymous successor on the site of St James's Square, but as far as any sophisticated sense of style was concerned it might as well be a thousand years. How do we explain this apparent descent into life-denying anti-architecture? How did a structure like New St Andrew's House come to be located alongside Robert Adam's exquisite Register House? As you might have guessed, it was all thanks to the chicanery of certain politicians and civil servants.

For those in the know, 1960s Edinburgh was a lucrative development opportunity waiting to happen. The council was well weighted with property and construction interests. A 'progressive' (which, paradoxically, meant laissez-faire right-wing) ruling party dominated by money-churning entrepreneurs was predictably in favour of clearance and reconstruction, but it would be a mistake to assume that the Labour opposition was restraining them. Labour councillors, too, often had their fingers in the construction pie, either as trade-union activists or building workers.

As in most other parts of 'twilight' Edinburgh in the 1960s, the environs of Calton Hill were fair game for comprehensive redevelopment. The Murrayfield Real Estate Company, much involved in the university's plans to blitz the historic Southside, had financial problems and merged

with Ravenseft, and after winning an invited competition
the architects Ian Burke, Martin & Partners were hired
to design a replacement for eighteenth-century St James's
Square and its precincts.

St James's Square, built in 1779 on the site of a ham-
let called Moutrie's Hill, had been an early New Town
development in the style of pioneering George Square, in
the Southside, but more monumental in conception. It had
had illustrious beginnings, as the high quality of interiors
indicated. Robert Burns had stayed there for a time in
the house of the High School's classics master, William
Cruickshank, whose daughter ('young Jenny fair') picked
out melodies on the harpsichord for some of his songs. The
artist who painted Burns's best known portrait, Alexander
Nasmyth, was another resident.

With the expansion of a more sophisticated New Town
of palace-block regularity the square declined and its smart
houses were subdivided to provide living space for much
of the workforce brought in to service the building boom,
the Old Town being more than packed to capacity. By
the middle of the nineteenth century, with the boom long
gone, the poverty of the square and the streets around
it was bad enough to feature in the famous 1865 report
of Dr Henry Littlejohn, the city's first Medical Officer of
Health. A century later little had changed, though many of
the overcrowded houses had been taken over as low-cost
premises by a number of small businesses, such as printers
and bookbinders.

As housing, it was dire, but as architecture it had extraordinary quality. The block with the elevated walkway
which started at the Register Tap pub next to Register
House and ran parallel with the plunging abyss of Leith
Street was as memorable as a print by Piranesi. Had it
survived it would, today, almost certainly be an Edinburgh
version of London's fashionable Spitalfields, but in the 1960s
it was people like the city sanitary inspector who had the
power to save or condemn buildings, and since his criteria
were restricted to questions of baths and lavatories, rather

than structural integrity, history or architectural merit, St James's Square could only be categorised as a slum worthy of demolition.

The area was also something of a blot on Edinburgh's respectable reputation. Not only had Burns conducted his famous Clarinda romance from Cruickshank's house, but the young Robert Louis Stevenson had later latched on to the morally suspect Kate Drummond and her friends at the Black Bull, in the shadow of his grandfather's lofty Calton arch. Similarly, the irascible poet William Bell Scott had taken up with a Rosabelle in Picardy Place, celebrating her in verses which later inspired his friend Dante Gabriel Rossetti to paint *Found*, a depiction of fallen virtue redeemed. The seediness and couthy charm had persisted into the twentieth century, though in less literary form, particularly in the proximity of Fairley's Dance Hall, a popular haunt of US naval personnel, and in the notorious trysting grounds of the hill. One reason given for the Royal High School's closure in 1969, indeed, was that this area of town was no fit place for young people. Low Calton was, in effect, a morally questionable Hyde which undermined the self-conscious social mores of its Jekyll other self, bourgeois Edinburgh. Almost certainly, St James's Square was the model for the 'square of ancient, handsome houses,' of Stevenson's famous psychological novel.

In the official mind, more accustomed to life in the leafy suburbs or smart West End, the urban townscape bounded by Greenside, Broughton and Register House was a squalid and unkempt land of vicissitude and depravity. For the resident population, who were mostly ordinary law-abiding souls, the virtue of being in a familiar central location more than outweighed any of the local vices, real or imagined. The official solution was obvious. Exile the inhabitants to peripheral housing estates, evict the small businesses, knock everything down, and build a massive office block for civil servants over a nice new shopping mall.

Edinburgh corporation obligingly issued its compulsory

purchase notices for St James's Square on 26 December 1967, inviting objections from any who might still be around to defend their homes.

Back in 1967 those who felt that the demolition of St James's Square and its remarkable adjunct, Leith Street Terrace, was unwarranted, however, had a technical right of appeal, and if they felt let down by Lord Provost Brechin's planners they could take matters up with a higher authority. The problem was that the higher authority in question happened to be the prospective occupant, Secretary of State Willie Ross, who was already eyeing up the sketch proposals for his glitzy new suite of offices on the same site.

The inevitable happened. Mr Brand of Dundee hung his company notice on the Adam-designed anthemion balconies of East Register Street and brought in the wrecking crew, while, in the Ainslie Place offices of Ian Burke, Martin & Partners, where a battered 'St James's Square' street plate was hung on the wall, the staff were hard at work designing not just a shopping mall, hotel, department store and offices, but a modernist cathedral to replace the old-fashioned crocket and lancet number at the top of Broughton Street.

As it happens, I went to school with Ian Burke's son, and we would occasionally find ourselves in the drawing office, where a personable young architect, Ron Sutherland, tolerated us looking on as he drew. 'Burkie' himself was a generous, cultivated man who enjoyed life and bought good paintings at Ricky Demarco's Gallery. He owned a baronial castle in Perthshire where he was a regular opera patron at John Calder's 'Ledlanet Nights', and a villa in Majorca where his friend and neighbour was the poet Robert Graves.

He suggested I should visit the site to see the last of the eighteenth-century square before it was swept away, and with the benefit of this introduction I went along. It was an awesome scene. Window sashes had been torn out of the first few blocks and thrown into the street below. Architraves, shutters, doors, fireplaces and flooring were being hurled out after them, and the whole lot piled on to a bonfire. As the dust and the smoke rose, shafts of afternoon sunlight filtered through, giving the deserted square an eerie kind of beauty.

'Our Bohemia, if it is anywhere, is round the Register House,' wrote one anonymous Edwardian commentator, who went on to provide a measure of the decline of St James's Square 'from the middle class to the lowest stage' by reference to its falling rents and condemned attics. I entered the block which William Cruickshank, Burns' host, had once occupied. A small plaster consul bracket had been knocked off the hallway arch. I picked it up. Perhaps Burns had looked at it once. In the upper floor of another block I found a stunning oval room with arched windows looking towards Calton Hill. It had done service as a printing workshop, and some of the old machinery was still in place, but it must originally have been the assembly room where Nasmyth's daughters, amongst others, had danced their elegant quadrilles.

But there was more to this visit than sentiment. In East Register Street the tenement with the anthemion balconies had caught my attention. The curved ones were identical to the balconies of Ainslie Place, where they decorated all but a block of offices then occupied by the National Galleries. The East End's loss seemed like an opportunity to make good this minor lacuna in the West End. I vaguely recall a hurried telephone call to Colin Thompson, the then director of the National Galleries. It was a brazen initiative, perhaps, but at the time it seemed like common sense, and both Ian Burke and Colin Thompson were happy to go along with the idea.

Another visit to the doomed square followed. The foreman of the demolition, whose site office was in the same building, was positively enthusiastic. He'd get a couple of men on to it right away. He even explained how the lead pockets could be melted with a blowlamp and the detached balconies slung from the windows above. A straight surgical procedure. They would load them on to one of their lorries

and deliver them for a few pounds. If I called back in a week
I could check on progress.

So this anecdote has a happy ending? Unfortunately
not. What I was to end up with was an object lesson
in bureaucratic obstructiveness, rather than three Carron
Ironworks balconies. The foreman shook his head as I
approached. An official had got wind of the plan and
instructed that under no circumstances should any time
be wasted on such frivolous activities. The balconies were
to be smashed up with the rest of the building. The basement
area was littered with broken cast-iron. So that was that –
but not quite. He went into his office and reappeared with
an end section of one of the straight balconies. This was
to be my consolation prize. It is now in the Museum of
Scotland. It wasn't the only relic saved from the wreck-
age. An original stone with the St James's Square name
and the date 1779 is now displayed in front of the shopping mall.

I've often wondered how a cultured individual like Ian
Burke came to be memorialised by a building celebrated
for its awfulness. The fee was an obvious temptation, but
it doesn't explain everything. Another Edinburgh architect
of the 1960s, the late Michael Laird, who also had decent
personal taste, once offered me his own slant. The role of
most architects designing buildings for government departments at that time tended to be one of damage control,
he maintained. The politicians and civil servants weren't
particularly interested in good architecture. The goal was
to achieve maximum exploitation of space for minimum
cost, and to the tightest possible schedule. The design
had to adhere to formulaic requirements and standardised
dimensions which couldn't be altered.

The architect receives the brickbats, but in the case of New
St Andrew's House the civil servant leading the project, the
latterly infamous George Pottinger, was eager to infill the
courtyard area in front of the principal façade with yet more
open-plan office decks, and the architects had to resist.
They went on to achieve what was asked of them, and

an essentially prefabricated structure (the concrete components were sent from Aberdeen) was finished on time, and within budget. Three hundred and twenty thousand square feet of office space at £6 million, even thirty years ago, was value for money, the £18.75 per square foot construction cost being rather less than the annual rental levels of modern city-centre offices today.

It was a well-engineered complex with some impressive internal open spaces, however grim its brutalist exterior, but it was one that should never have been built on such a site, and it rapidly became Edinburgh's most celebrated *bête noire. Evening News* editor Ian Nimmo held an opinion that was more or less representative. The 'cheapskate concrete monstrosities of New St Andrew's House and the St James Centre' were 'perhaps the biggest crime perpetrated in the area'; 'the hideous St James Centre . . . would have Craig, Adam, Playfair and the rest of the New Town architects in tears today at the way in which standards and aspirations have been discarded'.

Twenty years later my association with St James's Square and Ian Burke was to receive a curious postscript. I was telephoned by the editor of the *Observer* magazine, Angela Gordon, who asked if I could come to London to accept an award. The readership had voted the St James Centre 'Worst Building in Britain' (Scottish Category), but she'd been unable to persuade the architects to appear at the presentation, so I was being invited in their place. This may have been something of a double-edged compliment – I was then Scottish property correspondent of the rival *Sunday Times* – but curiosity had the better of me.

The trophies were to be handed out by the property developer and Mies van der Rohe supplicant Peter Palumbo. He was delighted to present splendid silver salvers to the Duke of Devonshire and the Bishop of Durham for their best buildings, but demurred nervously when it came to passing the 'worst building' engraved axes over to those such as myself and Ned Sherrin (accepting 'on behalf' of Lasdun's National Theatre). We had to be content with picking our awards up from an *Observer* staffer. This was possibly not unconnected with the fact that Palumbo had only just been given the go-ahead by environment minister Nicholas Ridley to demolish eight listed buildings, including the landmark Mappin & Webb department store, in a London conservation area.

The St James Centre and New St Andrew's House was an Ian Burke, Martin & Partners creation of its time which very quickly became universally unloved, yet it should never be forgotten that architects have clients, and clients can be demanding, or provide inflexible briefs. In the case of this contract there were no fewer than six clients, chief amongst them the government, represented by Secretary of State Willie Ross, without whose support the project would never have happened. New St Andrew's House was the product of a narrow political mindset, as much as a drawing office.

The problem, says Ron Sutherland, was that they were determined to get a quart into a pint pot, and for George Pottinger, who would have crammed yet more offices over the courtyard, even that wasn't enough.

# 14 On the Waterfront
## The Rise of Fortress Victoria

*What little town or river by sea shore*
  *Or mountain built with peaceful citadel is emptied*
*of this folk, this pious morn*
                John Keats: 'Ode on Melancholy'

WHEN NEW ST Andrew's House was opened by the Queen
in July 1975 it was already the Edinburgh building that
everyone loved to hate. It represented not just the by then
much disparaged 'New Brutalist' style of architecture of the
post-Festival of Britain era, but something much worse: the
brutish arrogance of the political establishment which had
ridden over public opinion in its determination to build its
own monument.

The justification for building it had been largely statistical.
The civil service workforce in Edinburgh had expanded by
some 400 per cent since the end of the Second World War. In
the private sector companies were beginning to embark on the
technological revolution, and clerical workforces were being
downsized, but Scotland's civil service was different. Despite
having set up its own computer service in west Edinburgh, the
administrative empire of Willie Ross and J. Dickson Mabon
had exploded exponentially. The sizeable Department of Agriculture and Fisheries had been exiled to rented offices in
Chesser House, but the space demands of the remaining army
of bureaucrats was still more than the original St Andrew's
House, built for a mere 1,000, could possibly cope with.

New St Andrew's House wasn't entirely the result
of Labour's traditional fixation with command-economy
planning, with its plethora of sub-departments and consulta-
tive bodies. Ted Heath had complained about there being

more civil servants in Edinburgh than there were in the European Commission, but even so when Labour lost the 1970 election it was an incoming Tory Secretary of State, Gordon Campbell, who set up the enormous Scottish Economic Development Department. When Labour regained office in 1974 Willie Ross's spacious rooms, complete with spectacular views towards the Ochils, Ben Ledi and the Bass Rock, were ready for use. Ross wasn't an unmitigated rebrander, for he was also delighted to reoccupy the splendid Adam residence at 6 Charlotte Square which had been leased for a very reasonable £1 per annum from the National Trust for Scotland during his previous incumbency, and is now the First Minister's official residence.

The move from Mary, Queen of Scots' 'Balmerino Walnut' panelled suite on Regent Road took place as soon as it could be arranged. With a building like this, it was obviously better to be inside, looking out, rather than the other way around. As William Morris had replied when asked why, in Paris, he always dined in the Eiffel Tower Restaurant, it was the only place in town where the view hadn't been ruined by M. Eiffel!

This fusion of East European Ministry of Truth and 1950s American shopping plaza was a well-engineered structure, but its heating and ventilation system soon began to show signs of failure. Staff dreaded the summer days, when the temperature behind the sealed glazed units could reach tropical levels. Blinds would be drawn and lights put on in the interests of survival. Anyone who displeased his superiors, it was rumoured, might even be allocated a south-facing room. Yet while the clerical staff had no great affection for the building, the majority, it seems, were satisfied, on balance, with its mid-town location.

By the end of the 1980s the novelty of New St Andrew's House was beginning to wear thin as far as the upper echelons were concerned. Individuals such as the government economist Gavin McCrone made little attempt to hide their dislike of the place, and Secretary of State Malcolm Rifkind moved back to the august splendour of the Balmerino

Walnut suite, for which tasteful gesture he was commended by the Secretary of the Cockburn Association. There was a gathering will amongst the First Division brigade to cut free from this grim legacy of the Ross and Dickson Mabon years, and the accommodation chief began to look around at other potential locations.

The sites considered included the Gyle, where HMSO would eventually spend some time, the former London Road Foundry site, halfway between St Andrew's House and Meadowbank House, at Jock's Lodge, and Greenside Place. The head of the Buildings Directorate, Dr John Gibbons, was keen on the Gyle, but first a credible case had to be made for abandoning New St Andrew's House.

The problem was the attitude of the clerical staff. Hideous or not, the building had an ideal location. The railway and bus stations were nearby, and as this was the hub of the city public transport provision was exceptional. The best shopping in town was on the doorstep, from Valvona & Crolla's cult delicatessen in Elm Row to Jenners, 'the Harrods of the North', on Princes Street, as well as John Lewis's and half of Britain's chain stores immediately next door. Princes Street Gardens, ideal for sandwich lunches in the summer, were two minutes away, while the traditional pre-weekend pint could be downed in comfortable brass and mahogany pubs such as the Café Royal and the Abbotsford.

In the late 1980s another possibility appeared: Leith. The Forth Ports Authority was in the process of becoming privatised and, as Forth Ports plc, were moving away from the traditional, and declining, port functions of freight handling, warehousing and the provision of dock facilities, activities that had, for several years, been increasingly concentrated at entry-points such as Felixstowe and Tilbury (another Forth Ports asset) for onward shipment by container truck.

The Forth Ports strategy, which was to prove enormously effective as soaring share values demonstrated only too well, was to develop its on-shore landholdings. Indeed, the company went even further when, in a joint venture with the GA Group (formerly the construction company Gilbert Ash), it formed Edinburgh Maritime and announced to an astonished world (or at least to an astonished Trinity and Newhaven) that it was planning to infill a sizeable chunk of the Forth Estuary at Wardie Bay, effectively landlocking the picturesque port of Newhaven, where the famous *Great Michael* had been built in 1511.

The idea was to create a 'unique waterfront environment – possibly unrivalled anywhere'. The first proposals were howled down, but a revised plan of 206 acres stayed on the tracks, offering such philanthropic benefits as 'accommodation for single-parent families' and 'pleasant public squares'. This, too, met with opposition from the massed ranks of residents, the local yachting club, and even Sir Peter Scott, who was horrified at the potential ecological damage which, in his view, the scheme would inevitably inflict. Edinburgh Maritime's Wardie Bay scheme was bounced out, but its resourceful and bullish chief, Terry Smith, stayed on to become Forth Ports development head.

At this point the civil service chiefs in New St Andrew's House had come up with a reason for abandoning their building: asbestos. Quite how much asbestos, and what level of risk it posed, was not altogether clear. A monitoring survey to detect airborne particles had been carried out by the East of Scotland group manager of the Property Services Agency in association with an asbestos removal contractor, but the results were said to be difficult to come by. Requests for 'hard evidence' by staff within the internal division responsible for government property, the Buildings Directorate, met with a cool response. The civil servant in charge of accommodation, David Kay, would not allow the directorate to conduct its own surveys because, in his view, such duplication was unnecessary, though at the same time he was reluctant to release the findings of the technical assessment that was said to have identified an asbestos hazard. Since the same David Kay was known to be an outspoken advocate of relocation from New St Andrew's House some found this response unhelpful.

That there was asbestos in the building was not disputed, nor that in certain circumstances it might prove hazardous. Ron Sutherland, the original project architect, recalled it being specified during construction in sprayed liquid form. While conceding that no architect would specify it today, he shared a general view that, left alone, asbestos applied by this method need not pose a major problem. He stressed that he was 'no expert', but his opinion appeared to reflect government guidelines of the time, which were to monitor, observe, and leave, unless there was a problem, in which case the priority option was to seal in the affected area or, as a very last resort, remove the asbestos altogether.

Meanwhile, there were changes afoot at the Sir Humphrey level. The senior mandarin, Robert Gordon, was moved from the Management, Organisation and Industrial Relations division of the Scottish Office to a new post as head of Administrative Services. Some highly placed sources have since suggested that this was a pre-emptive strike for an anticipated 1992 Labour election victory, in which event Gordon would be in charge of a Kinnock government's devolution brief, a speculation given a degree of credibility when he would later became head of the Constitution Group.

By the early 1990s there was considerable resistance amongst a section of the clerical staff when it was finally revealed that Leith was to be their destination. Forth Ports Authority had the ideal site at Victoria Quay. The halcyon days of Jenners, sandwiches in Princes Street Gardens, and unwinding in the Abbotsford were about to end, except for a few top brass who would stay in old St Andrew's House with their ministers.

A consummate mandarin, Gordon, it was said, had a particularly deep knowledge of Italian literature of the period of Niccolò Machiavelli. He had studied at Aberdeen University when, coincidentally, Donald Dewar had just made a spectacular entry into national politics by capturing the 'safe' Tory seat of Aberdeen South from John Buchan's

daughter-in-law, Lady Tweedsmuir. Gordon had entered
the Scottish Office in 1973 and quickly been identified as
a rising star, becoming Scottish Development Department
principal in 1979, and PPS to the Secretary of State in 1985.
In the run-up to devolution he was made head of the Constitution Group, and afterwards headed the Scottish Executive
Secretariat. Popular with ministers of all parties as a tough
operator who could get things done, he was one of two
senior civil servants who sat on the competition selection
panel that chose Enric Miralles' Holyrood design, the other
being Scottish Office chief architect John Gibbons.

For many of the lesser ranks in New St Andrew's House,
Victoria Quay's logistics posed something of a problem, for
the windswept post-industrial foreshore of Leith had abys-
mal public transport links. They were promised a shuttle
bus, but this didn't deal with some of their other reservations. While there had been something of 1980s 'renaissance'
in the Leith restaurant scene and co-ordinated attempts had
been made to mitigate the effects of deprivation, the area
had retained something of a *Trainspotting* reputation. The
poorly lit streets to the south of the proposed new development, indeed, formed Edinburgh's kerbside red light
district, and there was a recognised drugs-related crime
problem.

Asbestos, nevertheless, became the lever to move out
the more intransigent 'clericals' who continued to be
obstructive, and the Scottish Office chiefs found a useful
ally in the form of union convener Steve Cardownie, who
by a happy coincidence was also the Labour councillor for a
ward in Leith. Mr Cardownie (who has since become better
known to readers of the *Edinburgh Evening News* for his
alleged propensity for running up stiff mobile phone bills
during overseas visits) was naturally, on behalf of his rank
and file, somewhat concerned about this matter of hazardous
asbestos. Leith it was.

Victoria Quay Ltd was established in 1993 with the
London developer and former Lipton business partner
Godfrey Bradman as joint chairman. The contractors for

the £24 million project were Trafalgar House, the architects RMJM, and the civil servant in charge was Barbara Doig, a graduate in geography who had specialised in statistical research, and who would later become sponsor for the Holyrood project.

# 15 Alarums and Excursions
## The Countdown to Holyrood

*The sublime and the ridiculous are often so nearly
related that it is difficult to class them separately*
Tom Paine, 1795

HOLYROOD IS THE scene of a crime, or so we are led to
believe by Ian Rankin in Scotland's first post-devolution
political thriller *Set in Darkness*. A rich mix of seedy low-
life and not so glittering high politics, it evokes a sinister and
oppressive atmosphere in the shadow of ancient Queensberry House, where, legend has it, a particularly grisly
murder took place in 1707 when the insane son of the
Marquess of Queensberry disposed of the kitchen boy while
his father was disposing of Scotland's liberty in the old
parliament hall. When the leader of the union faction arrived
home with his armed entourage the lad was caught chewing
on the evidence, done to a turn on the kitchen spit. The
murders that inspector John Rebus investigated on the same
premises were mild by comparison.

With a nod in Rebus' direction, the train of events that are
set to bring Scotland's politicians to Holyrood merit the sort
of investigation that, to date, has been sorely lacking. The
difficulty is knowing where to start.

It has to be Calton Hill. The story of the parliament building to be, is also that of the one that won't be; the Callaghan
government's 'New Parliament House'. The existence of
the former is not possible without the denial of the latter,
which will for ever be Holyrood's predicament as a symbol.
The gesture was one of an anti-historic sentiment which is
currently fashionable amongst our politicians, much as it
was forty years ago.

In attributing blame, while New Labour's rebranding shock troops have a case to answer, it is fair to point out that, like the Millennium Dome, the anti-historical trend was begun by the Conservatives. Nicholas Ridley's legacy has already been referred to. Another indicator was the English Heritage *putsch* conducted by Sir Jocelyn Stevens in the early 1990s in which its regulatory role as an inspectorate charged with the protection of listed buildings received a lesser emphasis. This earthquake was largely resisted by Historic Scotland, but at a political level the Stevens effect was slowly filtering through.

If the 'modernity versus heritage' context was clear, the process of making decisions about Scotland's parliament building was exceedingly opaque, though there was known to be a school of thought gestating in the Scottish Office long before the general election that a move to Leith would be highly desirable.

The portents for John Major's government were not good in the mid-1990s, when Victoria Quay was nearing completion. A Labour victory two or three years down the line would obviously make a Scottish parliament a reality. Some forward planning was called for. If it could be in Leith, a number of criteria would be satisfied. First, it would vindicate the relocation of the Scottish Office to its magnificent new RMJM-designed megaplex at Victoria Quay. Second, it would keep elected types at a safe distance from the power that really counted, a St Andrew's House *nomenklatura* which had enjoyed much administrative latitude, and little meaningful interference, since the Scottish Office had come into being in 1885.

The old arrangement had been a stable one, well insulated from the rough world of adversarial Scottish politics. Secretaries of State would reach their decisions after due consultation with Scottish Office advisers. Scrutiny was not too much of a problem. It didn't mean that there weren't some outstanding Secretaries of State, such as Tom Johnston and Walter Elliot, or some talented civil servants, such as Sir Douglas Haddow and Sir William Kerr Fraser, or that some remarkable achievements hadn't been made. In essence, however, it was an administrative structure recalling the quasi-colonial tradition in which a governor-general ruled with the able assistance of a bureaucratic *corps d'élite*. To say that policies formulated in faraway London were discussed in closed ministerial meetings, refined over port in the New Club, and aired on the fairways of Muirfield, might be an exaggeration, but not much of an exaggeration, at least as far as some of the more traditional mandarins were concerned.

There were certainly senior civil servants who were openly sympathetic to devolution, but even in that group several allegedly had misgivings about the difficulties that might arise if MSPs had too much access at the top level. A little separation was thought a wise thing, and, *ipso facto*, Leith would be a splendid location. Once there, the elected members could take up whatever cause they chose with those in charge at Victoria Quay, leaving the top tier in splendid isolation with their ministers in Regent Road. An exaggeration? Perhaps, but not much of an exaggeration.

To make this desirable outcome a reality it was necessary, metaphorically speaking, to light a slow fuse under Calton Hill. It was obvious that the former Royal High School, even in its converted state, would need further upgrading if and when Labour's devolution policies became effective. The parliament of John Smith, Donald Dewar and the Scottish Constitutional Convention would be a more powerful entity than the proposed assembly of 1979, requiring more back-up for its committees and improved media facilities.

The debating chamber had already been put through rehearsals after the Major government, in 'taking stock', had introduced peripatetic Scottish Grand Committee sittings at venues throughout Scotland. While infinitely more 'parliamentary' than the likes of Selkirk's Victoria Hall, its failings were all too evident. The public gallery, at a push, held around sixty. The press and broadcasting media, a vital component of the 'more open and transparent Scotland' were less than adequately catered for. The best accommodation went to the MPs, each provided with one of 150 comfortable spacious seats upholstered in dark green leather, a 'club-class' improvement on the serried benches of the Commons.

On the face of it, the anti-Calton Hill faction could reasonably claim that these shortcomings, particularly in an A-listed building, would involve spending large sums of public money. It was suggested that the cost of digging out bedrock to create even more space might be prohibitively expensive. A quiet campaign was under way.

A closer look at all the available facts produced a rather different picture, however. Thomas Hamilton's former Royal High School, which had a total gross floor area of over 10,000 square feet, was only one of seven buildings on a 2½-acre site. The remaining six ranged from 700 square feet to 7,000 square feet, producing a total of just over 23,700 square feet in all seven buildings. More to the point, the main building was the only one that was of major historical value, the remainder being later pastiche additions scattered around the playground. They were of no great quality and could have been demolished and replaced. A doubling of existing floorspace was theoretically possible without detriment to the appearance of the original building, and probably without undertaking much 'prohibitively expensive' bedrock excavation.

But this was only the start. On the other side of Regent Road St Andrew's House was, in any case, due to have substantial sums of money spent on structural upgrading, and was an obvious candidate for inclusion in a parliamentary campus, as Glasgow-based architects Page & Park were to demonstrate in time.

Then there was Waterloo Place, and several hundred thousand square feet of commercial and local authority office space, virtually all of which was potentially negotiable into parliamentary use. Beneath the street itself the arches of Robert Stevenson's Calton viaduct offered scope for such secure institutional uses as data storage, while to the north the massive thirty-year-old extension to the city's Housing

Department could either have been demolished and rebuilt, or upgraded.

The former General Post Office headquarters building at Number 1 Waterloo Place would be a particularly tragic lost opportunity. A stunning exercise in the High Renaissance Italian style, it was built to a design by the government architect Robert Matheson in the mid-1860s, and much extended afterwards in a similar style. This was a building with remarkable townscape presence, and more than 100,000 square feet of floor space. Due to its enormous bulk, much of its internal volume was poorly lit, but where this would have produced a problem for most standard uses, such as hotel or commercial office, it offered a useful opportunity to develop the parliament's own TV and radio studio facilities.

Robert Adam's Register House was directly opposite, and alongside it more than 300,000 square feet in vacant New St Andrew's House. If any opportunity were wanted to create an image for 'the New Scotland' the demolition of the New Brutalist monstrosity would have been at the top of many lists. It had just the sort of Old Labour associations from which the new regime was eager to distance itself, as well as the Pottinger link, and while it was not now a crown building, the taxpayer was somehow committed to a massive programme of asbestos removal so that it could be sold on in a purified state.

At Greenside Place, on the north flank of the hill, was a sizeable site which had gone through several incarnations, from a proposed BBC headquarters, to a Holiday Inn hotel, to a Warner Village leisure 'n' pleasure complex, to a possible location where Edinburgh council could 'rationalise' itself. Though there was nothing visible above ground level, an enormous underground car park was already in use, and concrete building foundations were in place. This was the site that had featured as a possible substitute for New St Andrew's House, but had been rejected, partly because with its outlook over Leith Street it would have seemed too much like more of the same, minus asbestos.

Greenside Place was opposite Basil Spence, Glover & Ferguson's John Lewis 1987 extension which did much to relieve the severity of the New St Andrew's House complex, and already had its architectural footprint, but this would not necessarily have been a disadvantage.

With the ground engineering largely resolved and paid for, it would have been a relatively simple matter to put it out to the sort of open competition that any one of several younger Scottish practices could have happily coped with. As a block of land relatively unrestrained by historic context, it brought few of the aesthetic problems posed by Holyrood, in its medieval UNESCO World Heritage Site.

Further development opportunities were available at Lower Calton, beneath the cliff face of St Andrew's House, an area that had attracted the notice of John Gibbons' predecessor as head of development at the Scottish Office, Bruce Beckett, who had mooted a scheme for government offices on the site of the New Street bus depot, with a direct connection to St Andrew's House. There was also a substantial surplus of railway land, offering the possibility of a dedicated link between Waverley Station and the parliament complex.

In all, there was somewhere potentially in excess of 1 million square feet on or near Calton Hill which could have been brought into use over a period of years. With the starter pack, 'New Parliament House', already in place, it would have been possible to gauge the needs and funding of the new institution over time, running a phased construction programme suited to the requirements of MSPs, staff and visitors on the basis of rigorous assessment, and all at a fraction of Holyrood's costs.

Far from Calton Hill being merely the location of a single building which was now too cramped for a parliament, it was, in reality, a precinct in the very heart of the nation's capital with a magnificence that few other sites in Europe, let alone Scotland, could better. It was also the practical choice, with a debating chamber in place, a 'signature' already known across the world, and a railway station right next door.

It all made perfect sense, but not to those who were opposed to it. The combination of interests was formidable, headed by the Secretary of State, Donald Dewar, who was already disposed to play the part of patron for his own reasons. Add to that the rebranding obsessions of the Downing Street modernising contingent which had yet to burn its fingers with the Millennium Dome, the steely determination of the civil service élite which was guiding and advising Dewar, a Prime Minister who, with his official spokesman, had a neurosis about conceding more than the powers of a parish council, and it soon becomes clear why a parliament fit for a mature democracy was not an option. The real thing simply couldn't be tolerated. It was to be a Billy Connolly 'wee pretendy parliament' to satisfy some, an 'exciting new building for the new Scotland' to satisfy others, and anywhere but Calton Hill to keep the whole devolution deal in perspective.

We were entering a Michael Dobbs novel, though with one critical difference. With a book, whether by Rankin, Dobbs, Tom Sharpe, or whoever, you buy it, read it, then pass it on to a friend, give it to a jumble sale, or leave it to gather dust on a shelf. With 'big-signature' gesture architecture it doesn't happen that way, as Lord Falconer knows only too well.

The other problem was that the Scottish public, in general, might allow logic to intervene. If this was devolution, how come the centralised authority is telling us what we're going to get? Nothing daunted, the machine of state lumbered on. The decision to ditch Calton Hill and go for a symbol of the 'New Britain', rather than the existing Scotland, was a *fait accompli* before an election was even held, though by mid-July the Prime Minister, after a month of press criticism (and cabinet opposition) over his decision to endorse the Dome, and beset with problems arising from Lord Irvine's refurbishment scheme, was reported to be unhappy about the prospect of yet more extravagance. Naturally, Donald Dewar was able to point out that since London seemed to be the recipient of most of the projects which were then attracting criticism, it was only fair that Scotland, too, should get its bite of the *zeitgeist* cherry. It was confidentially agreed, provided costs were met entirely from the Scottish budget allocation. Upsetting middle England's voters was strictly forbidden.

The ground rules were now in place. In June 1997 the Scottish Office estates section compiled a list of three possible locations. The 'preferred' one was allegedly Leith, the others being Haymarket and St Andrew's House. The last mentioned had already had £25 million allocated for essential repair works. Thomas Hamilton's 'New Parliament House', while it might have an ancillary role in relation to a 'gut and stuff' proposal for St Andrew's House, was no longer the focus for any of the schemes under consideration, while Holyrood had yet to make its appearance.

The Holyrood site, at that point, was part of a proposed 'master plan' which had been drawn up by the Edinburgh architect John Hope. This anticipated a local scheme for urban regeneration with a particularly strong emphasis on housing, and a reintroduction of at least an element of the traditional Edinburgh street patterns. Scottish Brewers (later Scottish & Newcastle), who had successfully developed much of the Fountainbridge area which, to Robin Cook's alleged annoyance, it had picked up for a song in the early 1970s,* had set up the Holyrood Brewery Foundation in the 1980s as a vehicle for the use of a sizeable chunk of its landholdings at Holyrood. Dynamic Earth became the centrepiece, aided by the commercial development of the south-west corner, which was bought for the new *Scotsman* building.

By June 1997 word was leaking out that a 'ditch the Calton Hill' decision had been made. There had been anxiety in the Scottish Office about the reaction of some within the Labour Party, such as Edinburgh council leader Keith Geddes, who might be less than thrilled at the prospect of

---

* Fountain Park, a planned leisure scheme, was forward sold by S&N in September 1998 for £42 million.

asking his councillors to control their budgets while their
*arriviste* superiors were palace-building in Leith. Geddes,
councillor for Holyrood ward, was allegedly notified of the
First Minister's intentions at an early stage in the hatching
process – even before the election, according to one source.
If so, his initial response was not made public. An effective
silence was maintained throughout an upbeat referendum
campaign which was characterised by cheery *bonhomie* on
the part of the leaders of the three 'Yes-Yes' parties, and
a cleverly worded pre-referendum circular daringly mentioned the Royal High School alone by name, though on
closer inspection it was a form of endorsement that, interpreted differently, could equally have been a Calton Hill
exit strategy, which indeed it was. The cost of the exercise,
according to this flyer, was going to be about £8 per head of
population for the building, with running costs thereafter
set at £5 per head per annum, a construction total of £40
million.

Within days of the referendum result the press were on
to the story, and the longest-running architectural scandal
in Scotland's history was off the starting blocks. Edinburgh
City Council were deeply divided on the issue, and for good
reason. After the election, with devolution in the bag, the
council's development arm, Edinburgh Development and
Investment (EDI) had drawn up a £30 million parliamentary scheme based around 'New Parliament House' which
had reverted to council ownership after the failed 1979
referendum.

The majority of councillors were unhappy about the Leith
option, including Keith Geddes, the economic development
chief Donald Anderson, the city finance convener Brian
Weddell, and Angus Mackay, who would later become
an MSP. There was some astonishment when it emerged
that the Lord Provost, Eric Milligan, was amongst those
who supported Leith. Initially, the council was to take a
constructive attitude to the rival proposal, believing that
EDI's Calton Hill scheme could be sold on merit alone,
while it was a clear front runner with the public. Given

that the government had already allocated several million for repairs to St Andrew's House, and that, as a listed building, it would qualify for substantial VAT exemptions, it seemed, in commercial terms, a foregone conclusion. However, Leith, furiously promoted by Forth Ports as a Scottish answer to Sydney harbour front, was said to be the object of much behind-the-scenes lobbying by several civil servants.

The battle was not simply between central government pulling rank and a local authority defending the city's reputation. This was a clash of corporate giants, pitching EDI against Forth Ports. As more leaks appeared in the press relations became strained. Civil servants and Forth Ports chiefs were enraged by suggestions, which they claimed emanated from EDI, that their £40 million price tag was more likely to be £80 million. Nonsense, claimed the Leith faction, a waterfront parliament could be built for as little as £23 million. This deftly undercut EDI's £30 million plan, though Forth Ports had yet to produce a costed scheme, according to an EDI spokesman.

Some councillors were openly unhappy about a Thatcher privatisation success story like Forth Ports poaching a city development opportunity with the collusion of a Labour government in London and a Secretary of State representing a Glasgow constituency. Brian Weddell was measured in his on-the-record objection. 'My concern is that the Labour government does not take a decision it might live to regret,' he told the *Scotsman*'s local government editor, David Scott. His private views were said to be more robust, and this was not surprising, since EDI's scheme was more than simply an attractive venue for the coming MSP and his or her support staff. It was part of a wider strategy to infuse some prosperity into the east end of Princes Street.

Due largely, it must be admitted, to the council's own generosity with edge-of-town planning consents at Straiton, Kinnaird Park, the Gyle, and other retail prairies, it had triggered something which, half a century earlier, the American planner Lewis Mumford* had famously dubbed 'the donut effect'. The urban perimeter was booming, with Ikea the latest top retailer to work out that no parking meters meant more customers. The town centre, meanwhile, was in trouble. EDI's strategy addressed this problem by using the prestige of the parliament to promote a high-quality retail 'ripple effect' into the east end of the New Town, and the flagship, wrested from Glasgow after much wooing, was *Ab-Fab* icon Harvey Nichols, which was to be slotted into the redeveloped St Andrew Square bus station. EDI believed that Harvey Nichols would, in turn, generate more demand for retail space, and when the available outlets at street level ran out there would be a massive underground EDI shopping mall, Princes Street Galleries. The problem with Dewar's plan for a parliament in Leith was that Harvey Nicks might think again about setting up in Edinburgh and head off to booming Glasgow, thus pulling the plug on the whole city centre retail strategy. In the event Harvey Nichols agreed to stay on, but it required paying out £1 million from council coffers in May 2000 as a consideration.

David Begg, the city's transport supremo, soon to be seconded to John Prescott's new mega-ministry of Transport, Environment and the Regions, could see the wider implications at first hand. Leith foreshore was notoriously difficult to get to. The only route from Waverley Station was via Leith Walk, accessed from Princes Street by the dog-leg bottleneck of Leith Street, and ending up in the labyrinthine backwaters around Constitution Street, Henderson Street and Coburg Street – the latter a popular haunt of the kerbside brigade. It was the ultimate traffic planning nightmare. Begg was so furious he interrupted a visit to Washington to make a series of explosive telephone calls.

Labour's post-election conference at Brighton was, understandably, a celebratory affair, being the first occasion in almost two decades in which the platform party consisted of real government ministers, rather than opposition shadows.

---

* They should have known better. Mumford was a disciple of Edinburgh's own Patrick Geddes, 'father' of town planning.

There were, no doubt, many fulsome congratulations and much enthusiastic back-slapping. In this arena, amongst party friends and admirers, Donald Dewar had particular reason to feel satisfied. After quarter of a century, he had finally delivered devolution. How could he put a foot wrong?

Donald Dewar was minded to take it upon himself to commission a 'world-class' parliament for Scotland, and if he had his way (and few doubted he would) it would be at Leith. Signature buildings, according to the New Labour orthodoxy, were symbols of national redemption. At that point, the world's imagination had been caught by the Canadian architect Frank Ghery's brilliant Guggenheim in the Basque capital of Bilbao, a city only slightly smaller than Edinburgh. Barcelona, too, was a *cause célèbre*, having risen out of the torpor and oppression of the Franco years under the able leadership of the Socialist mayor, Pasqual Maragall, whose ten-year programme of architectural innovation had culminated in the staging of the 1992 Olympic Games. This had given Enric Miralles an opportunity to prove himself as an original and unusual architectural talent.

For many of the Scottish delegates at the conference, however, Donald Dewar's 'modernity versus heritage' vision was about something else altogether. Dumbing down. It was also about inconvenience. An hour in the train from Glasgow Queen Street for a nine o'clock committee meeting was manageable, but from Waverley to Leith waterfront in rush-hour traffic could, on a bad day, add on another half an hour each way. The Secretary of State was quickly appraised of the general sentiment, particularly by those MPs who, like John Home-Robertson, would be giving up the London job to become MSPs in Edinburgh.

It must have been a despondent Donald Dewar who came back to Scotland to tell his civil servants that, as far as Leith was concerned, the game was up. It was not Edinburgh councillors who had won the day, but Scottish MPs in general, and, ironically, a number of Glasgow municipal 'big hitters'. Despondent, but not, by any means, defeated. There were other sites, after all. There was, for example, Holyrood.

A few days later a new office block, Alhambra House, was opened in Glasgow. After a speech by none other than *Private Eye* editor Ian Hislop, the ninety-four guests mingled to chat about the latest news in the property world. One of these guests, John Clements of D. M. Hall, happened to be 'non-retained' estate agents for Scottish & Newcastle. According to his own account, it was on the train back to Edinburgh that evening, in the company of a number of Scottish Office civil servants, that he had the 'brainwave' that would rescue Donald Dewar's plan to ditch Calton Hill. Why not, he suggested, build the parliament at Holyrood?

It seems unlikely that those civil servants and ministers who looked out of their windows in St Andrew's House at the Holyrood site hadn't actually noticed it before; or perhaps they had, but simply didn't think it was available. In any event, Clements was soon in contact with S&N's Gordon Izatt, and before long, Donald Dewar and Sir Alistair Grant were talking by telephone. This was kept strictly confidential, though vague rumours began to circulate around the business community, the result, it was said, of some loose dinner-table chat.

There was an added plus to the link-up between Donald Dewar and Sir Alistair. Under its previous chairman, Sir Alick Rankin, S&N had been been a regular contributor to Conservative Party funds and a leading corporate critic of devolution. Sir Alistair Grant was from an altogether different mould. I interviewed him for a magazine when he was chief of the Argyll Group, and some months later was invited to lunch with himself and his wife at their house in East Lothian. Alistair Grant was, in his way, more like an academic than a top-ranking businessman, well read, and deeply interested in history. He also had a rather different slant on politics. At that time the Argyll Group board backed the Conservative Party, but, said Grant, if he had his way he would have been contributing to John Smith's Labour Party, for he greatly admired Smith's integrity and fundamental decency.

There was perhaps some satisfaction to be gained by

having devolution's once fiercest opponents, Scottish & Newcastle, come on board for the ultimate devolution symbol: the parliament building itself. It also matched the business-friendly philosophy of New Labour. The deal was allegedly set in place by mid-October, with an entry date fixed for April of the following year, by which time all S&N staff would have left.

Dewar and his advisers perhaps favoured minimum publicity for two strategically useful reasons. First, the SNP had commissioned an appraisal of the known sites: Haymarket, Leith and Calton Hill. It was vital that it knew nothing of the Holyrood dark horse. Second, the public was venting its spleen on Leith, although it was effectively out of the running, squashed by his own colleagues at Brighton. If they continued to work themselves up into a lather about Leith versus Calton Hill, Holyrood could be pulled out of the hat as last-minute compromise, giving the impression that he had 'listened', without conceding the 'shibboleth'.

It worked like a treat. The letters pages of the *Scotsman* and the *Herald* continued to fizzle with fulminations about Leith. A public meeting was held in the Museum of Scotland lecture hall in early December and was filled to overflowing. Broadcaster Colin Bell was in the chair, and the anti-Leith rhetoric was corrosive. On a show of hands, four brave souls opted for Leith. The best part of 300 gave a ringing endorsement of Calton Hill. No contest.

Three days later the Holyrood rabbit popped out as an 'eleventh-hour entrant'. This was to be the first of many lies. The idea was, it seemed, that everyone would accept that Dewar had capitulated on Leith, had listened to the 'settled will', had decided to play decent and move the show back to the city centre. It was that rare thing: a victory for both sides.

Only it wasn't. It was a botched compromise, resorted to in desperation without any thought for the planning implications of siting a massive institutional building in the heart of a medieval UNESCO World Heritage Site. It wasn't good for the area, nor particularly liberating for the 'signature' architect who would inevitably be limited by the sensitivity of its setting beside the oldest royal palace in Britain. It was, like Leith, difficult to access, while any attempt to improve through routes to it would clearly have a severe impact on both the medieval townscape and the environment of Holyrood Park and Arthur's Seat, with its bird sanctuaries, archaeology and sites of special scientific interest.

The official line was that the Secretary of State was considering all options and, of course, still listening. Even so, he was clearly taken with Holyrood, describing it as a 'smashing site'. It appealed, we were told, to his 'sense of history', which was *piquant*, given that we were about to witness the desecration of one of Britain's best known historic cities.

No one was in the least surprised when, on 9 January 1998, it was announced that Scotland's first parliament in 300 years would be built at Holyrood.

Transparent Democracy
*Homage to Caledonia*

*Look on my works, ye Mighty, and despair!*
                    Shelley: 'Ozymandias'

AND SO, HOLYROOD, and relief all round, or were we still in the real-life version of a Michael Dobbs novel? With much gusto, it was announced early in the new year that there would be an international architectural competition. There was great excitement, as you might expect, in the Scottish architectural community. The anticipation had been building up since the previous July, when the possibility of a new building had first been raised. An opportunity for a young star, perhaps, like Charles Barry, barely forty when he won the competition to design the Palace of Westminster?

New Labour's wonks, having lost old words such as 'socialism', incant certain approved buzz words in the endless cascade of literature, speeches, party pep talks and interviews: inclusiveness, openness, accountability, empowerment. As far as the Scottish parliament project was concerned, it was rapidly becoming apparent that these words had to be read and understood as their respective opposites.

There was no greater example of that than the 'public consultation' exercise which wasn't. Held, it appears, on the suggestion of the Royal Incorporation of Architects in Scotland, though not, it would seem, with the wholehearted enthusiasm of the Scottish Office establishment, it wasn't so much advertised as quietly put about that some sort of presentation was taking place somewhere in Edinburgh; a report in the *Evening News* identified the City Chambers. The city's principal amenity body, the Cockburn Association, heard nothing of this mysterious event until it was over.

One doughty lady who managed to track it down had made a journey from Dunfermline and duly arrived at the City Chambers, to be met with a blank stare. Exhibition? Council staff, all equally unknowing, appeared puzzled when told that an exhibition of parliament sites was taking place somewhere on the premises. A council employee offered to make inquiries, and came back with the news that she should perhaps try the old regional chambers on George IV Bridge. It was the only other possibility anyone could think of.

She made her way up the High Street and arrived at the destination. There was no notice visible, but she walked into the entrance lobby and was directed to an upstairs room, where there were three 'rather woolly interpretations of possibilities' and two or three people she took to be architects. Or had she stumbled into some revived mithraic cult? There was no sign of any book in which to record her comments.

The official designation for this hole-in-the-corner event would later be altered from 'public consultation' to 'public information'. For good measure, it was staged around Chistmas; shades of the infamous Boxing Day compulsory purchase orders sent out thirty years earlier, when Edinburgh corporation in cahoots with the Scottish Office had decided on a symbol for an older 'New Scotland', New St Andrew's House. *Plus ça change*.

Donald Dewar's 'New Scotland' vision, while it had left Leith foreshore, was still in heavy waters. The concession of Holyrood was being cynically interpreted in some quarters as a continuation of the waterfront stitch-up by another name. There were even dissenters in his own party urging a rethink, and not because of any appreciation of the finer points of neo-Greek aesthetics, but because democratic process was being usurped and, what was worse, it could be *seen* that it was being usurped. If, as Ron Davies had said before his moment of madness, 'devolution is a process, not an event' this process was being pushed through with unnecessary haste and no regard for public opinion or wider political participation, and the coming event was a Scottish parliamentary election.

The protests continued. An elderly lady in Peebles made up petition forms and spent a Saturday morning collecting signatures outside the Royal Scottish Academy. Every passer-by she stopped signed, she assured me, with only one exception, and he apologised profusely because he was a high court judge, and couldn't. The tone was less than incendiary: 'We respectfully request the Secretary of State for Scotland to reconsider his unrepresentative choice of Holyrood Road, Edinburgh, particularly as St Andrew's House is to be upgraded.' She was to deliver almost 1,000 signatures to the Scottish Office.

The Edinburgh Lib Dem MP and former councillor Donald Gorrie, horrified at what was being proposed for his city, was continuing to be unhelpful, unlike his colleague Jim Wallace, who had his eye on the power-sharing future. Gorrie discerned the hand of the mandarins, and was outraged. 'It is a question of whether the parliament is to suit the convenience of the civil servants or the public, and the civil servants can get stuffed.' As it happens, some civil servants were as horrified as he was, but they were wisely keeping their heads down.

Mr Dewar could be assured, however, that it was not all bad news. The Campaign for a Scottish Assembly, which had fought tirelessly for devolution for many years and faithfully backed Dewar's call for 'independence in the UK', were of two minds. The consensus view amongst the organising committee was that Calton Hill should be the location, but a number were of the opinion that the remit of their group had been to effect the devolution settlement. Nigel Smith, the businessman who had funded much of the CSA's work over the years, believed that it had achieved its end on the day the Scotland Act had passed into law, and should avoid any debate over buildings and sites that might be detrimental to the 'settled will'. Others, including Isobel Lindsay and Marian Ralls, suggested that this was essentially a Westminster decision which was being thrown in the face of the 'settled will', and the CSA should register a strong objection. Smith's view won the day.

Labour's dissenters, too, were to remain silent in public, if deeply unhappy in private. It was essential to close ranks behind Donald Dewar for the simple reason that he was virtually the only one of their number who commanded the respect and indeed affection of the voting public. The other 'big beasts' of the Westminster jungle had noticeably failed to show up. Robin Cook, who had let it be known during a TV interview that he would resign as a UK cabinet minister to stake his all as a member of the new parliament, announced in early January that he had other plans. George Robertson, who had pompously intoned 'it will be an honour to serve in a Scottish parliament' had discovered it was an even greater honour to be a peer of the realm and Secretary-General of NATO. As far as Labour's credibility was concerned, Donald Dewar was it. He was also one of the few performers who could see off Alex Salmond in the chamber and on TV.

Scotland's press, with one or two exceptions, was well disposed to devolution and keen that it should stay on track. Not only did Dewar have close friends in journalism, who were bound, in decency, to protect him, but he was unusual in that he had genuine character, and stood out from the grey mass of the Labour machine. While he could be cantankerous and conspiratorial, he was incapable of being dull. He also knew instinctively how to 'work' the press, and could deliver the sort of one-liners that added sparkle to an otherwise routine report. In time, many journalists would be disappointed in him – and, as the copy became more barbed, he in them – but even those who found Donald Dewar difficult agreed that he was 'value for money'.

The wider establishment, equally, were giving very little trouble. The heritage lobby was beginning to lose momentum. The RIAS, meanwhile, still looked forward with pleasure to the prospect of a worthy new building which, it felt, would reflect the best that Scottish architecture had to offer.

For Donald Dewar the best news of all came in February when an ICM poll of around 1,000 Scots found that over half favoured a new parliament at Holyrood. This seemed like a total vindication of the project, scattering those who had accused him of defying the settled will. He had all along, as luck would have it, been acting with the consent of the people. The problem was that the lead-in statement in this poll indicated that its findings would influence nothing: 'It has been decided that the Scottish Parliament shall be sited at Holyrood in Edinburgh.' It followed that since 75 per cent of voters had voted in the referendum for a parliament, and had got it, and that the government had in any case made up its mind about where it should be, there was little point in complaining. So was this support for Holyrood by default, or an enthusiastic endorsement of a building which, as yet, hadn't even been designed?

The ICM poll, as it turned out, would be something of a false dawn, but for the moment it allowed the Secretary of State to ignore the continuing flow of negative letters in the press and concentrate on other matters. Meanwhile, arrangements were being made behind the scenes. The architect Bill Armstrong, well respected for his proven ability to manage large projects, had earlier received an invitation to a private party. There, he had fallen into conversation with Robert Gordon, head of the devolution unit, who asked him to become involved in the site evaluation and construction of the parliament project. Though then on the point of retirement, Armstrong agreed, and joined a project team which, under the close scrutiny of Gordon, was led by Barbara Doig as 'project sponsor', aided by Dr John Gibbons and civil servant, Paul Grice.

Armstrong's own view was that in terms of getting a building ready for the tight target date of 2001, allowing for a lapse while the brief was prepared and the competition conducted, the site that made sense was Leith. It was flat, cleared and free. Holyrood presented several problems, not the least of which would be the awkward gradient, the demolition of existing buildings, and the restricted access, which, for a construction project generating several thousand lorry movements through city traffic, was an important consideration. Having been a brewing site since the twelfth century, it was also riddled with aquifers, tunnels and other unmapped subterranean underworkings. One source with military connections recalled that even the SAS had been bamboozled by it in the early 1960s when they were looking for a site for a nuke-proof command centre.

With the team assembled and the preliminaries under way, it was felt that a watershed had been passed and the public would come in behind the project as the 'world-class' entries began to pour in to the architectural competition. The voices of dissent, however, were not to be silenced. On 25 January a letter appeared in *The Times* from the Hereditary Keeper of the Palace of Holyroodhouse, the Duke of Hamilton. In the 'New Britain' the aristocracy has been largely sidelined, but this particular duke had a more interesting record than most. He had, for one thing, publicly supported devolution during the referendum campaign, and publicly endorsed Labour at the general election. Although technically a member of the royal household, and expected to maintain a low political profile, he was also a professional engineer with an interest in sustainability who had spoken out for the abolition of the hereditary peerage and hunting with dogs. Credentials, you might say, that could almost have entitled him to the label 'New Labour', had he wanted it.

On this issue, however, he was very much his own man, and politely suggested that the Secretary of State should think about public opinion, as well as John Smith's legacy, and reconsider Calton Hill. Although the letter was written entirely on the duke's own initiative, it was the nearest there would be to a palace pronouncement on a scheme that was set to dwarf Holyroodhouse itself. The Prince of Wales, who had already taken flak over an earlier competition project, the Museum of Scotland, was understandably apprehensive about wading into this particular constitutional squall.

Even cabinet ministers were developing serious misgivings about the negative propaganda fallout. Much hay had already been made. Brian Meek, of Edinburgh council's Tory group, accused Dewar and his civil servants of wanting to 'hive the parliament off to Leith, the prostitutes' capital of Scotland and about as accessible as a drainpipe'. The SNP could afford to take the relaxed view, merely snapping at the hapless Secretary of State whenever the project was developing problems. Although the nationalists had initially had their own dissenters on the question of location, with some, such as the journalist George Kerevan and George Adam of the party's youth wing, pushing for the old parliament building by St Giles, SNP policy had now been determined, and it was for Calton Hill.

It rankled with some in the Labour Party that Donald Dewar seemed to have achieved something the nationalists themselves had failed to achieve: uniting the SNP. On the Calton issue, the SNP's 'fundies' and 'gradualists' had found common cause, and one that was, moreover, in tune with the people.

According to Labour's strategy, devolution was meant to make the party of government appear competent and responsible, yet the new parliament wasn't even elected, and already the plan was in chaos. The SNP, with a potential front-bench team that looked perfectly capable of running the affairs of a small European state, made the party of government, with its palatial building plans, look self-indulgent, dictatorial and confused.

The matter, at any rate, was progressing. The site had been chosen, and now it was a question of getting on with the competition. The three woolly 'interpretations of possibilities' which had, nominally at least, undergone public scrutiny had consisted of an RMJM feasibility study of the Haymarket site, a Benson & Forsyth one of Leith, and a Page & Park assessment of the conversion of old St Andrew's House, plus another, done in a mere four weeks, of the 'eleventh-hour entrant' site at Holyrood, again by RMJM.

Unfortunately a nasty glitch had appeared in the form

of a Comparative Transport and Environmental Assessment commissioned by the Scottish Office from Scott Wilson Kirkpatrick which had annoyingly stated what everyone without buttons on the back of the head knew to be the case anyway. The only rational choice from the transport planning point of view was Calton Hill, which sat at the end of the A1 Euroroute to London and more or less on top of Waverley Station. This raised a further issue. How do you make a site tucked away in the far corner of a medieval townscape accessible? The answer, it seemed, was to commission a 'strategic access study' by another company, the Oscar Faber Group, with an altogether different brief, the objectives of which should include such motherhood-and-apple-pie comforters as 'the very best in terms of quality and innovation with an emphasis on reducing the need to travel by car with priority given to public transport and the slow modes of cycling and walking'.

For Bill Armstrong, the site with the fewest problems was still Leith, where Benson & Forsyth had come up with an imaginative scheme, while Page & Park's reworking of St Andrew's House was, he felt, both assured and achievable within the time frame. Haymarket, which had been promoted by the property duo of Sandy MacDonald Orr and Andy Doolan, was out of the question for security reasons (it was above operational railway tunnels) and Holyrood was, he advised, a tight parcel of land constrained by its setting. Even so, when Holyrood was selected he'd been sure that, given the support of the civil servants, he could deliver a parliament.

As January progressed it rapidly became evident that Scottish architects were unlikely to be flavour of the month for Scotland's most significant architectural commission in three centuries. There would be no 'Charles Barry' rising star. The method used was not totally to preclude them, which might invite an action under the Race Relations Act, but to orientate the conditions and introduce several hurdles. It was not, in fact, impossible that a Scottish architect might win, in the sense that it is not impossible that snow might fall in July.

The means of resisting home-grown applications was to geld them at the outset. The priorities were to be speed and reliability, a proven capability to deliver, and a track record of commissions of similar scale and complexity. The problem here was that, like young Charles Barry, precious few Scottish practices had ever had much of an opportunity to build on such a scale, even in Scotland.

Looking around at a decade or so's built evidence, there seems to have been little inclination to use Scottish architects on major public projects, with the notable exception of the Museum of Scotland by the London-Scottish practice of Benson & Forsyth. RMJM's Victoria Quay, with enough space for 1,500 civil servants, was certainly both Scottish and big, but it had won no top architectural awards, and hidden as it was between the Forth and a block of converted bonded warehouses, it was hardly a noticeable signature. The real 'sexy' projects – Foster's Armadillo, Farrell's Edinburgh Conference Centre, and Hopkin's Dynamic Earth – are by outsiders. It has been said that Glasgow should have hung its collective head in shame at the way it treated Mackintosh, but at least it allowed him to design a few significant buildings!

The *leitmotiv* of Scottish public architecture at the turn of the millennium would appear to be that Scottish architects – including those capable of designing award-winning buildings overseas – shouldn't be encouraged to produce too much of it in Scotland. This 'cringe factor' was to be embraced for the most important public building of all, the parliament, and it seems to have been a simple enough one to observe, for if an entry qualification is that you should have gained some experience from major commissions, and if you haven't been allowed near any, then too bad, matey, you're out. To reinforce the message, applicants were asked for guarantees of, for the vast majority, unrealistically high levels of professional indemnity insurance, effectively locking out most of Scotland's practices.

Some attempted to circumvent the barriers by joining forces, either holding on to the tailcoats of large international practices or forming syndicates. The message was clear, however. An 'international' signature was wanted, like, say, a big name from Catalonia, a semi-autonomous region of Spain which Donald Dewar felt had achieved the sort of 'locked-in' political balance Scotland might seek to emulate.

The response of the RIAS was muted, though many members were champing at the bit. The incorporation's council, however, had little choice but to take a non-disputatious line with the civil servants who were, after all, gatekeepers to some of the most important regular building commissions in Scotland. Several member practices were furious about the barriers to entry, while others, including some of the largest corporate firms, were entering the competition. A perceived need for balance was to limit any urge to make waves.

Whatever the predicament of the RIAS, the 'international competition' parameters appeared to be firmly fixed in favour of the fully verified delivered-to-deadline technical product, rather than a design-led creative outcome. Time was pressing. A competition had to be arranged, advertised and judged, buildings demolished, a post-industrial site investigated and prepared, and planning consultations undertaken. To facilitate the high-pressure schedule, and get a completed building out of it within the term of the first parliament, so many strictures had to be applied to entrants on the basis of their technical back-up, rather than any creative aptitude which might reveal itself in the course of the judging, according to one architect, that it could barely be called an architectural design competition at all. Even the usual European regulations covering public building procurement had to be negotiated around the margins to allow early completion.

Scotland had done without a parliament for almost 300 years, but now it had to have one in three! As another architect pointed out, a realistic and symbolically meaningful target for a new, custom-built parliament, wherever it might be, would have been the year 2007. This would have comfortably allowed MSPs enough time to debate it, a competition panel enough time to assess it, an architect enough time to design it, and a construction team enough time to build it. Even the public could have had its say. He had suggested this to a civil servant, but for some reason it hadn't been taken seriously. The priority, he'd been told, was to have the show on the road within the term of one parliament, and well in advance of the fixed 2003 election date. On reflection, he'd decided the tercentenary of the loss of an independent parliament, albeit a venally corrupt one, might point up the rather less independent nature of a new and transparent one ringed with reserved powers, 'joined-up thinking' from Downing Street, cross-border concordats, and all the other checks and balances that make the difference between devolution and full autonomy.

The competition was under way. Bill Armstrong's detailed 66-page building user brief for a design incorporating some 16,842 square metres plus car parking of 3,200 square metres was duly issued to applicants. There were seventy-one responses, thirty-three of which had at least some level of local input, with three of these being syndicates formed by Scottish practices.

For an international competition this was a less than overwhelming response. The 1991 Museum of Scotland competition had attracted a total of 365 entries from across the world, many of superb design quality – enough, indeed, for Edinburgh architect Ben Tindall to organise a Salon des Refusés for those not displayed at the official competition.

The constraints imposed by high indemnity levels and 'deliverability' safeguards had obviously precluded many smaller practices, but even so there were some surprising gaps. Richard Rogers intimated that he would not be taking part. He was then in the process of rebranding the Greenwich peninsula, and in his own words was about to start 'watching his backside' in Cardiff, where London's *leitmotiv* alternative to the City Hall was already enmeshed in some controversy. There was nothing from Frank Ghery, whose Bilbao Guggenheim, which had opened the previous October, had made him something of an international superstar. Norman Foster, too, was noticeable by his absence, though having delivered the Reichstag parliament for a government that seemed to see no conflict between heritage and modernity (even with a symbol of the 'Old Germany'), he had an intimate knowledge of the hazards of designing for nationhood.* He was also busy with his Thameside 'egg', a commercial project to be leased to Ken Livingstone's GLA.

One of the most interesting features of the competition was the composition of the five-strong selection panel. Donald Dewar took a close interest. The mandarin's representatives were the devolution unit chief Robert Gordon and Scottish Office development chief John Gibbons. Joan O'Connor, former President of the Royal Hibernian Institute of Architects in Dublin, added an out-of-the-country flavour. Andrew MacMillan, former Emeritus Professor of Architecture at Glasgow's Mackintosh School was an enthusiastic champion of 'big-signature' modern architecture, Kirsty Wark was well known as a *Newsnight* presenter.

The most noticeable thing about this group was not who was in it, but who wasn't. All Edinburgh interests had been meticulously excluded. Even Lord Provost Eric Milligan, so impeccably 'on-message' about the move to Leith and the retreat to Holyrood, and Labour group leader Keith Geddes, whose ward was Holyrood, were shut out of a process that was going to alter radically the character of the city they had been elected to serve.

A closer look at the talents being brought to bear on the consideration and selection of Scotland's most important architectural commission of the century is illuminating. It seems reassuring, at first, that three were qualified architects. Dr John Gibbons had trained in Birmingham before coming north to take up a research fellowship at Edinburgh

* Lord Foster and the German government ended up wrangling over his fees.

under Sir Robert Matthew. After a brief spell as a lecturer, he had joined the Scottish Office in 1972. 'I am not aware of John ever having designed and constructed a major building,' said one of his colleagues, 'though he can certainly understand drawings.' He had, in fact, been in private practice for two years in the early 1960s, and had long experience of work in relation to several Scottish Office projects.

Gibbons had known links with RMJM in a number of 'village Scotland' ways. During the 1980s he had occupied one half of a divided seventeenth-century mansion at Crichton, near Pathhead, while the engineer Brian Stewart, the managing director of RMJM, and his family had lived in the other half. The seemingly innocent, if close, connection was long established. He had lectured on architectural research under RMJM founder Sir Robert Matthew, and was friendly with the retired RMJM partner John Richards, who hailed from the same era. He had made no secret of his opposition to the use of the Calton Hill site, and had allegedly infuriated Historic Scotland chief, Graeme Munro, when he suggested at a meeting in St Andrew's House that a Calton Hill scheme might 'take substantially longer' because of listed buildings.

The Constitution Group chief Robert Gordon at least lived in Edinburgh, unlike the others, though he was an Aberdonian by origin and education. His meteoric rise attested to his skills as the consummate mandarin, and although his near contemporary Muir Russell had only recently been appointed head of the civil service in Scotland,* Gordon was widely regarded as a potential successor for the top post.

Joan O'Connor was a highly respected Irish architect, but her strengths were said to be in efficient project delivery, rather than creative design, while 'Andy' MacMillan was already attached to the Scottish Office as an architectural adviser. One Edinburgh architect regarded him as a 'hell

---

* 'New Broom' Russell had been appointed over the head of traditionalist Kenneth Mackenzie, causing some friction.

of a risky choice' as a panel member. A former partner in the Glasgow practice of Gillespie, Kidd, and Coia, MacMillan was an ebullient and outspoken member of the Glasgow arts scene.

The most intriguing choice was Kirsty Wark. A friend and neighbour of Dewar's, she was drafted in as the lay member with media glamour who had an interest in architecture and buildings, and had fronted the BBC's *One Foot in the Past* series.

Some suspected dark motives for this appointment, though no one suggested Ms Wark was herself a party to any conspiracy. There was rumoured to be a joke doing the rounds in the BBC canteen: 'Well, that should spike the awkward questions on *Newsnight*, then!' She openly subscribed to the in-house agenda: 'The new building should not be classical or modernist on the grounds that these styles are too closely associated with dictatorship.' Even modernism was too staid here, suggesting a post-modern deconstructivist symbol of chaos might be in the offing – a case of *One Foot in the Future*. It was to be a wonderfully democratic future, naturally; in which the people would have the chance to make further comments as the design developed, she assured the *Daily Record*.

Time was ticking on. The site had been secretly agreed upon in October 1997 and was brought into the running on 8 December, when RMJM had been appointed to do the feasibility study; it had been formally selected on 9 January, and the international competition announced on 26 January. A little over a month was allowed in which the applicants could develop the outline schemes in accordance with the requirements of a demanding brief. On 3 March the panel of judges was announced, and just over three weeks later the short leet of twelve was made public.

The process of arriving at a decision had been assisted by a 'sift through' to separate the unlikely from the possible. Bill Armstrong looked at the submission of a 43-year-old Catalan architect, Enric Miralles y Moya. His entry was unconventional, and his practice back-up, based in a small office in the heart of Barcelona's *bario gothico*, seemed no more substantial than that of many of the Scottish practices that had failed to meet the entry criteria. Armstrong rejected it without so much as a second thought. RMJM, which had submitted a solo scheme, was knocked out of the running in the first stage of selection.

The short leet of twelve included some well-known names, such as that of Peter Kulka, architect of the Dresden parliament and Kohn Pederson Fox Associates, who had designed a parliament for Cyprus. It was also noticeable by this stage that the budget was becoming fluid. The project which, shortly after the referendum, had been costed at 'between £10 million and £40 million' was suddenly being described as a £50 million scheme, and rising.

By 7 May, when the final short leet of five was announced, Holyrood had become a '£60 million contract to create Scotland's Westminster' but attention was focused on the exciting quality of the 'world-class' architecture, rather than costs. There were certainly some 'sexy' names on the list.

Richard Meier (in association with Keppie Design of Glasgow) had a megastar reputation based on an international portfolio of work, including the new Getty Museum in California and museums in Barcelona and Frankfurt. Michael Wilford & Partners had produced a celebrated Cool Britannia essay, the new British Embassy in Berlin. Denton, Corker, Marshall International (in association with Glass Murray architects of Glasgow) had also designed a parliament scheme, as well as the world's tallest building, in Melbourne. Rafael Vinoly of New York had designed the world's most expensive building complex to date, the £1 billion Tokyo International Forum.

The wild card seemed to be Enric Miralles, a conceptual designer relatively untried in the world of serious megaplex architecture. While his design abilities and innovative approach were widely admired, and he had created numerous ambitious, if unbuilt, schemes, there was nothing that brought him into the Vinoly or Wilford league. Alexander Linklater described him in the *Herald* as the 'slick

European alternative to the slick American work of Meier. The kind of ambitious architecture which looks good in glossy magazines,' citing the much admired Olympic Archery Pavilions in Barcelona, and the 'new town hall' in Utrecht. (The latter was, in fact, officially a 'Utrecht Town Hall Renovation Project' suggesting a reuse of existing buildings, as well as new additions.)

Dundee's Professor of Architecture, Charles McKean, had criticised the short list of twelve as 'a snub for the reputation of Scottish architects' firms', but now *Herald* political correspondent Frances Horsburgh obligingly highlighted the Scottish contribution, mentioning that two of the five teams included Scottish associates. She also quoted John Gibbons' assertion that although this was an 'incredibly important' commission it was 'not a large one in international cost terms'. However, rather more convincing efforts were being made to keep the public informed, with a series of ten public exhibitions, and there were even comment forms available.

This would be a parliament, said Kirsty Wark, that would have 'no dark corners', but there was much that seemed less than clear, such as the match-up of Miralles and RMJM. Despite having been pulled out by Bill Armstrong in an early sift Miralles had been brought back in and made it to the final list of five entirely on his own under the name Enric Miralles y Moya. There was no associate, not even his second wife and business partner, Benedetta Tagliabue, and no sign whatever of RMJM, which had given up its own connection with the competition after failing to reach the first short leet.

Michael Wilford & Partners, too, were running solo, as was Rafael Vinoly, although in the latter case a partnership with Reiach & Hall was tied up shortly after the final list had been prepared, and the joint team was identified as a single entrant for almost the entire phase leading up to the selection of the winner. At some point during this process, however, Enric Miralles y Moya was transmogrified into Miralles-Tagliabue/RMJM (EMBT/RMJM). Whether this hook-up was made before the selection panel had gravitated towards its choice of Miralles, or while it was gravitating, or after it had more or less decided, is largely a matter for speculation, but it was something of a 'dark corner' none the less.

No matter. On 6 July the winning entry was announced, and it was, as many had expected, EMBT/RMJM, headed up by Enric Miralles, 'one of the world's most avant-garde young architects'. This seemed, in some ways, like a complementary pairing of the no-nonsense technocratic approach of a large Scottish practice with worldwide experience and a dynamic and creative poetic visionary with an intuitive grasp of random, loosely formed ideas. Bill Armstrong would come up with his own description: the marriage made in hell. He would also write a frank letter to John Gibbons. 'I did not agree with Miralles' appointment but said that I would do the best I could. But if I felt the project was going off the rails then I would opt out. What I found most upsetting about the whole thing . . . was the lip-service paid to the Scottish architectural profession.'

For the moment, however, the spin was all positive. There was still no clear idea in the minds of many politicians, never mind the Scottish public, about how the costs were to be met, although the white paper Scotland's Parliament, which had identified a cost of £10 million to £40 million, had indicated that 'the start-up costs will be met from existing expenditure plans'. Miralles produced his 'upturned boats' proposals in October 1998. There was a widespread consensus amongst architects that, as a designed form, Enric Miralles' well-crafted model provided a unique signature while respecting the open space behind it. It was also clear that, in so far as anyone could have shoe-horned a vast public building between Holyroodhouse and the bottom of the Canongate, Miralles had at least made an effort where others had simply blustered. He had even thought about retaining the Edwardian Scots baronial frontage of the old Abbey Brewery until informed by John Hume, project team adviser on historic buildings, that they were of 'no historic merit whatever'.

On closer examination it was apparent that much of this compatability with the context had been achieved at the expense of the brief. Though, as always with Miralles, it was an 'evolving form', open to a variety of interpretations, it clearly missed out on a substantial proportion of the specified floor area. The chamber shape, too, was decidedly off-spec.

An *Evening News* ringaround of forty well-known Scots was broadly supportive of giving the design a chance. Even Donald Gorrie, later to become one of Holyrood's fiercest critics, was prepared to concede the benefit of the doubt: 'The panel has chosen this guy who is incredibly whizzo, so let's give it a try.' Margo MacDonald, who would also end up opposing the project as its costs spiralled, was cool, but not totally dismissive, merely asking that the architect should 'listen to the planners and the people of Edinburgh who want something a bit more harmonious with the natural surroundings'. Some were not impressed. 'As far as I'm concerned, an upturned boat has all the wrong symbolism,' said SNP councillor Eddie Malcolm. Donald Findlay QC, driving force of the 'No-No' campaign, deployed deadpan humour. 'I think it's a very nice model and with the assistance of a box of Swan Vestas it would make a very nice bonfire.'

The press coverage in general was positive, but qualified. Jonathan Glancey in the *Guardian* described Miralles' style as 'rich, complex, and subtle, like a conjurer pulling rabbits from a hat' but again called into question the project's underlying dynamic, arising from a decision that recalled 'nineteenth-century nationalism'. In the *Scotsman*, the architectural writer Hugh Pearman placed Miralles as 'first by quite some distance' adding that he had 'taken a risk with modifying the brief – wasn't a circular debating chamber specified?'.

The Scottish architectural profession nominally gave a public welcome to the panel's 'courageous decision', notwithstanding that, as Pearman noted, the contest might almost have been structured to exclude most of them.

RIAS spokesman John Pelan chose his words carefully: 'Enthusiasm was slightly tempered by the fact that some of our members felt that other Scottish architects should have been on the list.' The incorporation was certainly in an invidious position, with some of its more powerful members, including corporate giants RMJM and Reiach & Hall (the firm of its recent president, John Spencely) being closely involved in the competition, while others were outraged that their professional 'trade union' had been conspicuously ambivalent in looking after their interests.

Individual architects, while observing the unwritten code that you don't let the side down by badmouthing the other chap's work, at least not publicly, were anything but pleased. 'On the record, I welcome the panel's brave decision to select such an innovative and exciting young architect,' said the head of a well-known west of Scotland firm. 'Off the record, they've obviously taken leave of their collective senses with this reckless gamble. If it works, fine, but if not, it won't just damage political reputations. It will damage the reputation of the profession.'

From the beginning, Bill Armstrong was uneasy about Miralles' approach to the job, but decided to give it his best go. The first project meeting took place two months after the appointment. Miralles arrived with sketches and models which were difficult to interpret; indeed Joan O'Connor, despite her experience, had complained about the difficulty of comprehending the Miralles style even during the competition process. After the final selection, she had said to Gibbons, 'We know we've handed you a difficult test.' Miralles' initial technical sketches, says Armstrong, were more or less a rehash of RMJM plans and he suggested to Gibbons that the only way to deal with the situation was to 'get the concept to a certain stage and send him away'.

If the Armstrong-Miralles chemistry was a touch on the acidic side, the same couldn't be said of MacMillan's high regard for the easy-going *wunderkind* of Barcelona's architectural revolution. One architect, driving home from work, had been astonished to hear MacMillan praising the competition entrant fulsomely in a radio interview before the process was complete. 'I had a feeling then I knew what the outcome was going to be. With the exception of Joan O'Connor, this panel seemed out of its depth, and Andy MacMillan's attitude was dominated by the idea that he, personally, was nurturing a superstar talent.'

That was now history. The competition over, the winner was hard at work. Or was he? As time ticked by the Miralles' ideas factory fell behind schedule. Edinburgh's RMJM staff were waiting patiently for data to arrive, clocking up hours with very little to do. It wasn't simply a problem for RMJM. Steve Fisher, of the engineers Arups, had taken a team off a job in London, and they were looking for throughput on the project.

The costs began to climb as the 'concept' fluctuated. Miralles had initially indicated that he had some idea of reducing the bulk of the buildings. 'We do not want the parliament to be high. It is too high at the moment,' he had suddenly announced a mere ten days after his appointment, somewhat to the alarm of those who prefer their parameters to be technical, rather than conceptual. Later he decided to up the size of the service areas. Bill Armstrong needed another £8 million, and was informed, 'We can't tell the Secretary of State. He has an election coming.'

Doubts were also growing about the architect's disinclination to spend time in Edinburgh. There had been an understanding at the outset that the competition winner would establish a base in the city, but initial reports that Miralles was looking for a flat turned out to be unfounded. A number of local architects such as Nicholas Groves-Raines had offered accommodation and workspace, but had been rebuffed.

Further difficulties arose with the allocation of a contract that was self-evidently going to be a complex and challenging one. In early December Armstrong and the design team considered the construction management tender bids that had come in. The lowest was from McAlpine, with

Bovis moderately higher. Armstrong recommended either McAlpine or HGB, and even named a construction manager who could be released from a Standard Life contract to direct work on the parliament. As with the Miralles appointment, his advice was to be ignored. Bovis Lend Lease was added back on to the list, and its tender offer was accepted. A source in the industry suggested that the Scottish Office had 'felt comfortable' with Bovis over the duration of the troubled Museum of Scotland project, where there had been a 'bit of give and take' over costs.

Project consultant Bill Armstrong, meanwhile, was giving advice, but no one was taking it. Exasperated and worn down after six months of frustration, he had quite simply had enough. He could see the gathering storm clouds and was making his warnings clear, but the civil servants seemed more interested in hushing up the problems than tackling them head-on. Politics were beginning to get in the way of the project, and that wasn't in the job description. Bill Armstrong felt he had no alternative but to resign.

Which is precisely what he did.

# 17 Into the Vortex
## *Cascading Rocks*

> *Events, dear boy, events*
> Harold Macmillan

AS HOLYROOD'S PROBLEMS deepened, along with the unsightly crater which was, so far, the only visible evidence of work on the site, the Scottish election, due in May 1999, looked less than in the bag for Labour. Holyrood apart, Donald Dewar was being assailed on all sides by problems.

Many of these were not of his making, such as the arrest of Mohammad Sarwar on corruption charges and the suicide note left by MP Gordon McMaster which accused fellow MP Tommy Graham of hounding him. Others undoubtedly were, like the blocking of Sean Connery's knighthood, a story that had broken in late February 1998, but which kept on running as Labour developed a tendentious spin about Connery being vetoed not because of his politics, but because of his 'reputation with women'. Poor Miss Moneypenny, apparently, just hadn't been aware of the risk she'd been running. The Connery smear campaign would culminate in a *Daily Record* front page showing the harassed, and no longer young, actor in an angry pose after being badgered by paparazzi snappers on his own doorstep, an intrusion that overwhelmingly engaged public sympathy for the victim.

The repercussions of the Connery story reverberated around the world. Why was the most famous living Scotsman being hounded by a government that had the biggest majority in modern British history? As overseas journalists picked up on it the telephones began to ring in Alastair

Campbell's press office. Tell us more, they asked: so Sean Connery is being given grief because he supports some small party in Scotland? What is this party called? Is it like the Québecois then? Caught on the hop, Labour's reaction was to imply, just outside the limits of a libel action, and on the evidence of an old throwaway remark which the rebuttal unit had clearly dredged out of its Lotus databank, that Connery condoned violence against women. The ennobled George Robertson, ermine still fresh in the wardrobe, then waded in and suggested waspishly that Connery was simply furious because he'd missed out on a knighthood. Brian Wilson assiduously peddled the 'attitude to women' line. The damage-limitation exercise was as fruitless as it was desperate.

The reaction at home was no better than the reaction overseas. The 'open-handed slap' remark which Sean Connery had once made was hardly on a par with the public perception, real and imagined, of some of Labour's own bruisers. The suspended MP Tommy Graham, though cleared by an internal party inquiry of any part in the suicide of Paisley MP Gordon McMaster a year earlier, was under investigation over allegations (subsequently withdrawn) that he had offered a compromising gay photograph of an influential trade union official to two prospective MSPs. The party hierarchy, meanwhile, was deeply embarrassed by its futile attempts to oust Glasgow Lord Provost Pat Lally. Another west of Scotland MP, Jimmy Wray, who had once had a tussle with model New Labourite Derek Draper at a party conference, was being sued for divorce on the grounds of violence, which he denied.

Sean Connery, by contrast, was not only a popular and highly regarded unofficial ambassador for Scotland overseas, but he had sunk much of his own wealth at home into an educational trust for deprived children. He was, himself, a man who had risen from humble beginnings in Fountainbridge, working at a variety of occupations, among them delivering milk to Tony Blair's old boarding-school. To cap it all, he had even campaigned alongside Dewar and Brown as part of the 'Yes-Yes' team in the referendum campaign.

He was also dignified in his reaction to a campaign of vilification which was proving singularly counter-productive. The whole world, as well as the whole of Scotland, now knew that, off-screen, James Bond was really a *Braveheart* figure valiantly seeking the freedom of his nation. The more Labour attacked, the more secure Connery's reputation became, and the more cussed and mean-minded Donald Dewar and Sam Galbraith looked, for it was now public knowledge that the blocking of the nomination had been their idea.

A diversionary tactic was called for, anything to take the heat out of the Connery story. London was beginning to panic at publicity that might yet, by association, tarnish the Prime Minister's 'golden boy' reputation overseas. The Blair government was already suffering from mid-term unpopularity after a round of council budget cuts and welfare reforms, and it didn't need to take on Hollywood into the bargain.

Dewar had to act, and act fast. Rumours were coming in that London journalists were looking into the personal details of other MPs. Whatever the truth of such rumours, London was determined to put a lid on the affair before it got out of hand.

Another story, even a negative one, was needed to bump Sean Connery out of the Scottish tabloid headlines. It was all sorted out by the following week. While Holyrood was being constructed temporary premises would have to be made ready for the elected members, and that was going to be in the former Strathclyde Regional Council headquarters in Glasgow. It certainly grabbed the headlines, though, as it turned out, the press was losing interest in the Connery story in any case.

Some, including the then leader of the SNP Alex Salmond, believe that the Glasgow decision was merely hinted at initially. However, those journalists at the briefing given by Robert Gordon were told, unequivocally, that a decision had been taken to site the temporary chamber in Glasgow. The news that Glasgow had been chosen had been greeted with delight in the city, but in other parts of Scotland the old spectre of 'Strathclyde writ large' was fearfully projected. The civil servants in Victoria Quay, faced with the gruelling prospect of shuttling between their remote waterfront and central Glasgow for meetings and consultations, were filled with horror.

Then, on 16 March, it was announced that this wouldn't be happening after all. Glasgow councillors were predictably livid. The Edinburgh establishment, it appeared, were stitching them up again.

The mind-change sent Glasgow's city bosses into a fury, but, for London, at least, all the problems were now ring-fenced in Scotland. It was no doubt with some relief that Peter Mandelson put through his call of abject apology to Sean Connery and waited for the row to abate.

Labour's problems in Scotland were far from over, however. In its disarray, the party had been steadily shedding support, and it had slipped from being ahead in the polls to level pegging with the SNP. It was to get worse. In May, Labour's new spin-doctor, former Gordon Brown aide Paul McKinney, walked out after seven weeks in the job. With the election now a year off, it wasn't a good start, particularly since McKinney's brief had been to organise the campaign. In June, applicants falling foul of the selection rules for Labour candidates began to rebel, citing 'New Labour control-freakery' and 'Stalinist procedures' aimed at purging the left. By July Alex Salmond and the SNP were on the brink of an 'epochal' breakthrough, according to the *Scotsman*. The SNP were already in discussions with senior business leaders about the shape and style of their new Scotland.

But at least there would be the 'New Scotland' buzz of the Holyrood project to suggest that the nation was moving towards the millennium with a renewed sense of purpose. Serious attempts had been made to bring an end to Labour's political mayhem. Helen Liddell, Labour's 'nat-basher general', had been seconded as a deputy to Donald Dewar with instructions to sort things out. The annual conference was put off, as were the executive committee elections, avoiding a repeat of the previous year's embarrassment. Gordon Brown had begun moonlighting from the Treasury shortly after the Connery affair and was licking things into shape, keeping a safe distance, naturally, from the Holyrood crater. That was entirely Donald's responsibility. The Chancellor's job was being generous. Schools, hospitals, crime-fighting, nursery places, all came in for top-up funding. The nationalists had conveniently taken on the 'party of high spending' mantle by endorsing a penny-for-education policy, which meant implementing the tartan tax to raise £700 million.

There were changes, too, with the parliament project. Enric Miralles had decided to dump the much derided 'upturned boats' symbolism for 'tumbling stones'. A cascade of rocks, he explained, would have rolled down from the Salisbury Crags, as it were, and been reassembled as a parliament complex. A model of new shapes, as exquisite as the earlier one but radically different, had been unveiled in October 1998. Building work was to start by mid-1999, and it was still being claimed that it would be finished by 2001. When Bill Armstrong walked out in December the costs were around £80 million. By January, the *Scotsman* estimated that the total cost, including site clearance, would be £111 million.

The press was beginning to take notice again, and the civil servants were desperately trying to talk it down. David Steel stirred the pot with an attack on the shape of the chamber which, as Hugh Pearman and others had pointed out months before, had nothing to do with the competition brief. Miralles' visits to Edinburgh were episodic. He would fly in, check in at the Balmoral, attend a few meetings, make some site visits, perhaps give a lecture or take part in a presentation, then fly off. The visits were of short duration, and took place about once a month. There were other visits which were non-technical, and other Barcelona staff involved, such as his assistant Joan Callas, but RMJM architects were increasingly either taking data over the fax, or flying out to Barcelona.

As the election loomed public and press attention was focused on the coming campaign. In April, Salmond spoke out against NATO airstrikes on Belgrade, calling them 'unpardonable folly'. Although many Labour MPs publicly agreed with him, three out of four Scots didn't, according to a *Sunday Times* NOP poll. Robin Cook went for the jugular. He portrayed him as 'the toast of Belgrade'. The *Daily Record* advised against voting SNP on the tenuous if sensational premise that it might trigger Balkan-style atrocities in Britain. The SNP crashed in the polls. This had become a khaki election.

Gordon Brown had also announced a penny income tax cut, which the nationalists had refused to endorse, emphasising yet again an SNP 'high-spend' image which had little voter appeal. The results of the May election were mixed, but Labour, though it fell some way short of its hoped-for minimum of sixty seats, had achieved its aim of staunching the nationalist surge. The Liberal Democrats had already agreed the coalition terms.

Donald Dewar was safe, for the moment, and so was Holyrood.

The Impossible Dream
*Fixing the Odds*

*The enemy forty years ago was Ruskin and Morris.*
*Today I see the enemy here – government*
Frank Lloyd Wright:
speech at Hull House,
Chicago, 1940

THERE IS A sense beginning to emerge, or at least a hope, that the Holyrood project might be rescued from its rudderless and storm-tossed predicament and be brought home to a snug berth. A new captain has been hired to take up where Bill Armstrong left off after he'd lost all confidence in the officers' mess. This man is young, but not too young. His name is Martin Mustard, and he spent twenty years working around the country on Department of Social Security buildings before settling in Edinburgh in 1995. He'd been assigned by Project Management International to work to Barbara Doig on the Victoria Quay project, which was completed with efficiency. A staid and moderating influence on the architect, undoubtedly, he is even married to the facilities manager for the Scottish parliament.

But hey, what have we here! This is one funky guy! 'I became the archetypal hippie. I had the long hair, the Afghan coat, beads, and' – Rebus' ears prick up – 'drugs were certainly available.' Mr Mustard is, in fact, promoting his book, a novel about digging, which seems wonderfully appropriate, and he is describing a past that he has left behind. His next book will be called *The Chattering of Dead Sunflowers*. Who wouldn't warm to such a man? His name alone demands it. But can it be the same Martin Mustard who wears the hard hat and the day-glo jacket around the bomb site that will be the parliament? Surely not? Surely yes! The mind boggles at the thought of all those impeccably attired mandarins, serenely ensconced in their offices, reading the full-page splash that is Martin's book promo. One can almost hear the teacups rattle.

The scene is one of some devastation. Much of the demolition rubble has been cleared and a great hole dug out not far from the south façade of Queensberry House. The area that, in the Edinburgh Old Town Report of 1989, was called Canongate Square – a pleasant little housing precinct opening out towards the Palace of Holyroodhouse with a statue of King Edward placed in the middle – will never be. Its excavated subterranean bedrock will provide car parking spaces for 141 cars for staff and MSPs. What was that they said in 1997 about the prohibitive cost of digging out bedrock on Calton Hill?

The thought of 141 car parking spaces immediately introduces the dimension of environmentalism. The UK government's policies certainly looked pretty good as far as its declared views on the future of the planet were concerned. Tony Blair had spoken to the ERM Environment Forum in London in February 1996, setting out the New Labour stall. He was 100 per cent for the Brundtland Commission, Agenda 21, Rio protocols, Kyoto declarations and all the other paraphernalia of good intentions. This, in part, was reactive, since the Green Party, which had done surprisingly well at one European election, drew much of its support from Labour's own fringes, but Tony Blair did show genuine concern for the issue by, for example, committing the UK to a higher percentage cut in the emission of greenhouse gases. This was a concern shared by most of the human race. Even John Selwyn-Gummer, when not making his daughter eat hamburgers for the cameras, fought his environmentalist corner hard in the Tory cabinet. Most of us, after all, would prefer, on balance, that Venice and the Maldives were still around in a hundred years, and that our great-great-grandchildren might have enough oxygen to breathe.

Being eco-friendly is all very well, but we have to be realistic. While many businesses from the Body Shop to Proctor & Gamble to the world's largest carpet manu-facturers, US-based Interface (suppliers to Victoria Quay) pursue exemplary 'closed-loop' policies based on principles of sustainability, many are a little less discriminating, and apply political pressure in the other direction. Texas Utilities were hardly bankrolling George Bush junior because they liked the cut of his suit. The old heavy-industry unions, too, are not always sweetly disposed to the 'greenies' who have permeated the ranks of the left.

The not particularly sexy environment portfolio in pre-devolution Scotland had passed by the Commons and been subcontracted out to the unelected. In some ways this wasn't a bad thing. The Conservative Lord Lindsay and his Labour successor Lord Sewel were both able men who were largely free from the rancour of adversarial politics. A Secretary of State's Advisory Group on Sustainable Development had been set up, chaired by the leading businessman Sir Charles Fraser, who was also director of the charitable trust controlling nearby Dynamic Earth. Its members included the deep-green Kevin Dunion of Friends of the Earth, Scotland and the well-motivated Lord Lindsay.

In *Down to Earth: A Scottish Perspective on Sustainable Development* Lord Sewel wrote of the parliament's wish to 'protect and develop our unique environment and natural and built heritage' which was reasonable enough, given that one of the principles enshrined in this document was 'the maintenance of cultural diversity represented by the historic character of settlements and landscapes'. Sewel had given an address along much the same lines within a week of the referendum result at the Royal Society of Edinburgh entitled 'The Realities of Change' in which he had advanced the sustainable development case at length. At the same time Donald Dewar had decided to dump heritage and cultural diversity and go all out for big-gesture internationalism for the nation's parliament building.

The decision to abandon an existing parliament building

and order up an energy-gobbling brand-new one certainly made Lord Sewel's worthy sentiments seem futile. What's the point in persuading the business community to undertake 'best practice' sustainability audits when your own boss does something as crass as that?

None the less, a great play was made on the intention to observe all the latest benchmarked standards as far as construction processes, materials, embedded energy and other factors were concerned. This 'world-class' signature building was certainly going to be a good bit greener than its Palmerstonian counterparts. 'We are pleased that sustainable development played a central part in your selection of the site for the parliament building,' Sir Charles wrote to Donald Dewar, turning logic on its head, since the most sustainable building of all, self-evidently, is the one you don't have to build in the first place.

Part of the sustainability ethos was to be the retention of materials for recycling, and it was hoped that some of the stone from the demolished buildings would be salvaged. This wasn't an unqualified success. A carved stone panel which was to be relocated to S&N's Fountainbridge empire was smashed in error by the Bradford demolition crew hired to clear the decks ASAP. Vast quantities of stone were also being trucked off-site for dumping. Sir David Steel, tackled on this by the SNP's Kenny MacAskill, replied that 390 pallets of stone had been set aside. This much of a brewery, proportionately, was lamentably small beer.

At least the architects RMJM had a 'best practice' track record in sustainable building, although whether this would prove to be a match for the oddly shaped volumes of the upturned boats (tumbling stones would never catch on; nor would scattered leaves) was another matter. The National Farmers' Union building in Stratford-upon-Avon, for example, was a naturally ventilated RMJM building, as was Victoria Quay. This was a reputation that RMJM were careful to guard, for obvious reasons.

But the question of whether the Holyrood parliament

would be built at all was beginning to overtake any consideration of how it would be built. After the brouhaha over Glasgow's here today, gone tomorrow temporary parliament, and still stiff with terror at the thought of doing the sensible thing, which would have been to use the Calton Hill building, Donald Dewar had opted to ignore the anti-clerical Tom Nairn's scurrilous remark about Scotland not being free until the last minister had been strangled with the last copy of the *Sunday Post*. He'd settled for the Church of Scotland's Assembly buildings on the Mound as the parliament's temporary home.

Unlike Hamilton's Calton Hill chamber, which simply needed sprucing up, Bryce's Assembly Hall needed a radical reconfiguration in double-quick time. Edinburgh-based Simpson & Brown burned the midnight oil and came up with a scheme which was widely admired. The schedule was demanding, but work progressed with only a few minor hiccups. An anticipated visit by Donald Dewar on 16 January meant that a quantity of bricks and timber which had just been unloaded, with the usual difficulty, through the back door at the Lawnmarket had to be taken away again. Dewar had then failed to arrive. By the time he appeared some days later John Prescott had popped in. Dewar and his devolution minister, Henry McLeish, had a photo-op on 8 March. Both approved. 'We might be quite sorry to leave,' the Scottish Secretary conceded.

Then the day came. On 12 May 1999 the woman who had put the Hamilton frighteners on Harold Wilson thirty-two years earlier and kick-started the devolution process, Winnie Ewing, stood up in Bryce's wonderfully refurbished Assembly Hall and uttered the magical words: 'The Scottish parliament, adjourned on the 24th March 1707, is hereby reconvened.'

There would be the distraction of the ceremonial opening some time later, but the rough business of politics was under way. Donald Dewar's first cabinet meeting was overshadowed by the sacking of Brownite Scottish Labour's General Secretary, Alex Rowley. This was widely attributed to the

Millbank-approved machinations of Dewar's own newly appointed chief of staff, John Rafferty, in collusion with the west-central Scotland Blairite faction.

Holyrood, too, was soon on the agenda. As MSPs began to settle into their Mound chamber, which had just undergone a £7.7 million refit, it began to take on a certain appeal. Some began to question the necessity of Holyrood, by then known to be touching £100 million. Even Labour's Malcolm Chisholm risked disapproval by calling the Mound a 'brilliant building. After Westminster, it's like heaven', while, as usual, the critical letters had been rumbling along in the press. David Whitton, the First Minister's spokesman, insisted that Holyrood was now 'well advanced' and would continue.

Some had different ideas. 'The chamber at the Assembly Hall is a great success,' enthused Alex Salmond, who then repeated his view that Holyrood might be the wrong site. There was also a cross-party dynamic duo in the making. Lib Dem Donald Gorrie and the SNP's Margo MacDonald had tabled a backbench motion calling for a review of the Holyrood decision. A debate was fixed for 17 June 1999.

As mentioned earlier, this first debate on the Holyrood project was more about the politics of the New Scotland than it was about architecture. It also revealed much about the culture of the civil service. Donald Gorrie's computation, derived from official statistics, was that the cost of the entire enterprise would be in excess of £111 million. Donald Dewar, it seems, had gained an altogether different perspective. He had been informed by his Scottish Office staff that the £50 million approved cost which had applied at the time of the exhibition was likely to rise by about £12 million. This was a substantial additional sum, but it was one that an imaginative internal accountant could have coped with. But it was not the whole story. There were extras left out of the first approved cost such as VAT and road realignments. He finally admitted to £109 million. As early as October 1998 the project team knew that it was already £19 million over budget and rising, despite appeals to the architects to control costs, but apparently had kept this fact under wraps. By June, even Donald Gorrie's figure was an underestimate.

Labour's chiefs set about instilling order. This was a vote of no confidence in the First Minister. The line had to be held. With hindsight, the party was probably about to trip itself up on the previous year's Stalinist selection procedure. If they had allowed a few doubters into the ranks such as Dennis Canavan, or Edinburgh councillor Mark Lazarowicz, then perhaps Donald Dewar would have been prevented from taking a step that could only end in disaster. The facts were available. No major contracts had yet been signed. Cancellation penalties would have been due, certainly. These were estimated by Sir David Steel prior to the debate at around £1 million, a figure that Donald Dewar redesignated as £3 million during the debate. No one seemed very clear about anything.

A professional view had been offered by one of Scotland's leading commercial land experts, John Brown of DTZ Debenham Thorpe. He was reported as saying the site value was probably more than the price paid for it, and the excess might even equate with the penalty liabilities; in other words the politicians, at that point, could have walked away from it with containable losses, or perhaps even none. He also believed the alternative – to go ahead – was fated to become Scotland's equivalent of the Sydney Opera House débâcle.

Even the result was a lie, and not a very good one at that. I rang the parliament office to ask about Nick Johnston's pro-Gorrie vote which had failed to register on the electronic system, and was told that he obviously lacked the necessary competence. It seemed unlikely that Mr Johnston was a techno-phobe. He sold Mercedes-Benzes for a living. In light of the executive's subsequent decision to ignore a parliamentary vote in March 2001, of course, one wonders if Holyrood would have gone ahead anyway.

After the debate I was standing in the Lawnmarket when the First Minister and his press spokesman came striding down the street. Trying not to sound too much like a soothsayer I stopped him to point out that this could only be a Pyrrhic victory. 'Are you an architect?' he asked brusquely. I assured him I wasn't, but that the scheme he'd just pushed through on a minority vote with the help of a few Liberal allies was going to do enormous damage to himself, the Labour Party and devolution. 'Don't be silly,' he said, and walked on.

But the spin was unspinning, and Donald Dewar was becoming deeply worried. He could cope with an article in the *Telegraph* headlined 'DONALD DEWAR: DESIGN DICTATOR', or Jonathan Glancey's barb about the building that represents the lie that Scotland is to govern itself, or even Piloti's scathing 'Nooks and Corners' polemic in *Private Eye*. The majority of Scotland's Labour voters didn't bother much with London film-flam, no doubt. But criticism in the Scottish press was different. Margo MacDonald had a column in the *Evening News* and wasn't holding back, and it was no secret that she had overwhelming public support. Cool Britannia, meanwhile, was going off the boil down on the Greenwich peninsula. The letter columns continued to hurt. The architect and editor of *ARCA*, the Scottish journal of architecture, Peter Wilson, a champion of modernism, if a frequent thorn in the side of the RIAS, was writing erudite critiques about the 'weird shapes' and chaotic mismanagement of the project.

Scotsman Publications was in a bit of a double bind. Its proprietors, the Barclay twins, had built its new headquarters opposite the parliament site, and had other holdings nearby. From a commerical point of view it was clearly in their interests to promote Holyrood. On the other hand, as a juicy scam it made good copy for a readership that largely considered Holyrood to be simply the Dome with a kilt on it. The quandary was resolved with the occasional preachy editorial urging support in both the *Evening News* and the *Scotsman*. 'The whole area around Holyrood is involved in massive redevelopment, tying up millions of pounds of private investment. People have legitimately sunk their

savings, as well as their hopes and their dreams, in surrounding projects with reasonable expectations of making
a fair profit,' boomed the *Evening News*. If this were France,
opined the *Scotsman*, 'The philistines and doomsayers would
not be in full cry – we would have pressed on with the
"Grand Project" style and panache which has given Paris
daring structures such as the glass pyramid at the Louvre.'
On the other hand, both newspapers' journalists, as well
as others on *Scotland on Sunday*, seemed to have had free
range over the subject, and where a critical coverage was
warranted, it was run. The *Evening News* reporters Ian
Swanson and Karen Rice were even compared to the tenacious 'Woodstein' duo of the *Washington Post*.

Meanwhile, down by the Watergate, there was no sign
of the symbol of democracy. In July, after the ceremonial
opening, Dewar visited Europe to see how things were
done there. On his return, not much had changed. The
laid-back Miralles style, with its emphasis on the building
evolving out of the land, was driving the quantity surveyors
to distraction. Whatever Mr Mustard's literary inclinations,
his more demotic operatives wanted boring site drawings
rather than wistful Iberian delphic utterances along the lines
of 'a building is never finished' and 'the best way to be on
time is never to finish'.

Architects who had welcomed an original design which
had shown flair and imagination and coped with a sensitive
urban context by dividing the building mass into separate
elements now despaired. The profession had been given
a lift by the success of the Museum of Scotland and the
choice of Glasgow as European City of Architecture. The
executive's 'Development of a Policy on Architecture for
Scotland' was due to be launched by deputy culture minister
Rhona Brankin in September. Now, thanks to Holyrood,
these advances were being jeopardised. 'I can't imagine
we'll be seeing many more commissions for important
Scottish public buildings after this bloody mess,' said one
architect ruefully.

There was a continuing will to stick with 'the concept'

in some form, if only because abandoning it would make Scotland look inept in the eyes of the world. In a letter to the *Herald* Joyce Nicoll, the director of Euroscope, a company that had previously published an integrated proposal for a parliamentary precinct based on Calton Hill, Waterloo Place and the Waverley Valley, proposed setting up a review committee. Her approach was non-confrontational, restating the land experts' view that the Holyrood site value was sufficient to recoup all costs to date, and that the 'expertise of Señor Miralles' could still be used.

Others were taking a more critical look at the exact nature of the 'winning team' of EMBT/RMJM. 'There is a growing awareness that this has been driven all along by determined people who were selectively advising Donald Dewar,' suggested one architect. 'Perhaps it's time to explain exactly how and when this marriage between RMJM and Miralles was brokered, and by whom.'

Miralles' suitability for a technically complex large-scale commission was also coming under scrutiny. His buildings at the time of his appointment had consisted of uncomplicated structures such as sports halls, a meditation pavilion in Japan, the 'renovation' of Utrecht town hall, and the cemetery near Barcelona, many of these designed in conjunction with his first wife Carme Piños and business partner. His *atelier* working methods were unconventional, involving the input of students with enthusiasm, rather than experience. On the evidence available, he seemed no better resourced than dozens of Scottish practices. There was also growing resentment that, capitalising on the prestige of the Holyrood commission, he was now working on other projects across the world, including a new architecture school in Venice. The demanding workload, claimed some, wasn't helping with progress at Holyrood.

Miralles himself was losing patience. He could cut costs, he said, but it would be at the expense of energy efficiency and the use of cheaper foreign materials. The sustainability benchmark was sliding off the bench, but the clincher was the threatened use of linoleum in place of carpets. Since many ordinary Scots 'benchmark' social progress at that point in the 1960s when fitted carpet began to replace lino in the nation's front rooms, this chilling thought signified not so much a millennium future as an austerity past.

There was also growing concern that the scheme, which now bore little relationship to the competition entry, was losing the Miralles signature and becoming more recognisably a product of the RMJM style. Architects, reluctant as ever to be identified as critics of their rivals,* were none the less seething about an outcome in which the 'court architect' to the Scottish Office, as one called it, seemed to be winging in on an architectural competition which they'd failed on entry. While none would condemn the design of their Victoria Quay building in the lurid terms that the *Scotsman* journalist Albert Morris had used ('a structure that resembles a cross between a barracks of the People's Liberation Army of China and a Croatian hypermarket'), few considered it a particularly outstanding example of post-war Scottish architecture. Some were concerned that Gibbons was an adviser to the parliamentary body that disbursed honours, though there was no suggestion of wrongdoing. 'Giving the senior civil servant with responsibility for procurement a role in the awarding of gongs isn't an idea we should be comfortable with,' suggested one architect. Gibbons himself was to be awarded a CBE in the next New Year's Honours List.

As the year progressed, there were increasing signs of activity on site, but Holyrood was none the less falling behind schedule (Sir David Steel blamed problems with the concrete). In the meantime there were other crises to distract Donald Dewar. In September the 'Lobbygate' scandal broke in the *Observer*. A reporter posing as a businessman had secretly filmed two employees of the PR firm Beattie Media boasting of their access to ministers, and one of them happened to be the son of the Scottish Secretary. Tony Blair was furious when the scandal hit the

---

* A *New Yorker* critic was ruined after comparing the modernist Delmonico building to a grain elevator. The memory persists.

party's Bournemouth conference. There were sharp words on the telephone and a Dewar-Reid turf war led to a media feeding-frenzy. The affair rumbled on throughout October. By mid-November Donald Dewar, showing the strain of the pressure he was under, attacked MSPs for criticising himself and the executive. In early December his Blairite chief of staff John Rafferty was sacked after a press briefing that appeared to suggest that health minister Susan Deacon had received death threats from anti-abortionists. Rafferty refused to go quietly, blaming a mandarin's conspiracy for his departure, and forcing the normally circumspect Muir Russell to break silence with a firm denial.

There hadn't been much space in the prints for Holyrood, but it wasn't going away. In early December Enric Miralles gave a lecture in Edinburgh about his work in Barcelona. At the reception afterwards I exchanged a few words with Barbara Doig and former Historic Scotland head John Hume, who jointly informed me that Queensberry House, the A-listed mansion on the north side of the site, was in a much worse condition than they'd ever suspected. I replied that since Historic Scotland had the restoration of ruinous Chatelherault* to its credit Queensberry House should be manageable, then went off for a chat with Enric Miralles, to be told all about his 'near impossible' Holyrood site.

The next day the _Evening News_ front page carried the story: 'HISTORIC BUILDING MUST GO'. Edinburgh's vocal conservation lobby was traumatised. It was already concerned about aspects of the proposed restoration. On 17 May the Architectural Heritage Society for Scotland had put out a press release headed 'Destruction of Queensberry House', followed by another a month later: 'Expensive Butchery at Holyrood/Queensberry House'. Plans for the interior, it was argued, would destroy 'one of the country's most advanced suites of apartments for its date and type' while the exterior

---

* Chatelherault was the shell of a William Adam mansion near
  Hamilton which had been restored as the centrepiece of
  Strathclyde Country Park.

would be 'a fantastic Disney-style reconstruction'. This had been a vociferous objection to the proposed manner of its restoration. Never in their wildest dreams had the city's conservation bodies contemplated the total destruction of one of the most important A-listed urban mansions in the country.

Historic Scotland's team of consultants working on the job were gagged under secrecy rules and could only fulminate in private, but 'sources' within the Scottish executive's own administration even thought demolition was over the top, and were quietly saying so. The problem was that the 'main feature', the Miralles scheme, was going haywire again, and a bit of supporting distraction was necessary. On the basis of the figures, Queensberry House's destruction seemed hardly necessary. Simpson & Brown, architects of the Mound scheme, had carried out a survey some time before costing the restoration at upwards of £7 million. The building had then fallen into the care of EMBT/RMJM and its contractors, and a reassessment carried out which suggested a figure of around £4 million. By December 1999 this had become £8 million. In other words, the original study had been more or less on the mark, and adjustments to the new survey had simply brought it up to the same approximate area.

News was also leaking out about the soaring costs of the main project. It was now heading towards a dizzying £230 million, compared to which a mere £4 million extra from the reassessment for Queensberry House was of little consequence – less than 2 per cent of total contract value.

But Gibbons and his team had not only taken on Edinburgh's heritage lobby and incited rebellion in the government's own statutory agency for the protection of listed buildings. It had also taken on the Hereditary Keeper of Holyroodhouse. On 19 December the Duke of Hamilton wrote to the Prime Minister, Tony Blair. Sent in a purely personal capacity, but mentioning his role as Hereditary Keeper, the letter began with a reminder that he had been a supporter of both Labour and its devolution proposals, and went on to suggest that the proposed demolition was 'causing widespread dismay'. If the Scottish executive, guardians of the built heritage, were seen to be destroying a building of importance in a UNESCO World Heritage Site, he asked, how could they credibly enforce their own legislation when others chose to flout it? He then suggested that since the problem arose from a UK cabinet decision in the first place it might be a 'wise and constructive intervention' on behalf of HM Treasury to make a funding pledge which 'would take the heat out of the matter'.

The Prime Minister's ten-line reply arrived in late January. It was curt and to the point. 'The Scottish parliament assumed responsibility for the Holyrood building complex, including Queensberry House, on 1 June 1999 so the issues you raise concerning conservation and funding for the project are therefore entirely matters for the parliament itself.' And there we had it, from the horse's mouth: whatever the *Scottish Daily Express* had said in 1997 about HM Treasury footing the bill it was a different story now.

Another entering the lists was James Simpson of Simpson & Brown, the firm that had produced the original survey of Queensberry House. He had already stuck his head over the parapet by producing a master plan for an integrated permanent Mound complex which was released to the press the day prior to the June debate. The Simpson scheme, in effect, undermined Dewar's argument that the Mound was unworkable because the buildings were scattered around the Lawnmarket. The First Minister, indeed, had got 'fair droukit' crossing the road to his office. There had been some irritation in Victoria Quay at this incursion, and there was to be more when Simpson had articles in the *Scotsman* and the *Evening News*.

These were essentially a summary of Queensberry House's history and qualities, and a critique of the general restoration approach being proposed, but one contained a reference to the architectural consortium. RMJM deemed this actionable, since it appeared to question the abilities of those involved in the project to deal sensitively with a listed building. In fact RMJM had previously undertaken listed-building renovation work and at that point it was involved in a 'design-build' project for the Roxburghe Hotel in Edinburgh. It also had at least one qualified conservation architect on its staff, though it was not accredited with the RIAS as a conservation practice. A writ was issued, and Simpson was advised to retract and apologise, which he duly did. Many of his fellow architects, however, sympathised with his predicament, and felt that a public showdown did little for the profession's esteem, already suffering in the wake of Holyrood.

The Queensberry sideshow was kept running as the main feature deteriorated. The *Herald* ran a leader worthy of a 1960s iconoclast in support of razing the historic building. Six months later, the *Scotsman* was still taking soundings on the proposal. Majority opinion was strongly in favour of saving it, with only Magnus Linklater and Lord Provost Milligan conceding that it could go – a case of the 'great and the good' toeing the establishment line, it seemed.* The *Evening News*, meanwhile, was on to a demolition contractor who claimed he had been asked twice about knocking the building down. This was described as 'utter bilge' at Victoria Quay.

Meanwhile, the Holyrood project was running out of control again. At a ministerial visit to the Borders I asked John Gibbons if the inside rumour that the costs had now risen to £230 million was true, and he made no attempt at a denial. I also put it to the culture minister, Rhona Brankin, who merely smiled, saying, 'You know I can only give one answer. I couldn't possibly comment.' And, indeed, under the ministerial code, she was right. Within weeks, however, the figure had found its way into the press, and it was becoming no longer tenable to heap the blame on a £4

---

* Linklater's £22,000 part-time post as Scottish Arts Council
  director was politically sensitive. An alleged offer of a
  peerage to Eric Milligan had become a tearoom joke amongst
  some Tories in the City Chambers.

million predicted rise at Queensberry House. MSPs were demanding action while, in London, MPs were beginning to worry about the possible electoral repercussions, and Ken Livingstone was launching himself as a mayoral candidate. The Welsh, too, were still proving troublesome. Mr Blair needed a Holyrood crisis like a hole in the head. Enric Miralles was now telling friends that Holyrood was 'the worst commission' of his career.

Sir David Steel had little choice but to concede some sort of inquiry. He spoke to the RIAS, who recommended its former president, John Spencely, to head it up. Sir David's letter to MSPs announcing Spencely's independent assessment indicated that its remit was to be restricted to the Holyrood contract itself and its management systems. The site was no longer an issue. Steel even chided those who had had the temerity to suggest that it was too small: 'That is nonsense.' It was a statement that not only appeared to pre-empt the report; it also conflicted with a view that Enric Miralles himself had expressed only a few weeks earlier, when the Queensberry House issue had been about to blow.

John Spencely was the mild-mannered former head of Reiach & Hall, a leading Scottish practice. An architect who had once worked with him was sanguine about the appointment: 'I hope to hell he knows what he's letting himself in for.' Others were uneasy about the link with the original selection process, when his firm had entered with Rafael Vinoly of New York. Reiach & Hall, with whom Spencely was still a consultant, had also picked up the contract for the structural restoration of St Andrew's House. 'He's as decent a man as you could get, but he's 100 per cent establishment, which some might not like,' said another former associate. Sir David announced that he and his team should be 'able to complete their task unhindered'. Another debate was promised.

The Spencely report was delivered 'amid tight secrecy' to MSPs on the Parliament's Corporate Body on the evening of 28 March. As per its remit, it could make no comment on the choice of site. Holyrood was fixed. The second debate on the future of Holyrood was scheduled for 5 April. It was widely believed that if the motion to continue with Holyrood, which was to be in Sir David Steel's name, were lost, the project would be doomed, and the parliament would probably stay at the Mound. It was also, once more, a *de facto* vote of confidence in Donald Dewar, and defeat might bring his downfall. The debate was scheduled to take place on the Thursday before the Easter recess, described by Green MSP Robin Harper as a 'typical executive ploy'. It was moved back to the Wednesday. The executive again stressed that it had 'no plans to approach the Treasury for extra cash'.

As the MSPs were mulling over Spencely, Brian Stewart, MD of RMJM, waded in with an attack on both politicians and conservationists. Described in the *Edinburgh Evening News* as an architect (which he wasn't), Stewart accused Historic Scotland staff of being the real 'wreckers' of Queensberry House. Historic Scotland staff, constrained from speaking out under their terms of employment, were furious, and began to consult their union representatives. The slur was vigorously denied. Stewart also lambasted MSPs for their 'ignorance', singling out the SNP as 'protagonists'.

Things were also hotting up in London. Glasgow Labour MPs Ian Davidson and Jim Murphy called for a reopening of the embarrassing issue of the rejection of the vacant Strathclyde Regional Council buildings as a temporary home. 'Many of the decisions were taken before devolution,' said Murphy, 'and we want to investigate whether we got those decisions right.' You bet. Mr Murphy's seat was one of the few in Scotland the Tories had realistic hopes of recapturing, and the Ayr by-election result had doubtless concentrated his mind wonderfully. George Galloway had already suggested Dewar might think about resigning. The official response to this prospect of spillage of the issue into the Westminster arena, with its English backlash implications, was firm: 'The Comptroller and Auditor General Sir John Bourne has no powers to undertake value-for-money

studies into the Scottish administration or any part of it.
Whether spending involved was pre or post 1st July 1999
is not relevant.' Hadrian's Wall, rather than Holyrood, was
becoming Scotland's symbol.

The report, which was released on 30 March, was damning, but it could have been worse. Spencely claimed that it
would cost between £27 million and £30 million to abandon
the site, which had a possible resale value of between
£8 million and £11 million, leaving a shortfall of around
£20 million. He went on to suggest ways in which the
design brief could be changed to reduce the cost from £230
million to £195 million. One of these was the demolition
of Queensberry House, the restoration of which he estimated at £10 million. He also named a probable completion
date: New Year 2004, some two and a half years behind
schedule.

The outcome of the debate was a foregone conclusion.
Labour were solid, except for John McAllion who, while he
didn't support Donald Gorrie's amendment, which sought
a review, voted against his party on another two. I had been
told a day earlier that the majority was now a guaranteed
eight. In the event, it was nine.

On the previous evening there had been another event.
This was a meeting in the Museum of Scotland to which the
public had been invited. A few weeks earlier, in anticipation
of the debate, the Cockburn Association had decided it
might be a good idea to hold an open meeting to give the
subject a public airing. I was on my way south when I had
a telephone call asking me to speak from the platform with
others. This seemed like a reasonable idea. After all, the
association is Edinburgh's civic trust, set up at the beginning
of the nineteenth century by the judge, Lord Cockburn, to
protect the amenity of the city, and the Holyrood project was undoubtedly one of the most significant single
developments to happen throughout the entire period of
its existence.

When I returned to Edinburgh a few days ahead of the
debate I was astonished to discover the meeting was off.

With Queensberry House still at risk it obviously wasn't such a good idea to rattle the establishment's cage. I could only assume that the Cockburn Association had seen the wisdom of not holding the meeting. It was probably a wise decision, given the nature of the establishment machine.

With only a couple of days to go I booked the museum lecture theatre, and rang a few journalists. Lesley Riddoch kindly agreed to chair it, and Sebastian Tombs of the RIAS and Peter Wilson of ARCA, agreed to speak. Considering the short notice, a remarkable number of people turned up. The architect Ian Begg even made a special journey down from his home in Plockton. But, of course, all our efforts amounted to zilch, since the following day's debate wasn't about architecture at all. It was about Donald Dewar's position as First Minister.

There could have been no greater illustration of this than the bus convoy parked outside the MSPs block, ready to take 129 MSPs for a look at the site. Seventeen bothered to climb aboard. The culture of denial was kicking in. MSPs wanted to close the door on the episode, which was probably understandable. It had already taken a chunk out of parliament's time, and generated virtually nothing but bad publicity. It had damaged Donald Dewar's reputation, and brought him much anguish.

It had been decided to set up a 'progressing group' to monitor and report on the project, but it was proving difficult to find candidates. The Conservatives refused to have anything to do with it. Deputy Presiding Officer George Reid of the SNP had been lined up as a potential chairman but his party were unhappy about this. He had swung in behind the Miralles project, it was said, largely to protect what remained of the parliament's credibility over the issue. He pulled back after his colleagues voted against him taking the position on the grounds that it would be unwise for any senior SNP parliamentarian to be identified too closely with the Holyrood 'poisoned chalice'. His SNP colleague Linda Fabiani agreed to go on in his place.

Labour was criticised for keeping its ministers out of the

new 'progressing' group. During First Minister's questions David McLetchie, the Tory leader, raised this, and was accused of sniping. Dewar also insisted that not only was this not his responsibility any more, it wasn't even the executive's. It was technically a problem for the entire parliament. This from the man who, in 1997, had agreed to 'carry the can'. Exculpation was becoming a fine art.

Margo MacDonald had other views: 'The problem is that Donald Dewar says he is not responsible and David Steel refuses to answer questions.' Of course, much depended on the quality of the answers given. Donald Gorrie had already said that he hadn't been lied to so much in his life as he had over this issue. Eventually a Labour volunteer was found for the chairmanship: Lewis MacDonald, apparently a genuinely decent man, if not supremely well qualified. He had a doctorate in African Studies. Linda Fabiani could at least claim she'd done some work with housing associations. The Liberal Democrat Tavish Scott joined them.

The problems of Holyrood just weren't going away, however. Two days after the debate the *Evening News* dropped a bombshell: 'IS THE PALACE CRACKING UP?' Questions had been raised about the effects of intensive excavation and changes to the water table on the buildings around the site, and these included the oldest royal palace in Britain and one of the most important historic buildings in Scotland, Holyroodhouse, which stood only yards away.

Coming on top of the news that Enric Miralles was seriously ill, a fact that had been introduced as an aside into the previous Wednesday's debate by Sir David Steel, it was, to put it mildly, a bit of a scunner. Tory MP Brian Monteith – not a man to hold back where robust opinions were called for – was tabling parliamentary questions to find out more. It then emerged that, the previous week, the nearby primary school had been forced to close after its chimneys were found to be potentially dangerous.

This was about as bad as it could get. Or was it? The unfortunate Enric Miralles, buffeted remorselessly in the backwash of a scandal that was largely not of his making,

succumbed to his illness and died at his home in Barcelona
on 3 July. It seemed the MSPs, in the course of their debate,
weren't aware of quite how serious his condition was. Lewis
MacDonald had even insisted he was at work on the project
shortly after he'd visited a specialist clinic in the United
States, where he'd undergone brain surgery. In fact he had
never recovered, losing the sight in one eye and becoming
partly paralysed. His friends in Barcelona, distraught by
the turn of events, made their views clear, and let it be
known that even as he lay dying he had been the victim
of 'lies and dirty tricks' at the hands of the Scottish political
establishment.

Miralles' death was unfortunate timing for several reasons,
one being that the head of the Scottish Executive Secretariat, Robert Gordon, was in line for an appearance at
an investiture where he was to be made a Commander of
Bath by the Queen at around the date scheduled for the
architect's interment at the Igualad cemetery near Barcelona
which he had co-designed with his first wife, Carme Pinōs.
Thankfully, picking up the mandarin's gong turned out to
be a low-key affair as far as publicity was concerned.

Other matters received rather more coverage. Within a
week of his death, the *Sunday Herald* revealed that Miralles
had faxed a letter to RMJM in which he had said: 'We are
at the middle point, the project is ready.' RMJM had made
this public in an effort to demonstrate that the project had
reached the stage where the design input had come to an
end, and the construction could be left to the home-based
associate architects. But it was something of a double-edged
sword, for the date on the fax, which had been sent from
the hospital in Houston just before Enric Miralles had been
wheeled in for his operation, was 29 March – fully a week
before the debate in which Sir David Steel had said he
had only just heard of Miralles' illness. This left a rather
important question hanging in the air. Just who had been
hiding what from whom, here? And why?

The problem with this Holyrood stitch-up was that just
when it seemed to be under control it would become

unstitched again. A few weeks after the debate an exhausted Donald Dewar, worn down not just by the never-ending crisis at Holyrood, but by the Rafferty affair and other demands on his time, was diagnosed with a heart ailment which needed urgent treatment.

When Donald Dewar returned to work in August there were more problems bubbling up, including a spat over several million pounds that had somehow fallen out of Susan Deacon's budget as an 'underspend', only she hadn't quite seen it that way.

It seemed curious, in a country with western Europe's worst health and poverty indices, that the health service should have a surplus. People such as Danny Philips of Child Poverty Action Scotland had already been describing themselves as 'utterly gobsmacked' when the party that had traditionally preached compassion for the poor and underprivileged started setting itself up in expensive and unnecessary splendour. On 1 July Murray Ritchie of the *Herald* revealed that some of this 'end year flexibility' was to find its way into a contingency fund which might just develop a leak in the direction of Holyrood. Part of the Deacon underspend seemed to be heading in the direction of Historic Scotland, suggested another source.

Could this be the cost of Queensberry House? Unlikely. It appeared that Historic Scotland was being burdened with some of the costs of the landscaping around the late Enric Miralles' ill-starred parliament, though whether this was a valid part of the remit of an agency charged with the care of historic buildings was another question.

The First Minister was also becoming enmeshed in a horrific controversy over the chaos of the Scottish Qualification Authority. Teenagers all over Scotland were in despair, not knowing whether the exam results they were receiving, assuming they were receiving any at all, were valid. Scottish pupils were now apparently no longer certain of gaining places at universities.

Donald Dewar expressed his confidence in the two ministers involved, Henry McLeish and Sam Galbraith. The

SQA, it appeared, was an 'arm's-length' quasi-governmental body, and the politicians couldn't be held responsible. A bit like Holyrood, really. The precedent of the Critchley-Down affair which ended up with a minister's resignation, even although he'd been unaware of the mistakes of his civil servants, was now lost in the mists of time.

Holyrood was also bubbling up again. In the April debate Donald Dewar had pleaded innocence as his opponents insisted that he could not conceivably escape responsibility for a project that had risen from £109 million to £230 million in nine months. Having earlier described further questions over Holyrood as a 'witch hunt', he now claimed he simply hadn't been kept informed, adding that he had reported 'in good faith' in June 1999 that £109 million was the cost. His civil servants had kept the facts from him, and, he claimed, they had been perfectly right to do so. *Qué?* The figures included something called 'design risk', and it would have been contrary to good practice to tell him about this, so everyone was innocent. The parliament had not been misled after all. He had also mentioned that an investigation by the Auditor General for Scotland, Robert Black, was under way.

Beset by a mounting sea of troubles, the First Minister, who was still technically convalescing after his heart operation, struggled valiantly to cope with the mounting criticism over the Holyrood project. A report by the head of the civil service, Muir Russell, which had exonerated Donald Dewar and his officials, had been released in June, but this had been attacked by Margo MacDonald as a 'whitewash' which had focused the blame on one civil servant while her 'Teflon-coated' superiors had been merely protecting themselves. Even the 'scapegoated' civil servant involved, Barbara Doig, hadn't been disciplined, but had simply been moved sideways to another post. Dewar's spokesman David Whitton was not to give an inch: 'The claims made that there has been a cover-up are total nonsense.'

When the Auditor General for Scotland's report finally hit the desks in September its findings were devastating.

It contained an interesting 'Annex B', a restatement of a convoluted rationale lying behind the decision not to inform the First Minister of the full costs at the time of the first debate in 1999. Using rigorous accountancy, Robert Black rapidly despatched the nonsensical £195 million 'capped' figure in his report of September 2000 resulting from Gordon Jackson's amendment of 5 April 2000 by pointing out a) that the usual business practice is to factor inflation into one's forward projections, and that b) that there seemed to be an additional and uncapped budget of some £14 million, the responsibility of the Scottish executive.*

A quick computation on the back of an envelope indicated that if one included all the costs of avoiding Calton Hill, such as the reports by Spencely and the Auditor General himself, the cost of parliamentary time spent on the issue, the cost of researching and anwering almost 150 written questions which Sir David Steel's office had had to deal with between June 1999 and October 2000, the £7.7 million spent on refurbishing the Mound, the cost of hiring special advisers from outside the civil service at up to £750 per day each, the cost of all the knock-on effects of increased traffic circulation in the Old Town, and probably the £1 million which Edinburgh ratepayers had had to hand over to Harvey Nichols after EDI's initial Calton Hill scheme had been binned, then there was no realistic chance of seeing a penny change out of £300 million.

By late September it was all over the papers again, including *Private Eye*. Scalps were being sought. Labour backbench MSPs identified Muir Russell as the culprit for much of the mismanagement. There was a certain irony here. In his rise to the top Russell had been seen by many as a radical more in tune with New Labour culture than rivals

---

* Presumably Sir David Steel disapproved of the multiple suggested by the Auditor General's report. In the Edinburgh University Journal the following December, he wrote 'mischief makers have suggested that the Holyrood project costs have risen six times; his is nonsense . . .'

such as the more traditional Godfrey Robson or Kenneth MacKenzie. A Glasgow physics graduate, Russell had been something of a Scottish Office phenomenon, and was only twenty-six when he'd been appointed first secretary to the new Scottish Development Agency. He was even seen by some as a potential successor to Sir Richard Wilson in the Downing Street Cabinet Office.

Lining Russell up for a fall was risky. First of all, he was nobody's fool and his powerful friends were less than pleased at the attack on the heart of the civil service establishment. Second, mandarin discipline was a reserved power. If he was to get his jotters, or even a dressing-down, it would mean a visit to the Downing Street Cabinet Office. Once there, Muir Russell might just point out one little, salient fact: he hadn't even been in post when the decision to move to Holyrood had been made. That was the responsibility of the Cabinet Office. If Russell was to be censured, so too should Sir Richard Wilson or his predecessor, Sir Robin Butler. A bit of a sticky one for Messrs Blair and Campbell.

The Holyrood parliament was in crisis yet again, hanging around like a Medean curse. It had reached the point of being politically impossible to defend, however much its remaining architects tried to assure a sceptical press and public that matters were in hand, however hard the progress group and its ebullient secretary, Sarah Davidson, tried to persuade the world, or even the previously persuadable Donald Dewar, that it could all be brought home within the budget figure of £195 million without looking like a Formica and MDF hotch-potch with lino instead of carpets.

On 10 October Donald Dewar stumbled on the steps of his official residence in Charlotte Square. The following day, an emotional David Whitton held a press conference in the hospital and announced that Scotland's First Minister had died at 12.18 p.m. Holyrood had now outlived both its patron and its architect.

# 19 Postscript
## *After Donald*

*Anyone who has lived in Scotland will never live anywhere else. The democracy of the people, the sense of fair play is remarkable*

Victor Crolla

THE MONTHS FOLLOWING the death of Donald Dewar were not easy for Scotland. He was more than an interesting and skilful politician who would be missed. He was devolution's gravitas, the foundation of the whole enterprise. It didn't help that Alex Salmond, his long-time political counterweight, had already quit the scene as leader of the SNP. In devolution's probationary year and a half Donald Dewar had been the pivot of the greatest change in three centuries of British constitutional history. There was disappointment and a sense of anticlimax as the euphoria of the referendum had receded, but he had somehow provided continuity and reassurance.

Time moves on. After the fulsome eulogies came a change of style. This was publicised under the general heading 'dumping the crap', and suggested a realignment within the Scottish Labour Party between a Brownite faction with a more Scotland-specific agenda and a Blairite wing which favoured maintaining close ties with London.

Letting go of the Holyrood project was not part of the package. Redefined earlier as a memorial to Enric Miralles, it was now set to become a monument to the memory of Donald Dewar. Whether either man would have wished such a thing was doubtful. The pure spirit of the original Miralles' design had vanished under the distortions imposed on it and there could be no final touch from the master's own hand. For Donald Dewar it had always been a compromise on the first choice which his own party wouldn't back: a waterfront parliament at Leith.

Interviewed by Kirsty Wark after the First Minister's death, the architect Gordon Benson, whose company had drawn up the 1997 feasibility study for the Leith site, recounted a telling episode. On the day of the presentation he had arrived with his plans and model, to be greeted by Donald Dewar with the words: 'Gordon, we don't get everything we want in this life.' Dewar himself had wanted a signature parliament by the Forth. It ended up being somewhere else, and not even having a signature.

Scots were now paying more attention to the politics on the Mound than they had ever paid to the business of Westminster or their local councils. They didn't always like what they were seeing, and the benefit of the doubt was often under strain. One journalist, released to cover Guy Ritchie and Madonna's Sutherland wedding (one of the few up-beat stories of the new year) described it as an escape from Colditz. Sir David Steel's attacks had done little to soothe relations between press and politicians.* The crisis-ridden atmosphere and the continual tension made for hard politics.

The Holyrood project was now being monitored by the progressing group. This body also had another function. A sceptical public had to be brought on side. Holyrood had come close to bringing the image of devolution into disrepute as it had staggered from crisis to crisis and costs had escalated. It was a symbol all right, but not of the bright dawn of a new Scotland. It had become a metaphor for chaos, mismanagement, ineptitude, disappointment, and recrimination. It seemed to owe more to the old political culture of the municipal fix than to the new transparent Scotland which the wordsmiths had presented us with. The heady days of *camaraderie*, when Dewar, Salmond, Brown,

* His accusations of 'bitch journalism' were rejected by the Press Complaints Commission in October 1999.

and Wallace, with guest appearances by Sean Connery, had called for a 'Yes-Yes' vote of confidence in Scotland's future, seemed a long way off.

Lewis MacDonald and Sir David Steel struggled to inject some positive buzz into Holyrood. Yes, there had been problems, but the project was on course now and we should all get behind it to ensure its success. The difficulties had been dealt with, and everything was under control.

If only. The progress group had the unenviable, not to say impossible, task of keeping the right sort of gloss on the news, and drawing the flak off the politicians who simply wanted to get on with running the country. The Tory MSP Murray Tosh had sought to pin some accountability on ministers, but he was curtly informed that 'the bureau'* had decided that ministers would be taking no more questions on the issue.

The devil was in the detail. Despite the Auditor General's conclusion that the project, with inflation and other budgets factored in, was heading towards £250 million or more, the £195 million 'capped' figure of Gordon Jackson's amendment of April 2000 was repeated like a mantra, though ominously It was now referred to as a 'target figure' rather than a fixed cost. It was then topped up to a level just below the psychological threshold of £200 million, then inexorably crept towards £210 million.

The choreogaphy of blame-shifting continued. Miralles had been a mistake, claimed some: he had disregarded the brief, failed to meet the client's needs, and been cavalier with the budget. Others were adamant that he had been an internationally acclaimed architect atrociously victimised in the poisonous atmosphere of Scottish politics. In any case, asked Dundee's Professor McKean, is it actually a Miralles building we're talking about, or an RMJM reinterpretation of the concept? The critics also came in for a pasting. Many of the problems arose from 'ill-informed media comments'

---

* The bureau of parliament's business managers, dominated by the coalition, which decided on procedure.

claimed progressing group secretary Sarah Davidson. Civil servant Paul Grice took up the refrain, blaming some of the escalating costs on negative press coverage which had led contractors to top-load their tenders. A constantly running video in the £250,000 visitor centre which had opened shortly before the First Minister's death featured David Steel and Lewis MacDonald desperately urging the press and public to get behind the scheme.

The spinners fought an uphill battle as the controversy ground on. Squabbles over the possible use of granite cladding material from third world countries with employment practices that fell some way short of the International Labour Organisation standards became a live issue in *The Scotsman*. Granite supposedly had an ethnic value as a Scottish stone (albeit not one much used in sandstone Edinburgh) yet here we were apparently considering its importation from unregulated Chinese quarries or Indian workshops where it had been polished by four-year-old children. The point was finally conceded and a part order placed with Kemnay quarry in Scotland. The argument then moved to home-sourced timber. There wasn't enough Scottish oak to satisfy the parliament's requirements, it seemed, so it would have to be imported. At a question and answer session the progress group's Linda Fabiani stressed that there might be enough for use 'front of house', about 10 per cent of the total. The sustainable development lobby was aghast. The core value that you minimise the embedded energy deficit of tranporting materials over long distances by sourcing them locally was in danger of being lost. Earlier boasts about the government leading by example and incorporating environmental best practice into its own building procurement codes now had a distinctly hollow ring.

The news was little better as far as the treatment of the UNESCO World Heritage Site was concerned. Queensberry House was still being given a rough ride in the opinion of many archaeologists and architectural historians. There were differing views about the proposed removal of its late Georgian upper storey, but widespread unanimity on the unsuitability of pantiles for the roof. John Hume, the former head of Historic Scotland who had been seconded as a consultant to the project team, insisted that terracotta pantiles were in keeping with the character and age of the building, but this was much disputed. At a meeting of the Historic Buildings Council Hume gave his reasons and listened to the opinions of those professionals who disagreed with him. 'There was no on-site archaeological evidence at all for pantiles,' said one insider afterwards. 'You might find them on farm buildings and fishermen's cottages, but they would never have been used on an aristocrat's urban palace in the Royal Mile. It was the dingly-dell school of restoration.' According to the printed record, Hume rounded off the discussion by saying the exchange of views had been academic in any case. The pantiles had already been ordered.

This apparent technique of listening to others after the key decisions had been fixed had been identified as a characteristic of the debate over the site and the building from the start. One member of the EDI team that had made the 1997 Calton Hill presentation had detected the attitude then, during a meeting with Scottish Office officials at which Donald Dewar and Henry McLeish had both been present. 'We'd worked our backs off for weeks getting a proposal together, and thought we were on to a winner. Then at the meeting John Gibbons was asking all sorts of questions about security, and how difficult it might be to get chain-link fencing around a Calton Hill parliament.* It suddenly struck me we were simply going through the motions. We'd been wasting our time. The decision to scrap Calton Hill had already been made.'

Holyrood was also something of a cathartic experience

---

* The fixation with security, exemplified by the grim perimeter fence around Victoria Quay, had its farcical side. It was rumoured a group of civil servants had even thrown an apple at St Andrew's House from Calton Hill to ensure that it would be bombproof and bulletproof.

for architects. A fiercely competitive profession with an occasional tendency for backbiting, most architects none the less adhere to the general rule that architecture is a cause to be defended. Lessons had been learned from Prince Charles' criticisms a decade earlier. Architecture now had to be seen to be engaged with society's needs and aspirations.

The RIAS had been in a particularly difficult position, having pursued a policy of accommodation, with occasional constructive criticism, throughout the debate. 'The council should have been creating hell about the way the so-called competition was organised from the start,' claimed one architect in a country practice, eager, as usual, not to be identified. Others were more upfront. 'You can't have a signature building without a signature,' said modernist Edinburgh architect Richard Murphy, who had entered the competition with the larger practice of Law & Dunbar Naismith. The bond that held the profession together was sorely tested as those in smaller practices voiced misgivings about the power of the larger companies within the RIAS.

The hope that post-devolution Scotland would be a land of architectural confidence was also diminishing. In 1998 the environment minister Calum MacDonald had launched a policy on architecture, claiming: 'Scotland has some of the most talented architects in the world and the importance of promoting and protecting our architectural traditions is paramount.' The RIAS had taken up the theme, sending a pre-election copy of its *Agenda for Architecture in Scotland* to all candidates. The Scottish executive's 'Policy on Architecture' framework document was published in September 1999. 'When it arrived I couldn't believe it. The Miralles building was all over it,' said the countryman architect. 'We were asked for our views. The consultation report was even worse. Nothing but Miralles plans inside and out. Talk about selling us down the river – this was the Scottish cringe, and no mistake!'

The thrust of much of the thinking behind the 1998 selection was placed at the door of Professor Andy McMillan, an expert member of the panel. McMillan had argued that the parliament 'should be used as a chance to demonstrate the country's vision of its future'. He had linked 'change, renewal, and modernity' with the death of Princess Diana, when, in his view, 'a people united in grief at the loss of a symbol of contemporary life exerted a silent pressure to effect change, eschew pomp and protocol, and condemn remoteness in their rulers – the loss of a People's Princess and the gain of a People's Parliament has served to highlight a deeply significant universal desire for public participation in the ordering and determination of social priorities'.

Then had come the giveaway line, replete with its echo of 1960s renewalism. 'It must be modern and of our time, for our future, not merely the reuse of some existing, but unused, building laden with the values of a departed culture . . . It must be transparent – to reflect the spirit of open government, a People's Parliament providing access for people and information.'

Even consistent opponents such as Mike Russell of the SNP began to focus his energies not so much on the right and wrongs of the project itself, as on the art that should feature in the final fit-out. Another squabble had broken out on this issue, with National Galleries of Scotland director Timothy Clifford expressing his horror at the prospect of a parliament building being finished off with an airport lounge refit. Points of architectural detail were also being lambasted, with a proposed new entrance canopy being compared to a supermarket frontage or a bus shelter.

Margo MacDonald, whose opposition to the project now seemed fully vindicated, savaged the executive after it refused to pay any meaningful heed to the Auditor General's report. Damage containment had become a priority, Even Liberal Democrat Keith Raffan, who had initially opposed it, became conciliatory, suggesting on Radio Scotland that public buildings often exceed budgets. He cited the US government's Raeburn House office building in Washington, allegedly 1,000 per cent over target. This was news to Benjamin Forgey, architecture critic of the *Washington Post*: 'But that was put up in the sixties: it was maybe over budget, but certainly not by that much.' He suggested Mr Raffan might have been thinking of the Ronald Reagan building and International Trade Center, which after fifteen years had risen from around $350 million–$400 million to $850 million, closer to 100 per cent. 'And it's a fine-looking building.'

With foot and mouth disease sweeping rural Britain, the financial markets in freefall, and the election date now in dispute. Holyrood was left to simmer in the background. Senior minister Sam Galbraith resigned on health grounds, and Lewis MacDonald was switched from the progressing group into a a junior ministerial post. Henry McLeish himself took over the arts and culture portfolio. This caused a twinge of anxiety. In the search for a post-Dewar *zeitgeist* Alan Wilson had been appointed junior minister for culture and sport and his portfolio promptly redesignated sport and culture. The new First Minister, it was said, was a 'pie and Bovril' kind of a guy, never happier than when he was on the football terraces cheering on the lads, and indeed in his younger days he had actually played the beautiful game himself with some success. The First Minister, it was announced, would be unlikely to be opening any Cézanne exhibitions.

Holyrood was now a classic no-win situation. If the progressing group kept the lid on the budget, the quality of finish would inevitably suffer and it would fail to live up to its 'world class' billing. If costs began to escalate again in a drive for quality, the public would be up in arms about the public expenditure blow-out. It was a problem that the columnist Iain Macwhirter had already touched upon. How could politicians defend their own opulently appointed quarters when the headlines were thundering about old people dying in hospitals because the health service couldn't cope?

Nor was this the only question hanging over Holyrood. Just whose building was this exactly? The issue of liability was already poised to cause friction between Edinburgh and Westminster, promising more fireworks to come. Backbench

Labour MSPs could be relied upon to maintain a loyal silence until the UK election was over, but then what? If the impression had been given in 1997 that the Treasury in London would be footing the bill, how was it that all costs were to come out of the Scottish budget? This would hardly be an easy one to sell in the heartlands. Alex Salmond had already pointed out that the Treasury's tax take on the project was going to be significantly higher than the white paper's original £40 million costing for the entire project.

The Holyrood parliament was to be Scotland's gesture of confidence, the punchy, go-for-it equivalent of such world-beating schemes as Frank Ghery's Bilbao Guggenheim. History will interpret it differently. A Westminster-imposed scheme with an internationalist signature, it might almost be construed as an attempt to deracinate the Scots, rather than an assertion of their distinctive character.

As the late Michael Laird said, there are times when architecture serves the community, and times when the community serves the architecture. That, in all likelihood, is the difference between Frank Ghery's Bilbao triumph and Holyrood's catastrophic failure. There's a lesson for all of us in that.